THE INTERNET

Introductory Concepts and Techniques (UNIX)

Gary B. Shelly
Thomas J. Cashman
Kurt A. Jordan

An International Thomson Publishing Company

Danvers • Albany • Bonn • Boston • Cincinnati • Detroit • London • Madrid • Melbourne
Mexico City • New York • Paris • San Francisco • Singapore • Tokyo • Toronto • Washington

© 1996 boyd & fraser publishing company
One Corporate Place • Ferncroft Village
Danvers, Massachusetts 01923

 International Thomson Publishing
boyd & fraser publishing company is an ITP company
The ITP trademark is used under license.

Printed in the United States of America

For more information, contact boyd & fraser publishing company:

boyd & fraser publishing company
One Corporate Place • Ferncroft Village
Danvers, Massachusetts 01923, USA

International Thomson Publishing Europe
Berkshire House
168-173 High Holborn
London, WC1V 7AA, United Kingdom

Thomas Nelson Australia
102 Dodds Street
South Melbourne
Victoria 3205 Australia

Nelson Canada
1120 Birchmont Road
Scarborough, Ontario
Canada M1K 5G4

International Thomson Editores
Campos Eliseos 385, Piso 7
Colonia Polanco
11560 Mexico D.F. Mexico

International Thomson Publishing GmbH
Konigswinterer Strasse 418
53227 Bonn, Germany

International Thomson Publishing Asia
Block 211, Henderson Road #08-03
Henderson Industrial Park
Singapore 0315

International Thomson Publishing Japan
Hirakawa-cho Kyowa Building, 3F
2-2-1 Hirakawa-cho, Chiyoda-ku
Tokyo 102, Japan

All rights reserved. No part of this work may be reproduced or used in any form or by any means—graphic, electronic, or mechanical, including photocopying, recording, taping, or information and retrieval systems—without prior written permission from the publisher.

ISBN 0-7895-0003-5

SHELLY CASHMAN SERIES® and **Custom Edition**® are trademarks of International Thomson Publishing, Inc. Names of all other products mentioned herein are used for identification purposes only and may be trademarks and/or registered trademarks of their respective owners. International Thomson Publishing, Inc. and boyd & fraser publishing company disclaim any affiliation, association, or connection with, or sponsorship or endorsement by such owners.

1 2 3 4 5 6 7 8 9 10   BC   09876

This book was designed using Quark 3.31 for Windows and CorelDraw 5.0 for Windows.

Contents

The INTERNET
Introductory Concepts and Techniques I.1

▶ PROJECT ONE
Introduction to the Internet I.2

OBJECTIVES	I.2
INTRODUCTION	I.2
HISTORY OF THE INTERNET	I.3
THE INTERNET	I.4
CONNECTING TO THE INTERNET	I.5
Sending Information Over the Internet	I.8
Routing	I.9
Addressing	I.9
Domain Naming	I.9
SERVICES PROVIDED ON THE INTERNET	I.10
Internet Service Programs	I.12
Mail Courtesy	I.14
Finding People Using Finger	I.14
TELNET	I.15
File Transfer Protocol (FTP)	I.16
Software Packing	I.16
Rights and Responsibilities	I.17
INTERNET TOOLS	I.18
Archie	I.19
Gopher	I.20
Veronica	I.20
News Groups	I.21
Mailing Lists	I.22
WAIS	I.23
Internet Relay Chat	I.24
WORLD WIDE WEB	I.25
Netscape	I.27
ACCESS TO THE INTERNET	I.28
PROJECT SUMMARY	I.28
KEY TERMS AND INDEX	I.29
STUDENT ASSIGNMENTS	I.29

▶ PROJECT TWO
Accessing Internet Services from UNIX I.33

OBJECTIVES	I.33
INTRODUCTION	I.33
GETTING STARTED IN UNIX	I.33
Getting Help in UNIX	I.35
USING ELECTRONIC MAIL	I.36
Sending a Mail Message	I.36
Managing Your Mail Box	I.38
Managing Mail Messages	I.38
Saving Mail Messages	I.39
Including a Disk File in a Message	I.40
Reading Other Messages	I.41
Deleting a Mail Message	I.42
FINDING INFORMATION ABOUT PEOPLE	I.44
TERMINAL SESSIONS ON REMOTE HOST COMPUTERS	I.45
Managing TELNET	I.46
TRANSFERRING FILES WITH FTP	I.48
Starting an FTP Session	I.48
Displaying the Current Directory	I.50
Binary and Text Files	I.54
Changing File Transfer Types	I.55
Sending a File with FTP	I.57
Transferring a File with a New Name	I.58
FINDING FILES WITH ARCHIE	I.59
Displaying Information about a File	I.60
Setting the Search Type	I.61
Mailing Search Results	I.62
RETRIEVING FILES WITH GOPHER	I.64
Navigating Gopher Menus	I.65
Searching GopherSpace Using Veronica	I.68
Searching with Veronica	I.69
SEARCHING FOR DOCUMENTS WITH WAIS	I.70
Connecting to a WAIS Server	I.71
Selecting a Database	I.72
USENET NEWS GROUPS	I.76
Reading News Group Articles	I.78
Displaying a Summary of Articles	I.79
Changing to a Different News Group	I.80
Saving an Article to Disk	I.84
Posting News Group Articles	I.86
MAILING LISTS	I.89
Reading Mailing List Postings	I.91
Sending Mail to the List	I.91
Unsubscribing from a Mailing List	I.93
INTERNET RELAY CHAT (IRC)	I.94
Starting an IRC Session	I.95
Displaying Channel Names	I.96
Joining an IRC Discussion Channel	I.97
Changing to Another IRC Channel	I.99
PROJECT SUMMARY	I.101
KEY TERMS AND INDEX	I.102
STUDENT ASSIGNMENTS	I.102
HANDS-ON EXERCISES	I.106

▶ APPENDIX
Popular Internet Sites I.108

INDEX	I.111
PHOTO CREDITS	I.112

PREFACE

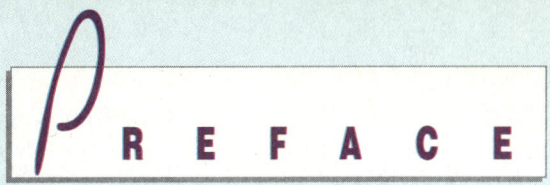

▶ SHELLY CASHMAN SERIES

The Shelly Cashman Series offers superior materials from which to learn about computers. In addition to computer concepts, programming, networking, and the Internet, the Shelly Cashman Series is proud to present both Windows- and DOS-based personal computer applications in a variety of traditionally bound textbooks. The table on page vii shows the available books in the Shelly Cashman Series.

If you do not find the exact Shelly Cashman Series book to fit your needs, boyd & fraser's unique **Custom Edition** program allows you to choose from a number of options and create a textbook perfectly suited to your course. This exciting program is explained and summarized in the table on page viii.

▶ THE INTERNET

One of the more popular topics of conversation today in all disciplines, the Internet links approximately 30 million people and thousands of organizations worldwide. Within just a few years, the Internet has grown from a limited number of networked computers accessible only to the scientific and academic communities to thousands of computers located all over the world available to millions of users. Nearly all post-secondary educational institutions and many businesses, governmental agencies, and industries use the Internet to communicate with one another, carry out research, transfer files, and connect to computers to access programs not available on their own computers. The Internet has undeniably become a worldwide web of computers within reach of anyone with a computer, modem, and the proper software. Thus, an up-to-date educational institution that teaches students how to use computers must teach Internet basics.

▶ OBJECTIVES OF THIS TEXTBOOK

The Internet: Introductory Concepts and Techniques (UNIX) is intended for use in combination with a variety of computer instruction. Specific objectives of this book are as follows:

- ▶ To teach the fundamentals of how the Internet works
- ▶ To expose the student to the various Internet services available
- ▶ To develop an exercise-oriented approach that allows the student to learn by example
- ▶ To help the student understand what can be accomplished using the Internet
- ▶ To encourage curiosity and independent exploration of Internet resources
- ▶ To serve as a primer on how to use the Internet

▶ ORGANIZATION OF THIS TEXTBOOK

The Internet: Introductory Concepts and Techniques (UNIX) consists of two projects that cover basic Internet concepts and the use of Internet services and tools and an Appendix that lists popular Internet sites categorized by topic.

Each project begins with a statement of objectives. A project summary and list of key terms are provided at the end of each project. The key terms are highlighted in bold when first introduced in the project. Questions and exercises are presented at the end of each project. Exercises include short answer, hands-on and research-oriented experiences. The projects and appendix are organized as follows:

Project 1 – Introduction to the Internet   In Project 1, students are introduced to the Internet and its components. Topics include how computers communicate over the Internet; the services and tools offered on the Internet; different discussion techniques available on the Internet; and accessing the Internet.

Project 2 – Accessing Internet Services from UNIX   In Project 2, students begin to explore the Internet. Topics include using the Internet services electronic mail, file transfer, and remote terminal operation; searching for files on the Internet using the tools gopher, archie, and veronica; and displaying and retrieving WAIS databases. Students learn how to subscribe to and use conversation techniques such as news groups, mailing lists, and Internet relay chat.

Appendix – Popular Internet Sites   This Appendix categorizes the listed sites by topics and provides a guideline for students to keep a directory of their own favorite Internet sites. Topics include Government, Pictures, Sound, Books, Games, Jobs, and Internet Resources.

▶ ## ANCILLARY MATERIALS FOR TEACHING FROM THIS SHELLY CASHMAN SERIES TEXTBOOK

  comprehensive instructor's support package accompanies all textbooks in the Shelly Cashman Series.

Instructor's Manual   The Instructor's Manual contains the following:
▶ Detailed lesson plans including project objectives, project overview, and lecture notes with page references and illustration references
▶ Answers to all the student exercises at the end of the projects
▶ A test bank of True/False, Multiple Choice, and Fill-in questions
▶ Selected master transparencies

ElecMan   ElecMan stands for *Electronic Man*ual. ElecMan is the Instructor's Manual on diskette. This diskette allows an instructor to use any Windows word processor to modify the lecture notes or generate quizzes and exams from the test bank.

Figures on CD-ROM   Illustrations for every screen in the textbook are on a CD-ROM. Using this CD-ROM, an instructor can create a slide show or print and make transparencies for a lecture presentation.

MicroExam IV MicroExam IV, a computerized test-generating system, is available free to adopters of any Shelly Cashman Series textbooks. It includes all of the questions from the test bank just described. MicroExam IV is an easy-to-use, menu-driven software package that provides instructors with testing flexibility and allows customizing of testing documents.

NetTest IV NetTest IV allows instructors to take a MicroExam IV file made up of True/False and Multiple Choice questions and proctor a paperless examination in a network environment. The same questions display in a different order on each PC. Students have the option of instantaneous feedback. Tests are electronically graded, and an item analysis is produced.

▶ ACKNOWLEDGMENTS

The Shelly Cashman Series would not be the success it is without the contributions of outstanding publishing professionals. First, and foremost, among them is Becky Herrington, director of production and designer. She is the heart and soul of the Shelly Cashman Series and it is only through her leadership, dedication, and untiring efforts that superior products are produced.

Under Becky's direction, the following individuals made significant contributions to this book: Ginny Harvey, series administrator and manuscript editor; Peter Schiller, production manager; Ken Russo, senior illustrator; Mike Bodnar, Greg Herrington, and Dave Bonnewitz, illustrators; Jeanne Black and Betty Hopkins, typographers; Tracy Murphy, series coordinator; Marilyn Martin and Nancy Lamm, proofreaders; Christina Haley, indexer; Dennis Tani, cover design; and Patti Garbarino, office manager.

Special thanks to the following reviewers of *The Internet: Introductory Concepts and Techniques (UNIX)*: Susan Conners, Purdue University, Calumet; Bill Ellison, Educational Consultant; Deborah Fansler, Educational Consultant; Lyn Markowicz, Purdue University, Continuing Education; Jeffrey Quasney, Educational Consultant; and Margaret Thomas, Ohio University.

Special recognition for a job well done must go to Jim Quasney, who, together with writing, assumed the responsibilities as series editor. Particular thanks go to Thomas Walker, president and CEO of boyd & fraser publishing company.

We hope you will find using this book an enriching and rewarding experience.

Gary B. Shelly
Thomas J. Cashman
Kurt A. Jordan

▶ SHELLY CASHMAN SERIES – TRADITIONALLY BOUND TEXTBOOKS

The Shelly Cashman Series presents both Windows- and DOS-based personal computer applications in a variety of traditionally bound textbooks, as shown in the table below. For more information, see your ITP representative or call 1-800-423-0563.

COMPUTERS	
Computers	Using Computers: A Gateway to Information
	Using Computers: A Gateway to Information, Brief Edition
Computers and Windows Applications	Using Computers: A Gateway to Information and Microsoft Office (also available in spiral bound)
	Using Computers: A Gateway to Information and Microsoft Works 3.0 (also available in spiral bound)
	Complete Computer Concepts and Microsoft Works 2.0 (also available in spiral bound)
Computers and DOS Applications	Complete Computer Concepts and WordPerfect 5.1, Lotus 1-2-3 Release 2.2, and dBASE IV Version 1.1 (also available in spiral bound)
	Complete Computer Concepts and WordPerfect 5.1, Lotus 1-2-3 Release 2.2, and dBASE III PLUS (also available in spiral bound)
Computers and Programming	Using Computers: A Gateway to Information and Programming in QBasic
WINDOWS APPLICATIONS	
Integrated Packages	Microsoft Office: Introductory Concepts and Techniques (also available in spiral bound)
	Microsoft Office: Advanced Concepts and Techniques (also available in spiral bound)
	Microsoft Works 3.0 (also available in spiral bound)*
	Microsoft Works 3.0—Short Course
	Microsoft Works 2.0 (also available in spiral bound)
Windows	Microsoft Windows 3.1 Introductory Concepts and Techniques
	Microsoft Windows 3.1 Complete Concepts and Techniques
Windows Applications	Microsoft Word 2.0, Microsoft Excel 4, and Paradox 1.0 (also available in spiral bound)
Word Processing	Microsoft Word 6* • Microsoft Word 2.0
	WordPerfect 6.1* • WordPerfect 6* • WordPerfect 5.2
Spreadsheets	Microsoft Excel 5* • Microsoft Excel 4
	Lotus 1-2-3 Release 5* • Lotus 1-2-3 Release 4*
	Quattro Pro 6 • Quattro Pro 5
Database Management	Paradox 5 • Paradox 4.5 • Paradox 1.0
	Microsoft Access 2*
	dBASE 5/5.5
Presentation Graphics	Microsoft PowerPoint 4*
DOS APPLICATIONS	
Operating Systems	DOS 6 Introductory Concepts and Techniques
	DOS 6 and Microsoft Windows 3.1 Introductory Concepts and Techniques
Integrated Package	Microsoft Works 3.0 (also available in spiral bound)
DOS Applications	WordPerfect 5.1, Lotus 1-2-3 Release 2.2, and dBASE IV Version 1.1 (also available in spiral bound)
	WordPerfect 5.1, Lotus 1-2-3 Release 2.2, and dBASE III PLUS (also available in spiral bound)
Word Processing	WordPerfect 6.0
	WordPerfect 5.1 Step-by-Step Function Key Edition
	WordPerfect 5.1
	WordPerfect 5.1 Function Key Edition
	WordPerfect 4.2 (with Educational Software)
	WordStar 6.0 (with Educational Software)
Spreadsheets	Lotus 1-2-3 Release 4 • Lotus 1-2-3 Release 2.4 • Lotus 1-2-3 Release 2.3
	Lotus 1-2-3 Release 2.2 • Lotus 1-2-3 Release 2.01
	Quattro Pro 3.0
	Quattro with 1-2-3 Menus (with Educational Software)
Database Management	dBASE 5
	dBASE IV Version 1.1
	dBASE III PLUS (with Educational Software)
	Paradox 4.5
	Paradox 3.5 (with Educational Software)
PROGRAMMING AND NETWORKING	
Programming	Microsoft Visual Basic 3.0 for Windows*
	Microsoft BASIC
	QBasic
Networking	Novell NetWare for Users
Internet	The Internet: Introductory Concepts and Techniques (UNIX Version)
	The Internet: Introductory Concepts and Techniques (Netscape Version)

*Also available as a Double Diamond Edition, which is a shortened version of the complete book

▶ Shelly Cashman Series – Custom Edition Program

If you do not find a Shelly Cashman Series traditionally bound textbook to fit your needs, boyd & fraser's unique **Custom Edition** program allows you to choose from a number of options and create a textbook perfectly suited to your course. The customized materials are available in a variety of binding styles, including boyd & fraser's patented **Custom Edition** kit, spiral bound, and notebook bound. Features of the **Custom Edition** program are:

- ▶ Textbooks that match the content of your course
- ▶ Windows- and DOS-based materials for the latest versions of personal computer applications software
- ▶ Shelly Cashman Series quality, with the same full-color materials and Shelly Cashman Series pedagogy found in the traditionally bound books
- ▶ Affordable pricing so your students receive the **Custom Edition** at a cost similar to that of traditionally bound books

The table on the right summarizes the available materials. For more information, see your ITP representative or call 1-800-423-0563.

	COMPUTERS
Computers	Using Computers: A Gateway to Information
	Using Computers: A Gateway to Information, Brief Edition
	Introduction to Computers (32-page)
OPERATING SYSTEMS	
Windows	Microsoft Windows 3.1 Introductory Concepts and Techniques
	Microsoft Windows 3.1 Complete Concepts and Techniques
DOS	Introduction to DOS 6 (using DOS prompt)
	Introduction to DOS 5.0 (using DOS shell)
	Introduction to DOS 5.0 or earlier (using DOS prompt)
WINDOWS APPLICATIONS	
Integrated Packages	Microsoft Works 3.0*
	Microsoft Works 3.0—Short Course
	Microsoft Works 2.0
Microsoft Office	Using Microsoft Office (16-page)
	Object Linking and Embedding (OLE) (32-page)
Word Processing	Microsoft Word 6*
	Microsoft Word 2.0
	WordPerfect 6.1*
	WordPerfect 6*
	WordPerfect 5.2
Spreadsheets	Microsoft Excel 5*
	Microsoft Excel 4
	Lotus 1-2-3 Release 5*
	Lotus 1-2-3 Release 4*
	Quattro Pro 6
	Quattro Pro 5
Database Management	Paradox 5
	Paradox 4.5
	Paradox 1.0
	Microsoft Access 2*
	dBASE 5/5.5
Presentation Graphics	Microsoft PowerPoint 4*
DOS APPLICATIONS	
Integrated Package	Microsoft Works 3.0
Word Processing	WordPerfect 6.0
	WordPerfect 5.1 Step-by-Step Function Key Edition
	WordPerfect 5.1
	WordPerfect 5.1 Function Key Edition
	Microsoft Word 5.0
	WordPerfect 4.2
	WordStar 6.0
Spreadsheets	Lotus 1-2-3 Release 4
	Lotus 1-2-3 Release 2.4
	Lotus 1-2-3 Release 2.3
	Lotus 1-2-3 Release 2.2
	Lotus 1-2-3 Release 2.01
	Quattro Pro 3.0
	Quattro with 1-2-3 Menus
Database Management	dBASE 5
	dBASE IV Version 1.1
	dBASE III PLUS
	Paradox 4.5
	Paradox 3.5
PROGRAMMING AND NETWORKING	
Programming	Microsoft Visual Basic 3.0 for Windows*
	Microsoft BASIC
	QBasic
Networking	Novell NetWare for Users
Internet	The Internet: Introductory Concepts and Techniques (UNIX Version)
	The Internet: Introductory Concepts and Techniques (Netscape Version)

* Also available as a mini-module

THE INTERNET
Introductory Concepts and Techniques

▶ **PROJECT ONE**

INTRODUCTION TO THE INTERNET I.2

Objectives I.2
Introduction I.2
History of the Internet I.3
The Internet I.4
Connecting to the Internet I.5
Services Provided on the Internet I.10
Internet Tools I.18
World Wide Web I.25
Access to the Internet I.28
Project Summary I.28
Key Terms and Index I.29
Student Assignments I.29

▶ **PROJECT TWO**

Accessing Internet Services from UNIX I.33

Objectives I.33
Introduction I.33
Getting Started in UNIX I.33
Using Electronic Mail I.36
Finding Information about People I.44
Terminal Sessions on Remote Host Computers I.45
Transferring Files with FTP I.48
Finding Files with Archie I.59
Retrieving Files with Gopher I.64
Searching for Documents with WAIS I.70
USENET News Groups I.76
Mailing Lists I.89
Internet Relay Chat (IRC) I.94
Project Summary I.101
Key Terms and Index I.102
Student Assignments I.102
Hands-On Exercises I.106

▶ **APPENDIX**

Popular Internet Sites I.108

Index I.111

Photo Credits I.112

THE INTERNET
Introductory Concepts and Techniques

PROJECT ONE

INTRODUCTION TO THE INTERNET

OBJECTIVES You will have mastered the material in this project when you can:

- Describe the history and background of the Internet
- Identify the hardware devices that comprise the Internet
- Indicate the data line types and media used with the Internet
- Describe how packet switching works
- Explain Internet Protocol (IP) and domain name addressing
- List and describe Internet service programs
- List and describe Internet tools
- Describe hypertext and browsers
- Connect to the Internet

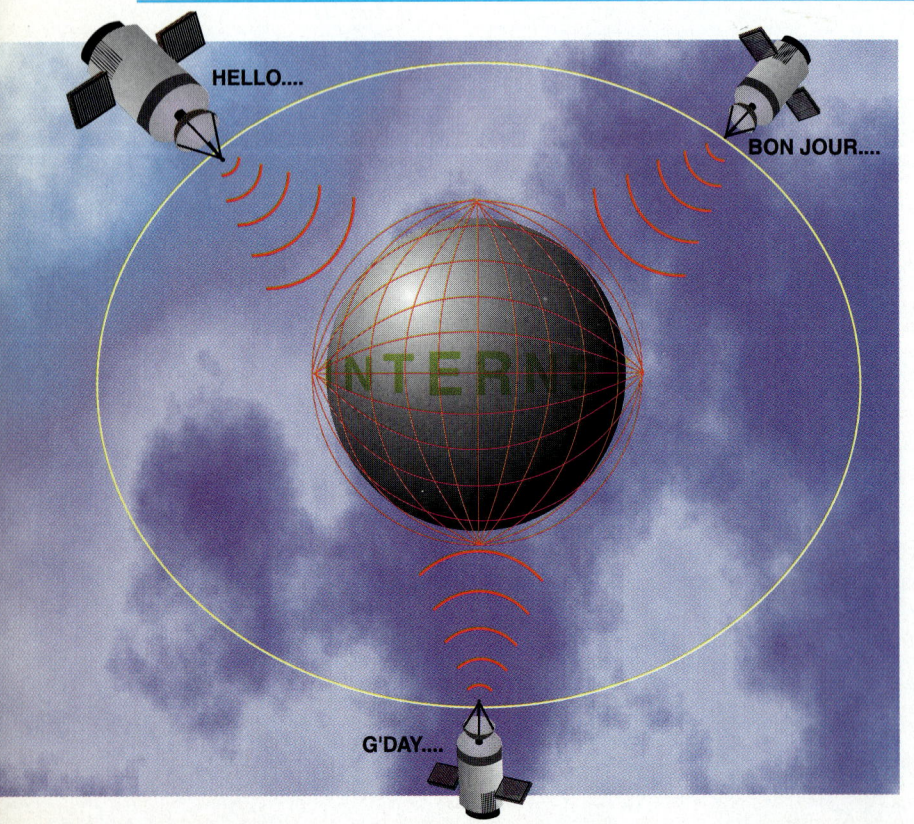

FIGURE 1-1 *The Internet allows you to converse with people all over the world.*

INTRODUCTION

One of the more popular and fast growing areas in computing today is the Internet. Using the Internet, you are able to do research, get stock quotes, shop for services and merchandise, display weather maps, obtain pictures, movies, and audio clips stored on computers from around the world, and converse with people on other continents (Figure 1-1).

Once considered mysterious, the Internet is now accessible to the general public because personal computers with user-friendly tools have reduced its complexity. To be considered knowledgeable about computer technology in today's world, being Internet-literate is almost a requirement.

History of the Internet

The Internet started as a method for the government's computers to communicate with each other for scientific and military purposes. The communications technique developed had to accommodate the different sizes and types of computers and software differences. It also had to adjust for the different speeds of the computers. The collection of connected computers that materialized from this effort was called **ARPANET** (**A**dvanced **R**esearch **P**rojects **A**gency **NET**work) and was developed in the late 1960s (Figure 1-2).

In the early 1970s, a government agency called **DARPA** (**D**efense **A**dvanced **R**esearch **P**rojects **A**gency), which funded the initial research on ARPANET, provided funding to make available to universities an inexpensive implementation of the TCP/IP communication technique. The letters **TCP/IP** stand for **T**ransmission **C**ontrol **P**rotocol/**I**nternet **P**rotocol.

TCP/IP is a set of protocols describing how computers will communicate with each other. A **protocol** is a set of rules governing the formatting of data. By following the same rules, each computer knows what format to expect when receiving data from another computer and what format to use when sending data to another computer.

In the early 1980s, universities started using TCP/IP to connect their computers together. As TCP/IP protocols became more popular, ARPANET protocols started to decline in use.

In 1989, the World Wide Web was created. The **World Wide Web (WWW)** is an arrangement of easy-to-access Internet resources from computer systems throughout the world. These computer systems are called **Web sites**. In 1993, the Mosaic software made the World Wide Web easily available to millions of computer users. And in 1994, the Netscape Navigator software simplified access even further for those outside the scientific and academic community.

The Internet today, which now consists of hundreds of thousands of connected computers, continues to grow with thousands of new users coming online every month. Businesses, newspapers, television stations, and even the White House are on the Internet; but just what is the Internet?

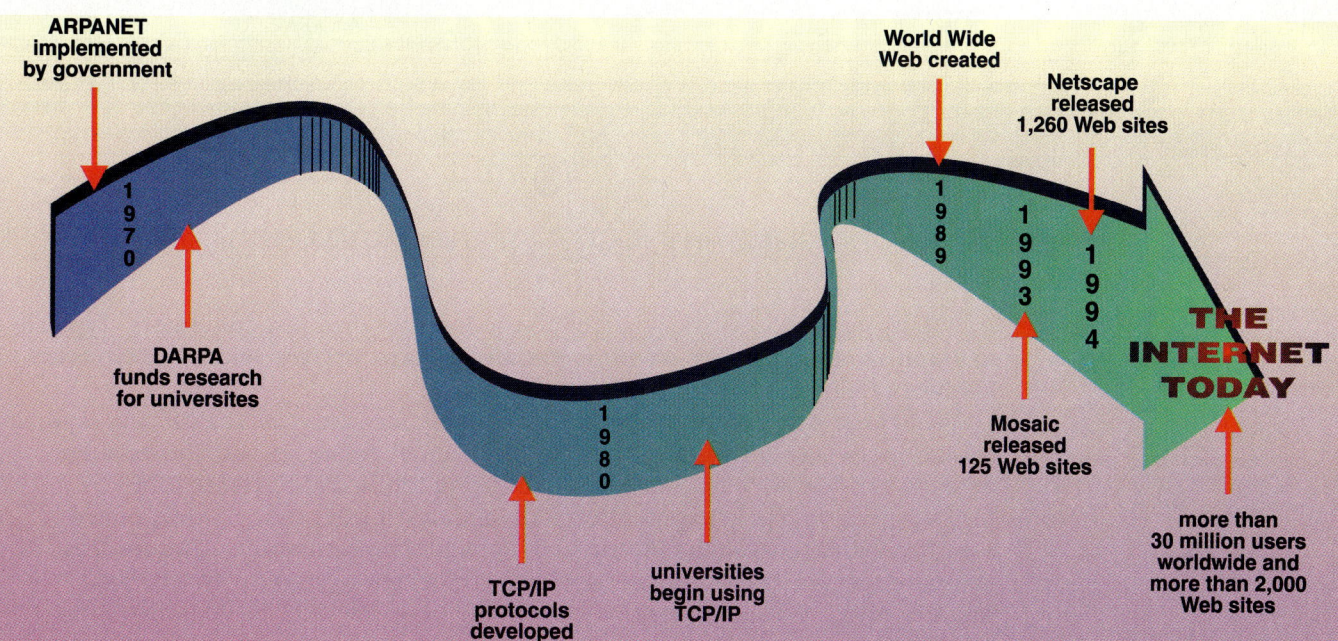

FIGURE 1-2 *The Internet development timeline.*

THE INTERNET

The Internet is a collection of networks (Figure 1-3), each of which is composed of a collection of smaller networks. A **network** can be defined as one or more computer systems, terminals, and communications technologies (such as cable and telephone systems) that allow the computer systems and terminals to communicate with each other, whether they are physically located in the next building or on the next continent.

The computers in these networks can be different types from different manufacturers and running different operating systems, such as MS-DOS or UNIX. As the term Internet implies, the Internet is composed of **INTER**connected **NET**works.

Networks are connected with high-, medium-, and low-speed data lines that allow data to move from one computer to another. The separate networks connect to the Internet through special computers called **gateways**. These gateway computers serve as pathways from one network to another, creating what many people refer to as the **Information Superhighway**.

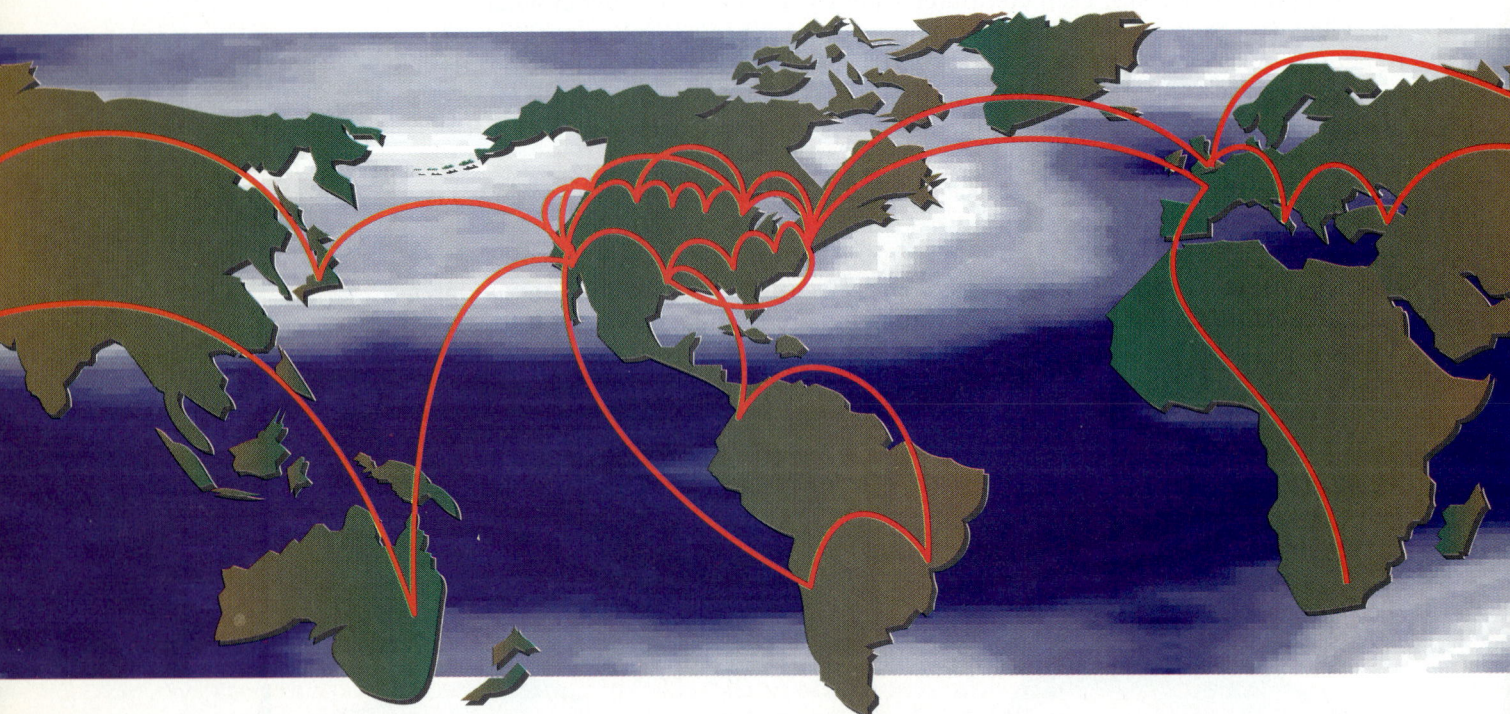

FIGURE 1-3 *The Internet has evolved into a global connection of inter-connected networks.*

Many more devices are attached to the Internet than just computers. Typically found in a college campus environment are printers, bridges, and other types of hardware (Figure 1-4).

A **bridge** is an electronic device that simply forwards the TCP/IP data on to another network. Bridges also can filter the data by letting in only the data that belongs in a certain network, thereby reducing traffic and response times.

A typical college computer network includes smaller subnetworks linked together with access to the Internet via the mainframe computer. The student computer lab and the faculty network are connected together with a bridge. Another bridge is used to connect the faculty network with the administration mainframe computer. High-speed telephone lines are used to connect the network to the Internet.

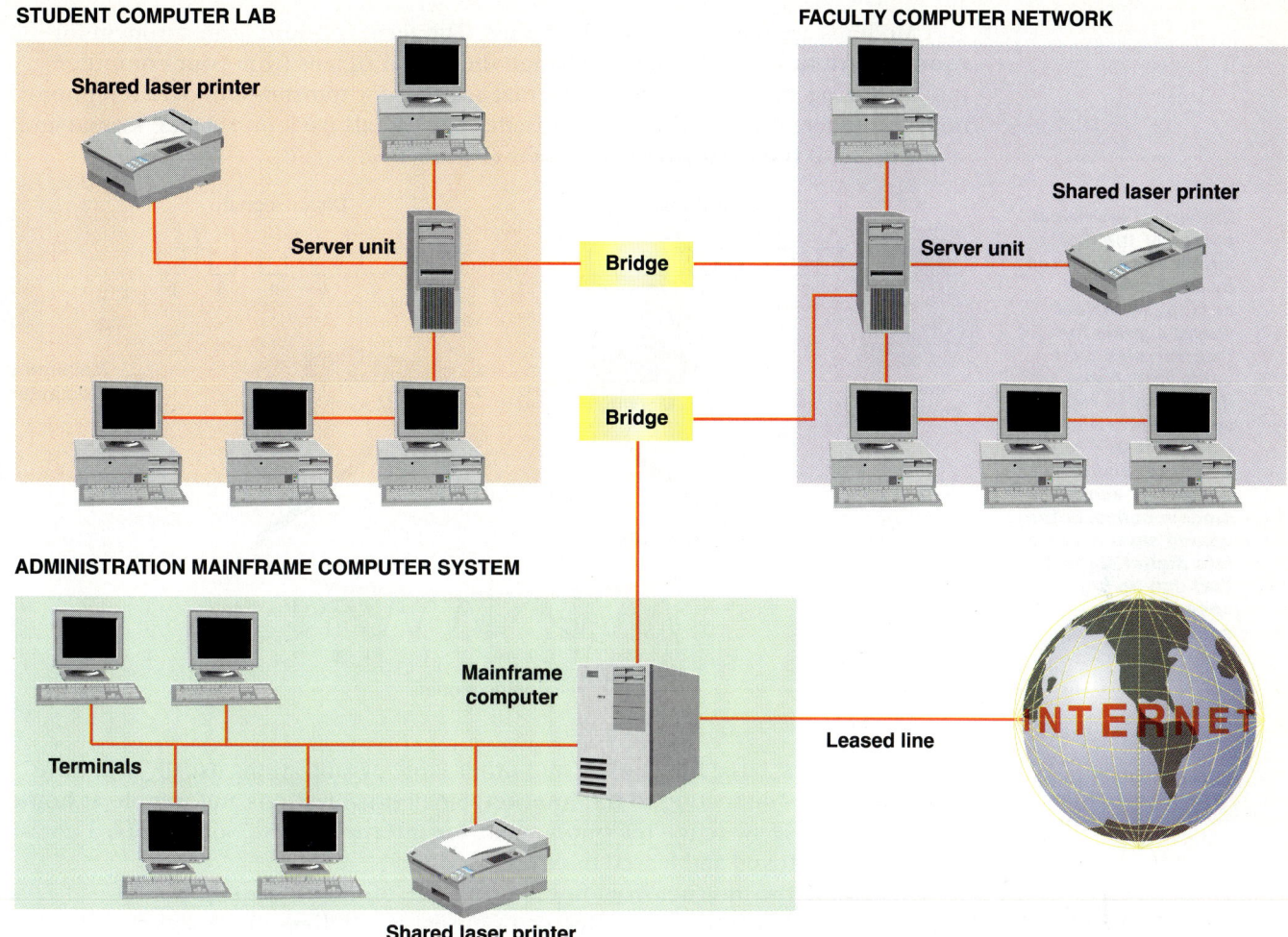

FIGURE 1-4 *A typical college computer network.*

All these different types of equipment seem to make the Internet very complex, as indeed it is. Fortunately, it is not necessary to know everything about the specifics of how the Internet works to take advantage of its services. To use the Internet, however, you must be familiar with certain terminology and how to connect to the Internet. The next section discusses these requirements.

▶ CONNECTING TO THE INTERNET

To access the Internet, you need a computer that is running TCP/IP. The computer must be connected to the collection of networks that make up the Internet. The connection will be over one of two types of data lines.

The two general types of **data lines** are leased and switched. A **leased line** is a medium- to high-speed line (5,600 characters per second) provided by the phone company that is dedicated for computer communications. A **switched line** is a dial up medium- to low-speed line (240 characters per second) that is the same as your home telephone line.

Modems are used with switched lines. The term **modem** is an acronym for **mo**dulate/**dem**odulate. Modems change the digital signals from your computer into an analog signal, which is the format suitable for transmission over telephone lines. A modem on the other end translates the signals back into digital format and sends them to the destination computer (Figure 1-5).

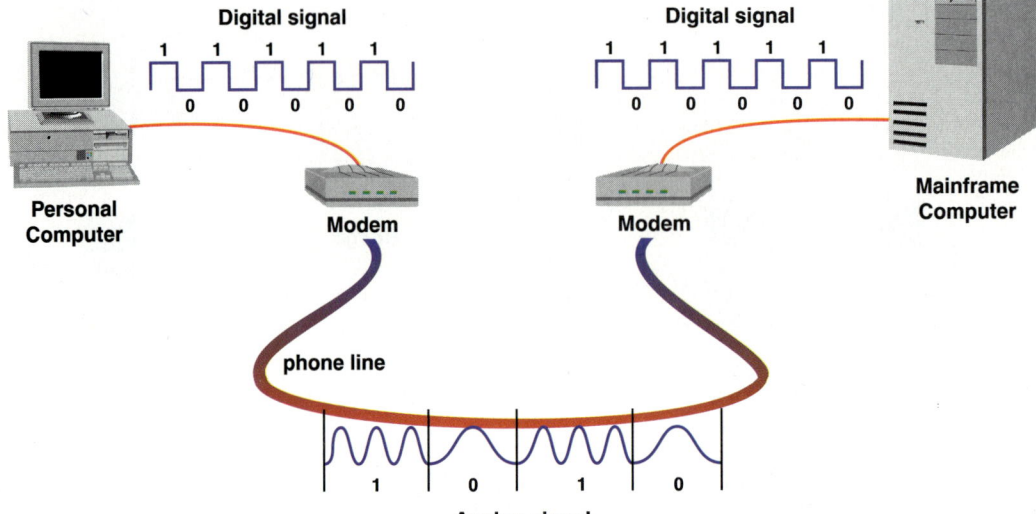

FIGURE 1-5
Individual electrical pulses of the digital signal are converted by a modem into analog (electrical wave) signals for transmission over voice telephone lines. The 1s represent ON bits and 0s represent OFF bits. At the receiving computer, another modem converts the analog signals back into digital signals that can be processed by the computer.

Universities, large businesses, and other large organizations usually will have leased lines for connecting to the Internet. Small organizations and people at home normally will use switched telephone lines for Internet access. Sometimes, a combination of switched and leased lines are used.

Accessing the Internet from home using one of the online computing **providers**, such as America Online or Compuserve, will require a switched line from your home to the provider's computer and a leased line from the provider's computer to the rest of the Internet (Figure 1-6).

FIGURE 1-6
Connections are available to the Internet using online service providers such as Prodigy, CompuServe, or America Online.

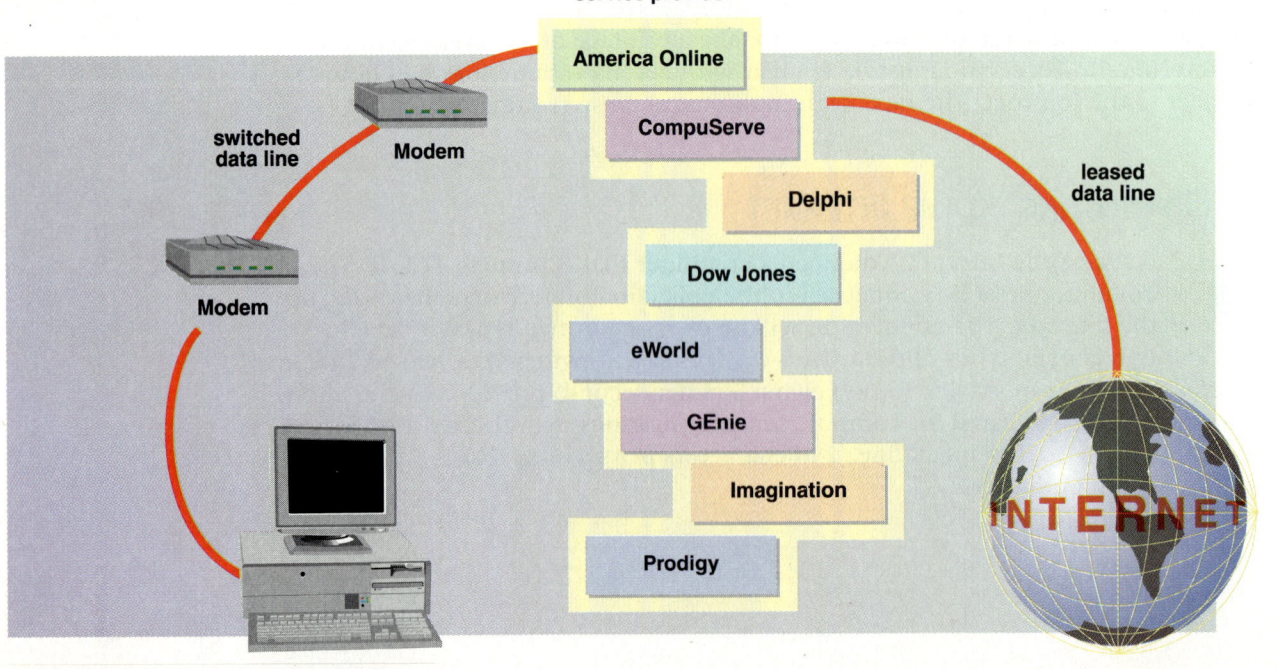

CONNECTING TO THE INTERNET **I.7**

A data line can use several different media for transferring information. The media can be **twisted pair wire**, which is a pair of copper wires much like telephone cords; **coaxial cable**, which is a heavy cable with a thick wire in the middle surrounded by a wire mesh shield; **fiber-optic cable** (Figure 1-7a), which is a thin strand of glass through which light signals travel; or **microwave** and **satellite** technologies, which use different frequencies of radio waves to transmit data. The messages and data you send and receive over the Internet probably will travel over all these different types of physical media (Figure 1-7b).

Several different possibilities for constructing a connection to the Internet are clearly apparent. The next section describes how data is sent over the Internet.

FIGURE 1-7a *A fiber-optic cable can transmit as much information as 1,500 pairs of copper wire cable.*

FIGURE 1-7b
When sending a file over the Internet from a computer in California to a computer in Florida, the data might travel over normal telephone lines (1), to a microwave tower (2 and 3), to a satellite (4 and 5), to a microwave tower again (6), and finally end up on normal telephone lines (7).

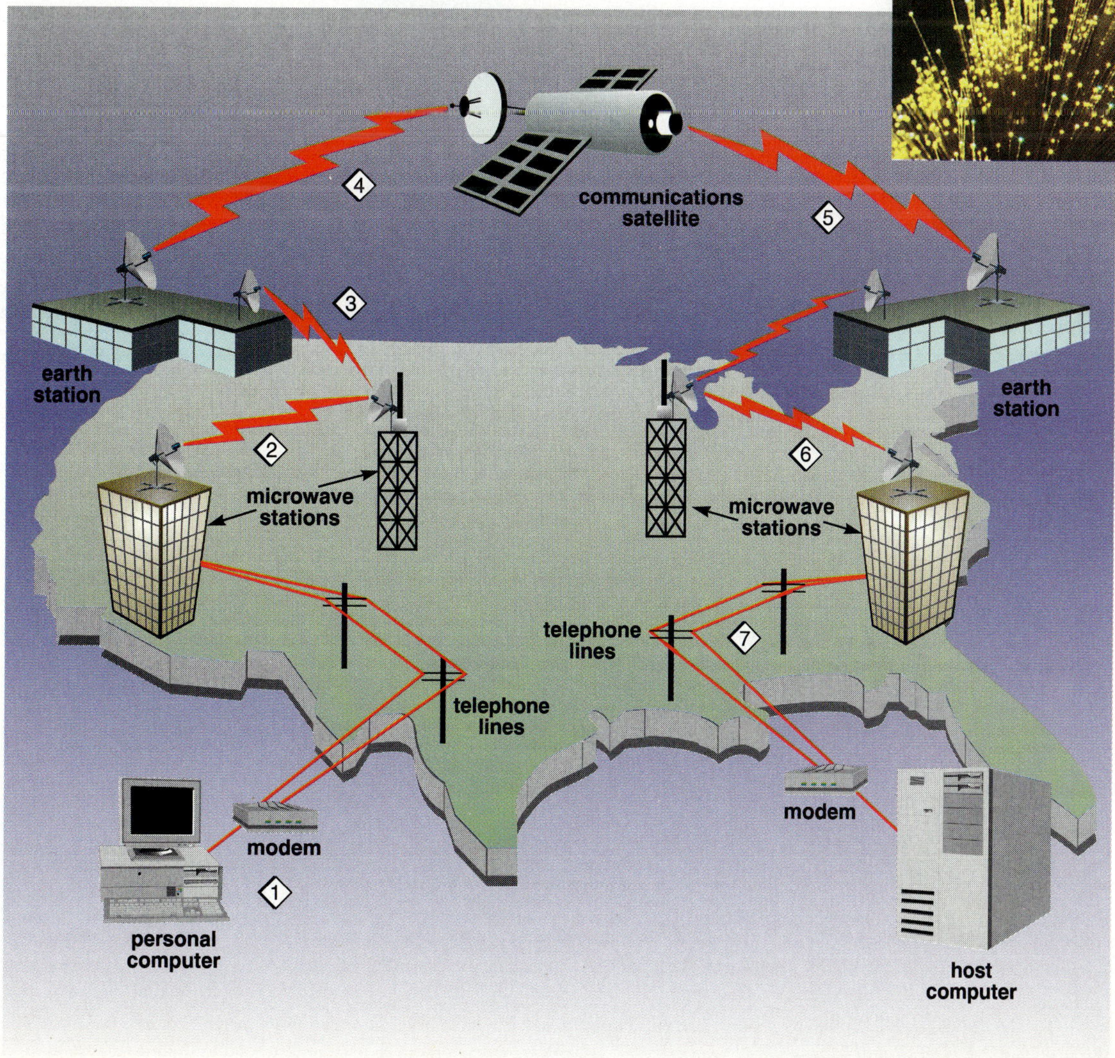

Sending Information Over the Internet

Suppose you had a file (program or data) on your computer you wanted to send over the Internet to a friend who was attending another school. How does that file get from your computer across the Internet to your friend's computer?

When you issue the command to send the file, the Internet software on the main computer (also called the **host computer**) to which you are connected, or in some cases the Internet software on your personal computer's hard disk, divides the file into small parts called **packets** (Figure 1-8). TCP/IP appends some extra information to the packet, such as source and destination computer locations and a sequence number, so the packets can be put back together in the right order at the destination computer. The packet is then sent out over the communication line. The Internet software makes the routing decisions to determine the fastest way to the destination. The process of breaking messages into small parts, transmitting them, and then reassembling the original message at the receiving end is referred to as **packet switching**.

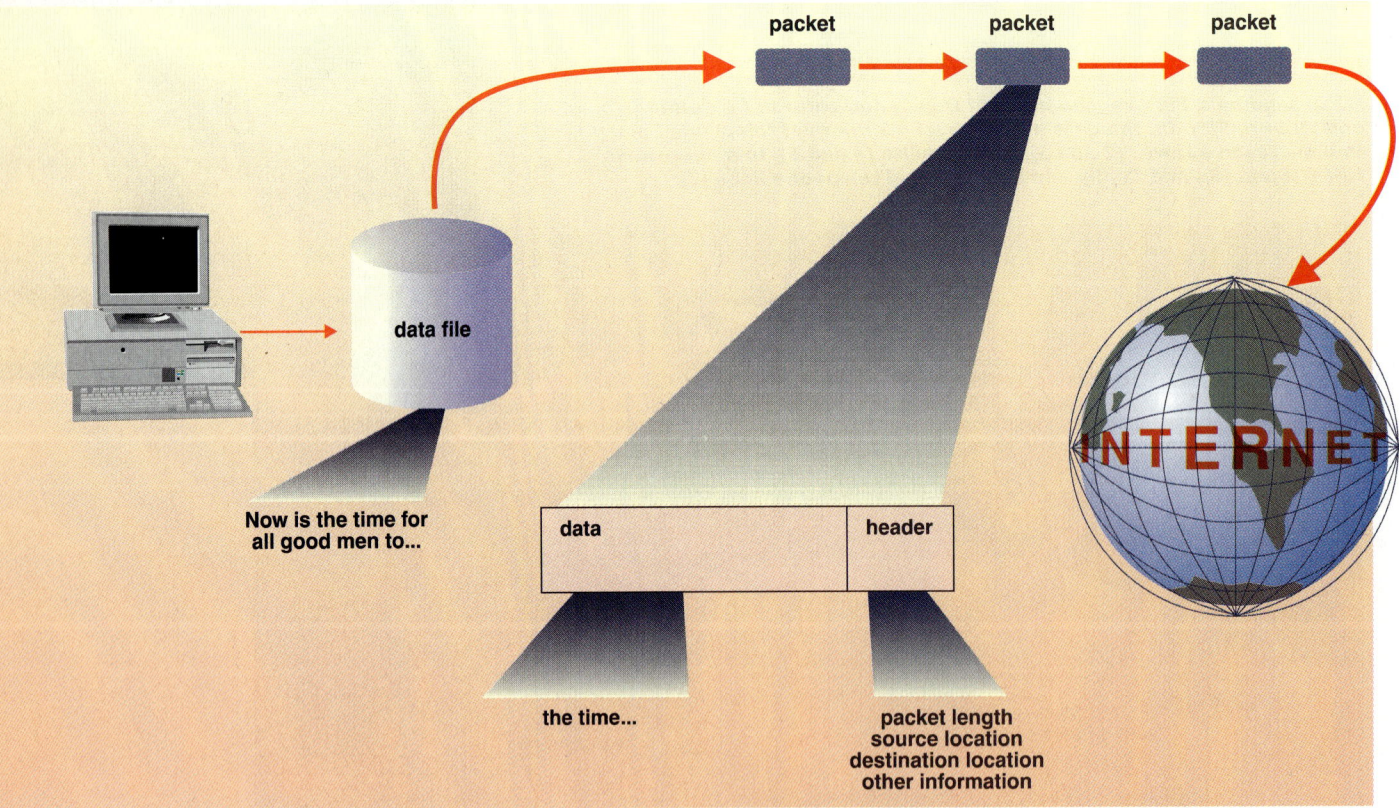

FIGURE 1-8 *In packet switching, files are divided into packets and sent over the Internet, where they are reassembled at their destinations.*

Routing

A college mainframe computer on the Internet will have the addresses of those computers on campus that are directly connected to it in a special table called a **route table**. The Internet software uses the route table (Figure 1-9) to see if it can deliver the packets directly to their destination. If not, it will use the default address where packets with addresses of computers that are not directly connected are sent. This way, the Internet software does not have to know the address of every computer on the Internet.

The computer at the default address, which serves as a gateway, will then look in its route table to determine if the destination of the packets is one of its directly connected computers. The process repeats itself until either the packets reach their destination and are reassembled or the Internet software determines the destination is invalid or unreachable. At this point, an error message indicating this problem will be received by the person who sent the file.

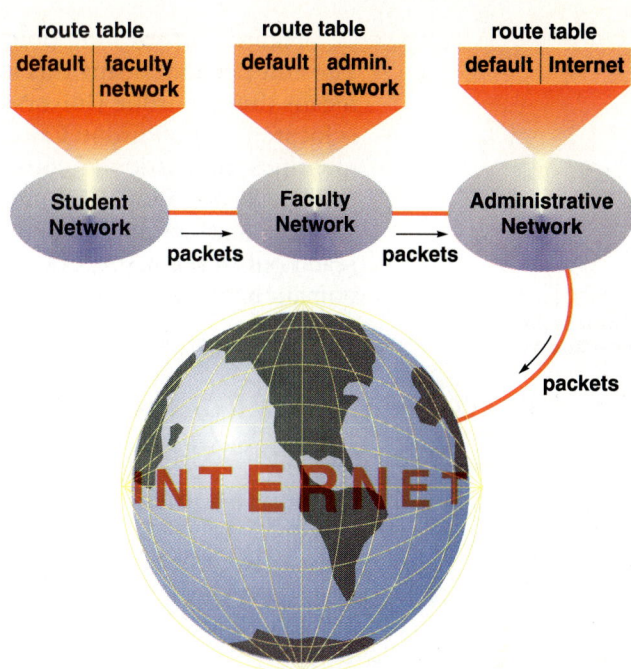

FIGURE 1-9 *Packets that cannot be delivered directly to their destination on the network are sent to the default location.*

Addressing

Each of the thousands of computers on the Internet has a unique identifier, called an **IP address**. Figure 1-10 shows this address is in the form of four groups of numbers separated by periods. Each number group ranges from 0 to 255. This format is referred to as the **dotted decimal format**.

FIGURE 1-10 *The dotted decimal Internet address is composed of four numbers separated by periods.*

Domain Naming

While computers work well with numbers, humans have a hard time remembering all but a very few dotted decimal addresses. In order to make it easier to handle Internet addresses, a technique was devised that allows a name to be associated with the address. This technique, called **domain naming**, makes it easier to navigate around the Internet by referring to computers using their domain names.

Domain naming uses a hierarchical technique to organize the hundreds of thousands of computers on the Internet. The network addresses are classified into one of a small number of groups, or top-level domains, and branch out from those domains.

The complete domain name is composed of several brief names separated by periods, or dots. A typical name begins with the highest level group, one of those listed in Figure 1-11, as the rightmost part. The name then builds to the left with that portion of the name that should uniquely identify the organization or network. Next, comes one or more names, separated by dots, that identify sub-networks, or the individual computers within the organization's network structure.

NAME	DESCRIPTION
EDU	Educational institutions
NET	Network support center
COM	Commercial organizations
MIL	U.S. military groups
GOV	U.S. government institutions
INT	International organizations
Country Codes	Individual countries

FIGURE 1-11 *Top-level Internet domain names.*

Figure 1-12 uses the domain name vaxb.calumet.purdue.edu as an example. The edu portion means this is an educational institution. The purdue portion means this is Purdue University's network. The calumet portion indicates this site is located at the Purdue Calumet campus in Hammond, Indiana. The vaxb portion identifies the particular computer at the Purdue Calumet campus, specifically, a Digital Corporation VAX computer system.

IP addresses and domain names are important because that is how you will reach out to the resources on the Internet. If you do not know the address or domain name, you cannot contact the computer on the Internet.

FIGURE 1-12
Domain name breakdown

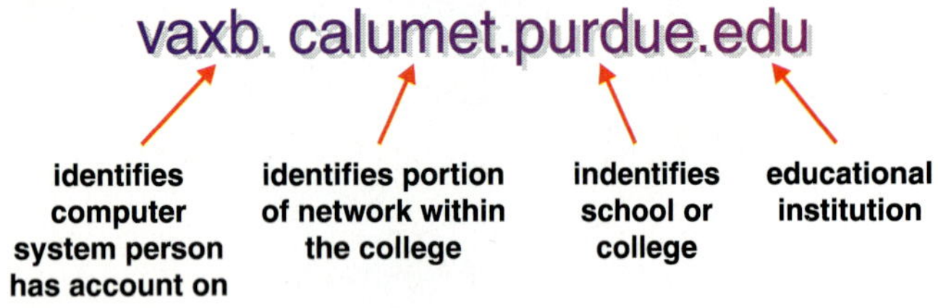

vaxb.calumet.purdue.edu

- vaxb: identifies computer system person has account on
- calumet: identifies portion of network within the college
- purdue: indentifies school or college
- edu: educational institution

Services Provided on the Internet

With an understanding of what the Internet is and how it is put together, you can begin to explore the capabilities of the Internet. The Internet provides a variety of services. Figure 1-13 shows some of the services available. These service programs are stored on the main computer to which your terminal (or personal computer) is attached, or in some cases they are stored on your personal computer's hard disk.

FIGURE 1-13
A large number of networking services and programs are available on the Internet.

SERVICE	DESCRIPTION
ARP	Displays hardware addresses for hosts
BOOTP	Supplies network address from hardware address
DOMAIN NAMING	Provides domain name services
FINGER	Displays information about a user account
FTP	Transfers files between computers over networks
HOSTNAME	Prints name of current host
KERBEROS	Provides security and user authentication
MAIL	Provides electronic mail services

SERVICE	DESCRIPTION
NFS	Provides access to remote disk storage
NETSTAT	Shows network status
NSLOOKUP	Queries Internet name servers
PING	Tests network connections
RARP	Displays hosts from hardware addresses
RCP	Remotely copies files
RDUMP	Provides networked backup facilities
REXEC	Provides remote execution services
RLOGIN	Provides remote login services
RPC	Allows programs to make remote services requests

SERVICE	DESCRIPTION
RRESTORE	Provides networked restore facilities
RSH	Provides remote shell capabilities
RUPTIME	Shows local host status
RWHO	Displays users on the network
SMTP	Mail transfer protocols
SNMP	Network management protocols
SOCKETS	Facilities for writing network programs
TELNET	Establishes a terminal session with a remote computer
TFTP	Simple file transfer facilities
WHOIS	User name directory service

SERVICES PROVIDED ON THE INTERNET I 11

You can correspond with other people on the Internet by using **electronic mail**, or **e-mail**, and transfer written documents, pictures, sound, and computer programs with **file transfer protocol**, or **FTP**. With **TELNET**, a program that establishes a terminal session with a remote, or distant, computer, you can use the computing facilities at that remote, or distant, location, which gives you the ability to run programs, attend classes, and go shopping. Doing research on remote, hard-to-access topics such as French Impressionists or the U.S. government becomes easy (Figures 1-14 and 1-15). You do not even have to leave the room (Figure 1-16). The Appendix contains several categories of popular and interesting Internet sites and the service programs used to access them.

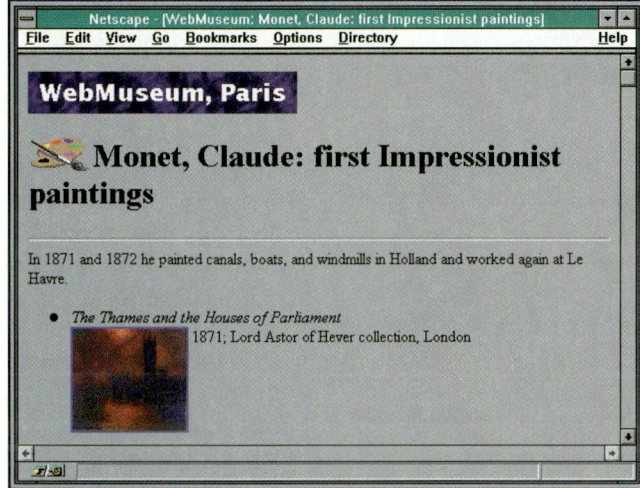

FIGURE 1-14 *French Impressionist paintings are easily accessible over the Internet.*

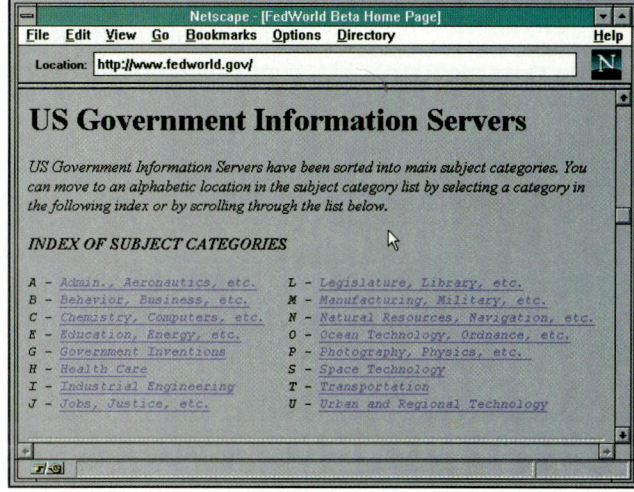

FIGURE 1-15 *The federal government has placed volumes of information online for retrieval by ordinary citizens.*

FIGURE 1-16
Access to the Internet is available in every dormitory room at some universities.

Internet Service Programs

One of the basic properties of proper communication is that a message has a sender and a receiver. As you interact with other computers on the Internet, your computer and the remote computer will alternate being the sender and the receiver. The sender will issue commands and requests. The remote computer (the receiver) will accept the requests and issue responses by becoming the sender. The receiver (previously the sender) acts on the responses. This type of interaction will continue as long as messages are being exchanged.

When you request services from a remote computer, a program, called a **demon**, exchanges messages with you. There are TELNET demons, FTP demons, and mail demons as well as others. Each demon accepts a request for service, executes a computer process to handle the request, and then waits for new requests. This exchanging of requests and responses over a network is a fundamental concept called **client/server computing** (Figure 1-17). The service programs are the server component that supply services when requested. The Internet programs you run from your computer are the clients that make requests of the service programs.

FIGURE 1-17
Client/server computing exchanges requests for services, and responses to those requests.

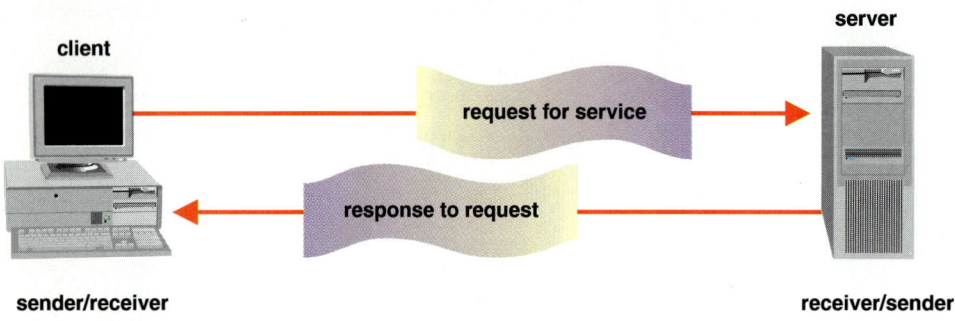

The next section explains the more important and more frequently used services, starting with electronic mail.

FIGURE 1-18
Electronic mail (e-mail) addresses have similarities to regular U.S. postal addresses, with a name and an address composed of parts that indicate where a person can be located.

Electronic Mail

Probably, the most popular service on the Internet is **electronic mail**, or **e-mail**. Using e-mail, you can converse with persons across the room or on the other side of the world.

Reaching a person who has an account on a computer on the Internet is simple. All you need to send mail is the person's account name and the Internet address (or domain name) of the computer on which he or she has an account.

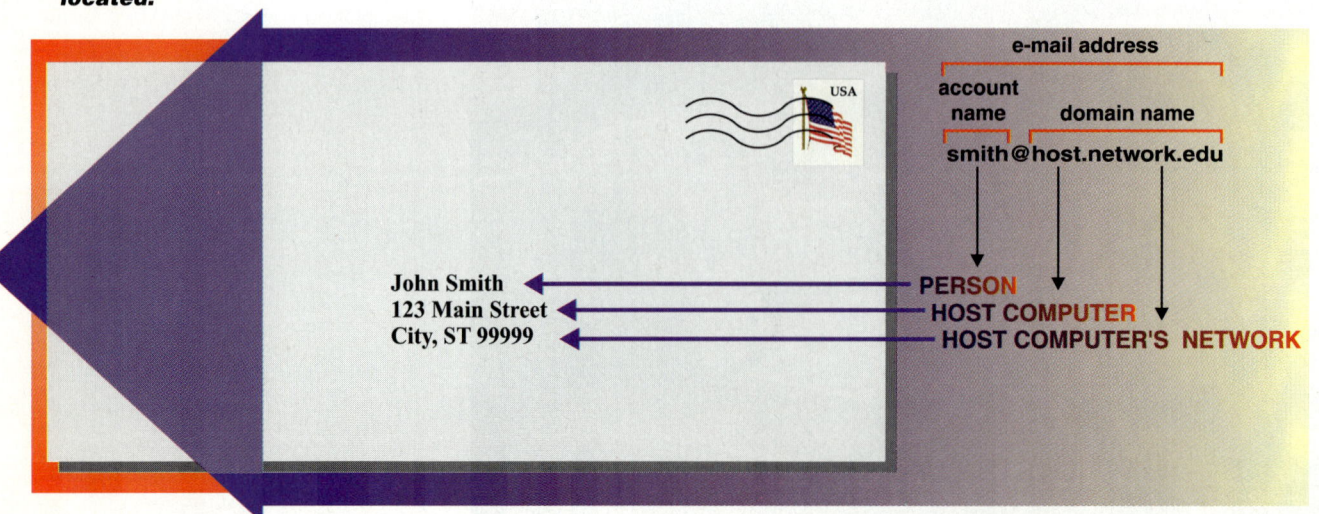

The complete **e-mail address** is the account name followed by the @ character, then the domain name where the account is located (Figure 1-18).

When sending mail, you use a special program, normally called mail, that allows you to enter the recipient's mail address, a brief one-line sentence that identifies the purpose or contents of the message, and the message itself.

Your message is then given to a mail service program that sends it over the Internet. When the message arrives at its destination, the mail service program on the destination computer stores the message in a special file using the recipient's account as the filename. This file is the **mail box** (Figure 1-19).

The messages will stay in the mail box until the receiver issues a command indicating he or she wants to read the incoming mail. The mail program will then open the mail box. The user issues mail commands to read (Figure 1-20), save, delete, reply, or otherwise manage his or her mail.

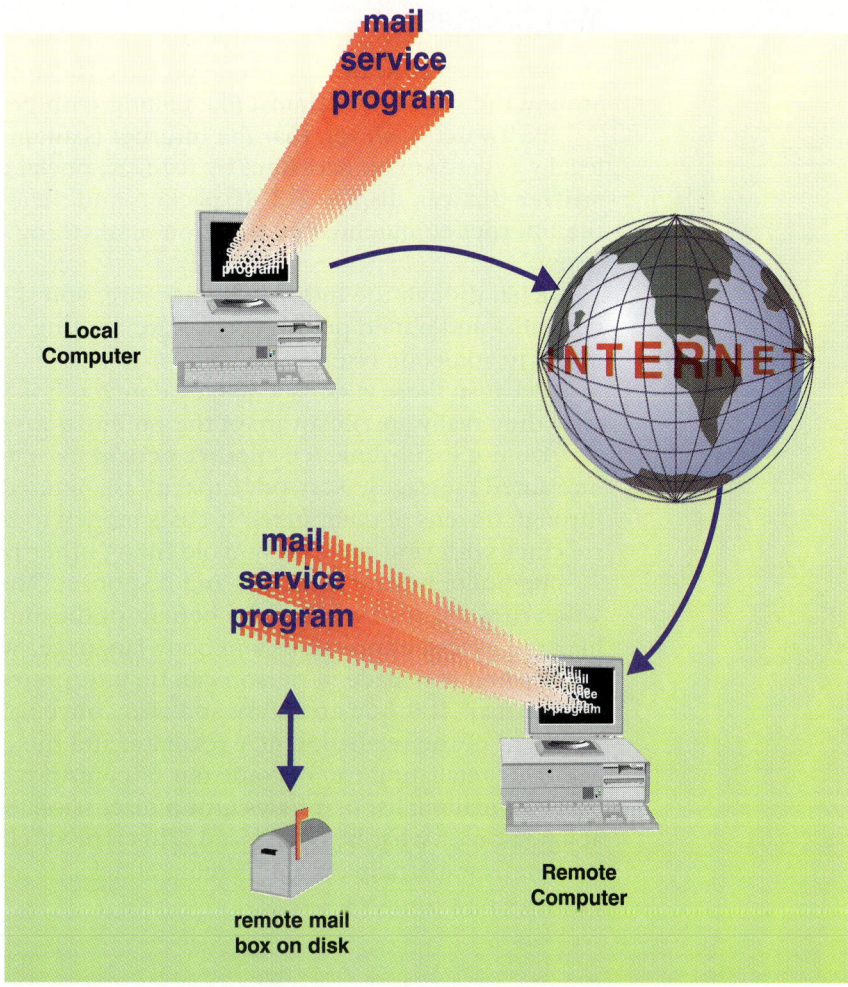

FIGURE 1-19 *The mail service program delivers mail over the Internet automatically. New mail is stored on disk in areas called electronic mail boxes.*

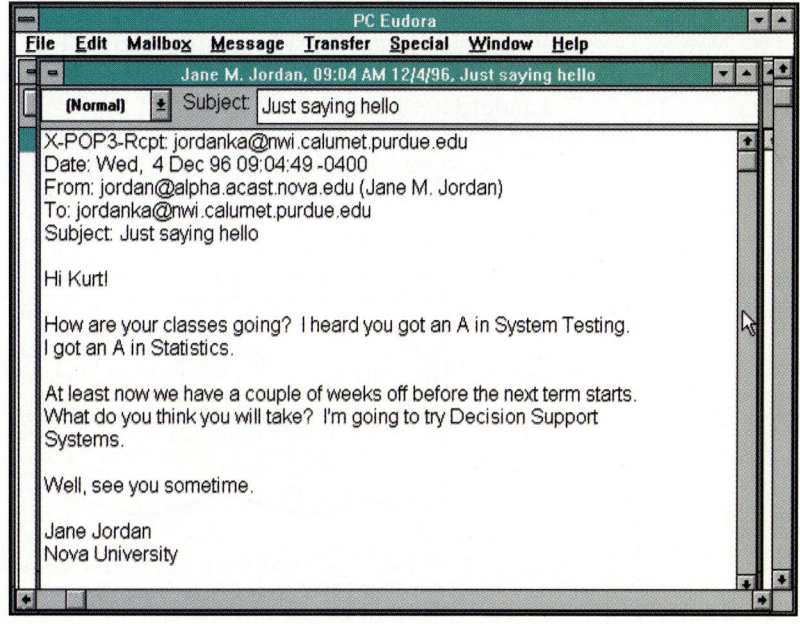

FIGURE 1-20 *Sending mail on the Internet is one of the more popular activities.*

Mail Courtesy

With access to the Internet, you have the ability to converse with others around the world. It is almost like talking with people you meet on the street.

Be aware, however, that the Internet is an unsecured medium. People can legally eavesdrop on data lines by using a special computer or a program called a **sniffer** that can display TCP/IP packets and their contents, so do not send over the Internet confidential information or anything you do not want everyone to know.

Even though the Internet is unsecure, you should still respect others' confidentiality and obtain permission before quoting what they say or forwarding their e-mail to someone else.

Because there is no face-to-face contact, it is very easy for people to disguise who they really are. Be aware of the potential for fraud or other illegal activities.

Do not inconvenience another person by sending very long or numerous unwanted messages. Network capacity is a limited resource. E-mail can travel through dozens of computers. It costs money to send and route mail. Be short and succinct with your messages. Avoid filling other people's mailboxes with garbage.

Be polite in your messages and responses. Messages can have a different tone when they are read without the benefit of the author's being there so you can see his or her facial expressions and body language. What could be a harmless statement when it is made in person can be interpreted as an attack or an insult when read as mail. It is human nature and also convenient to retaliate via e-mail. The recipient of the retaliation may retaliate, and the cycle can escalate.

This retaliation can become out of control when it is carried out in the context of a mailing list or a news group discussion. Several people send attacks aimed at a person or what he or she said. This type of electronic attack is called **flaming**. Refrain from participating in flaming attacks. It proves nothing and wastes networking resources.

Finding People Using Finger

Using a service program called **finger**, you can display information about someone else's computer account. For example, the finger program tells you whether the owner is using his or her account at the same time you enter finger. Some computer sites on the Internet will also indicate if the owner of the account has read his or her mail recently. Figure 1-21 illustrates using finger on a UNIX system to display information about a user account at Nova University in Fort Lauderdale, Florida.

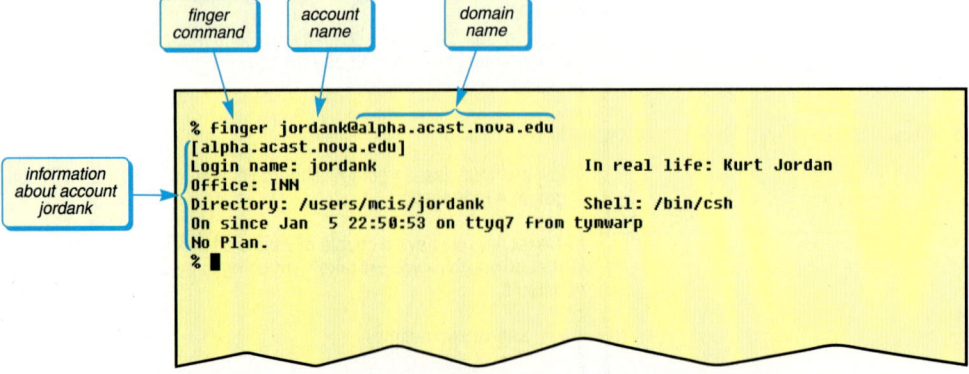

FIGURE 1-21 *Entering the finger command on a UNIX computer system returns information about a user on another computer system on the Internet.*

TELNET

TELNET is a program that allows you to start a terminal session on a remote, or distant, computer. The remote computer can be on another campus or on the other side of the world. You supply the Internet address (or domain name) of the computer you want to contact with the TELNET program.

When the connection is made, you can work on the remote computer just as if you were in the next room using a directly connected personal computer or terminal (Figure 1-22).

Figure 1-23 on the next page illustrates using TELNET in Windows. Notice the table of favorite Internet sites available to connect with TELNET. You double-click a choice, such as Legislation info on the Internet, and TELNET creates the connection. Some remote computer sites on the Internet have TELNET accounts you can use to access special resources such as university library catalogs and The Library of Congress.

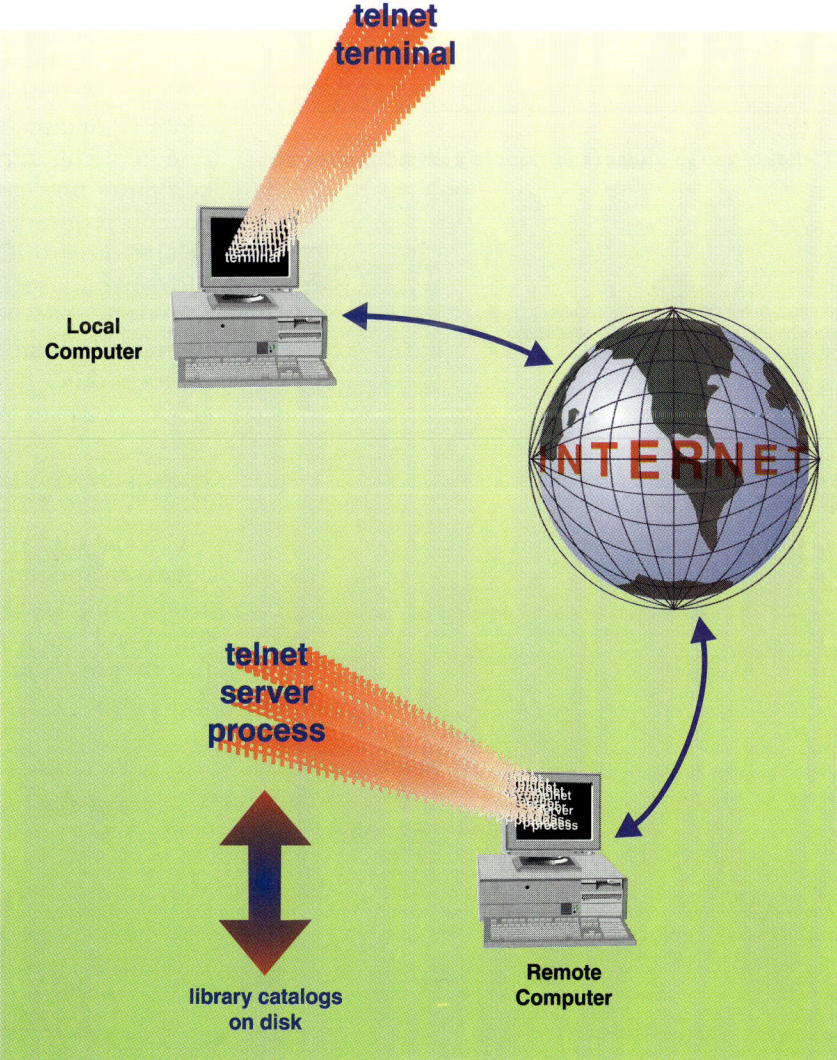

FIGURE 1-22
The TELNET service program creates a terminal connection on another computer system, allowing you to access special resources, such as university library catalogs.

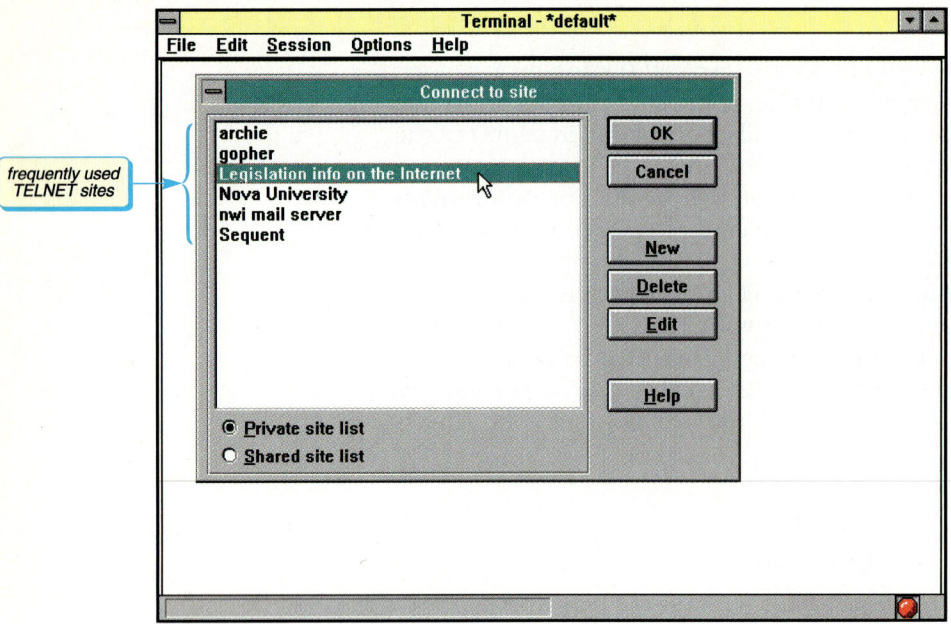

frequently used TELNET sites

FIGURE 1-23 *TELNET allows you to connect to remote computer sites on the Internet.*

File Transfer Protocol (FTP)

Another frequently used feature of the Internet is **file transfer protocol** (**FTP**), which allows you to send and receive files from one computer to another.

As with TELNET, you need the Internet address (or domain name) of the computer containing the files in which you are interested as well as the directory where they are located. You provide the address to a program called FTP, which will then contact the remote computer. The FTP demon on the remote computer starts a computer process that accepts requests from you to change directories, bring files to your computer, send files from your computer to the remote computer, and perform other functions (Figure 1-24).

Software Packing

Some files you may want access to at computer sites around the world are combined and compressed together into one file to save disk space.

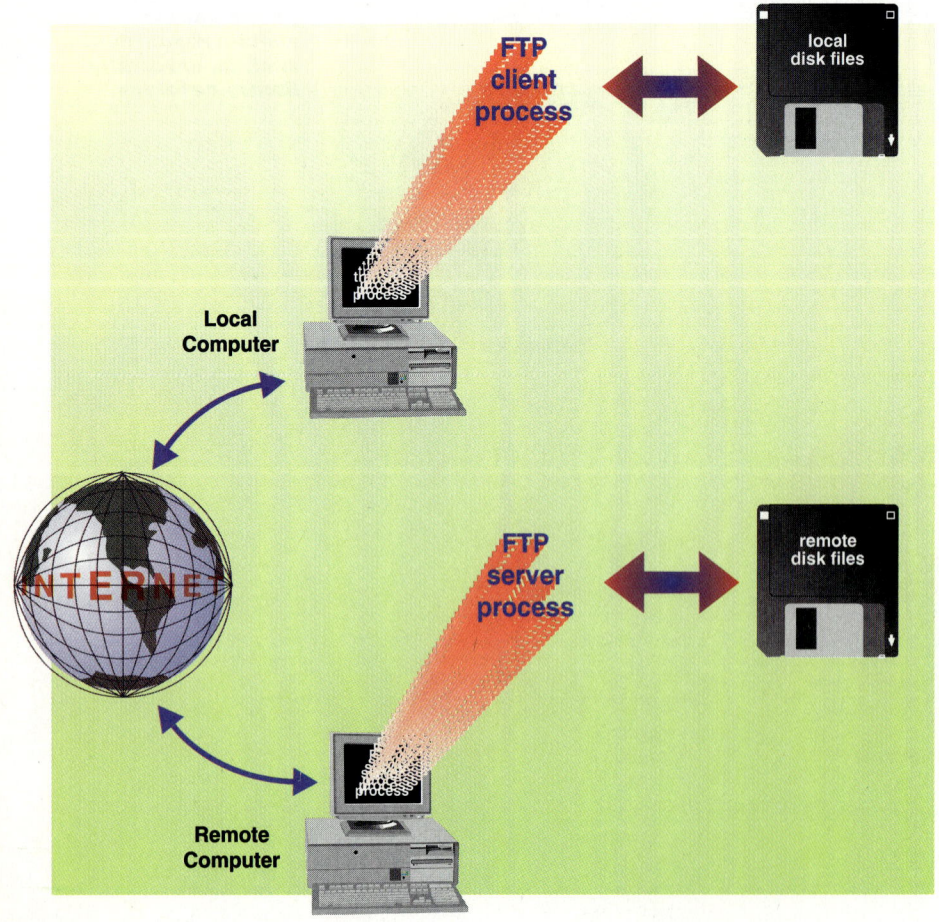

FIGURE 1-24 *Exchanging files with FTP.*

Figure 1-25 illustrates the process of using a free packaging program called **unzip** to extract the individual files from a single compressed file that contains Mosaic for Windows.

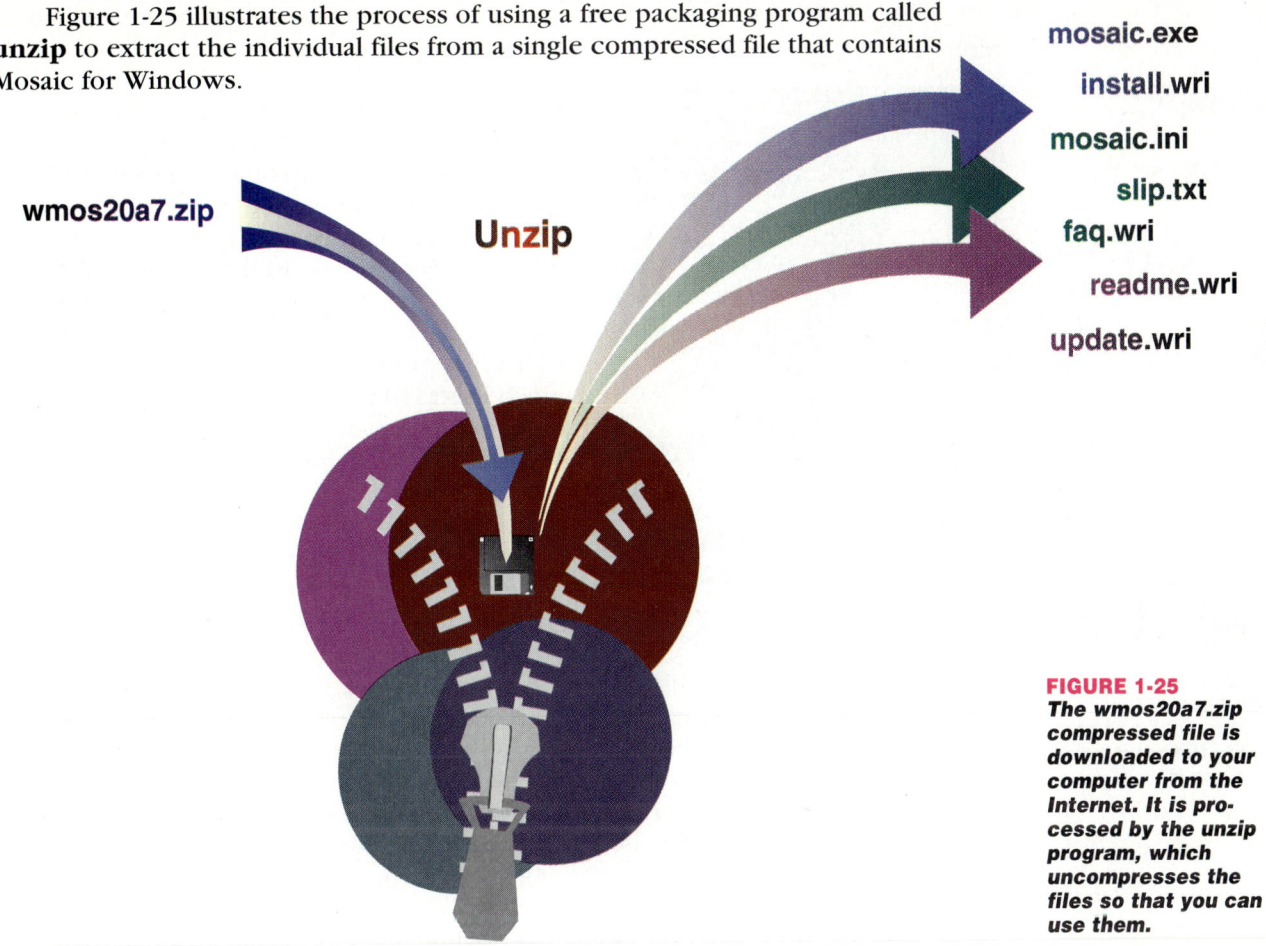

FIGURE 1-25
The wmos20a7.zip compressed file is downloaded to your computer from the Internet. It is processed by the unzip program, which uncompresses the files so that you can use them.

The names of the files you want to download usually indicate which programs are necessary to extract the individual files from the packages you get from the Internet. Figure 1-26 lists some sample files and their types.

Rights and Responsibilities

With the ability to obtain thousands of programs, text, and data files comes responsibility. Software is protected by United States **copyright** laws. This means that, just like a copyrighted book, you cannot make copies of the program to sell or give away. The author or owner of the copyright retains the rights to do those things. The four broad classifications of software are: commercial, shareware, freeware, and public domain.

Commercial software is normally purchased from a computer store, by mail order, or directly from the authors. You do not actually purchase the software. You purchase a license to use that software. A **license** is a right to use something. For the most part, the license says that the product is copyrighted, you can make one copy of the software for backup purposes, you can use only one copy of the software at a time, and lists other restrictions concerning use and liabilities. Figure 1-27 on the next page illustrates the license included with the WordPerfect software.

NAME	DESCRIPTION
archie1.4.1tar.z	Compressed UNIX tar file
readme.txt	ASCII text file
photo.zip	Zipped file
shuttle.gif	Graphical image file
manual.doc	ASCII text file
manual.ps	Postscript file

FIGURE 1-26
Some typical filenames you will find on the Internet.

Shareware can be acquired from software stores, by mail order, from someone else who has a copy, by downloading the file from a software repository, such as CompuServe or America Online, or from a computer on the Internet. The author usually retains the copyright. You may, however, make and distribute copies of the shareware to other people. You may use the shareware without charge, in order to evaluate it or determine if you want to keep it. If you decide to keep it, then normally, you send a small payment to the author or owner of the shareware product. This payment is usually much less ($10 to $35) than the cost of a similar commercial product purchased through retail outlets. You should pay for shareware if you decide to keep it. This gives the author recognition and incentive to keep up the good work. Most payments insure the user gets some small amount of technical support, a user's manual, and notification of any future upgrades, releases, or new products.

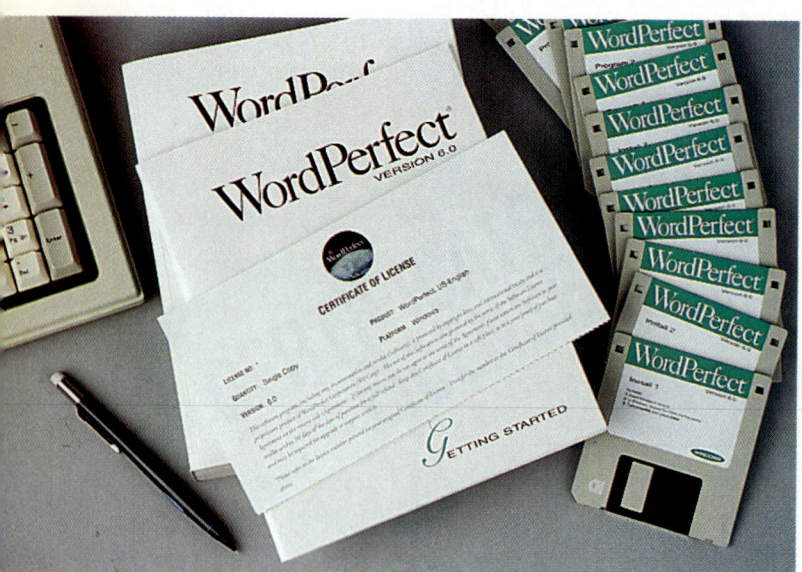

FIGURE 1-27
The license that comes with software limits the ways you can use it.

Freeware can be acquired from many of the same sources as shareware. The author may or may not retain the copyright. This type of software can be readily copied and distributed to others. You are allowed to use the software at no charge. One popular restriction to distributing freeware is that a special README file or other informational file that recognizes the author is to be included with all copies.

The last general category of software is called **public domain software**. You may read about or hear someone talking about software that is in the public domain. The author usually has given up the copyright and declares the software is public domain. No restrictions apply to copying, distributing, and using public domain software.

Be aware of the type of software you are using. Respect the copyright laws and the wishes of the author. Do not illegally make copies of and distribute commercial software. Pay for shareware software you decide to keep. Failure to do these things deprives the owner of recognition and revenue, can cause legal problems for the institution you attend or the business you work for, and is against the law.

▶ **TABLE 1-1**

TOOL NAME	PURPOSE
archie	Allows you to search for filenames and display the Internet address of host computers and directory paths of those filenames. Use when the Internet site containing the file is unknown. Retrieves no files.
gopher	Allows you to search and retrieve files, like FTP, but using a menu-driven user interface.
veronica	Allows you to perform a search for filenames, similar to archie, but from within gopher. Use when you want to use gopher to retrieve a file when the filename is unknown.
WAIS	Allows you to retrieve text documents by searching the contents of documents for key words you type. Displays a list of documents containing the key words and mails the document you choose.
News groups	Allows you to participate in discussions on thousands of interesting topics. Requires a news reader program and access to a news group host computer site.
Mailing lists	Allows you to participate in discussions on thousands of interesting topics. Messages are sent and read using electronic mail.
Internet relay chat (IRC)	Allows you to engage in live conversations with other people on the Internet.

▶ **INTERNET TOOLS**

Just as graphical interfaces such as Microsoft Windows were developed to make the computer easier to use for the average person, tools were developed to make using the Internet easier. Table 1-1 summarizes the Internet tools and their purposes.

Archie

The Internet is made up of hundreds of thousands of computers, with thousands of files on each one. How do you know where to go to find what you are looking for?

Some Internet sites have set up special software, called an **archie server**, that accepts search requests in the form of a string of characters. This character string is the whole or partial name of the file you are looking for. Figure 1-28 illustrates an archie search for files with the character string calculus in their names.

Archie performs the search and returns the Internet addresses and the directory paths of the files whose names contain the character string. You can then use FTP to retrieve the file. There are several ways you can search with archie. The easiest way is to ask for an exact match of a character string you provide.

The archie server performs its search on lists of filenames and their locations on host computers on the Internet. These lists are refreshed on a regular basis in an effort to keep up to date. Not everything on the Internet will be in the lists. That would require too much disk space. This means that archie sites keep only a limited number of files and a limited number of locations of these files in their lists. The number of filenames in the archie lists is very large, however.

There will be times you will not find what you are looking for. That does not mean a file does not exist, it just means that it is not in the set of lists for that archie server.

Having to know the name of the file you are searching for can be somewhat of a disadvantage. If you are searching for software about calculus and do not know the names of any files that contain calculus software, searching for the string calculus may not return anything, even though there may be several programs dealing with calculus in the archie lists. Archie can help you by providing a short description of a file using a command called whatis. Figure 1-29 shows an example of using the whatis command. The figure shows that although the word calculus returned no matches, the word math returned several possibilities.

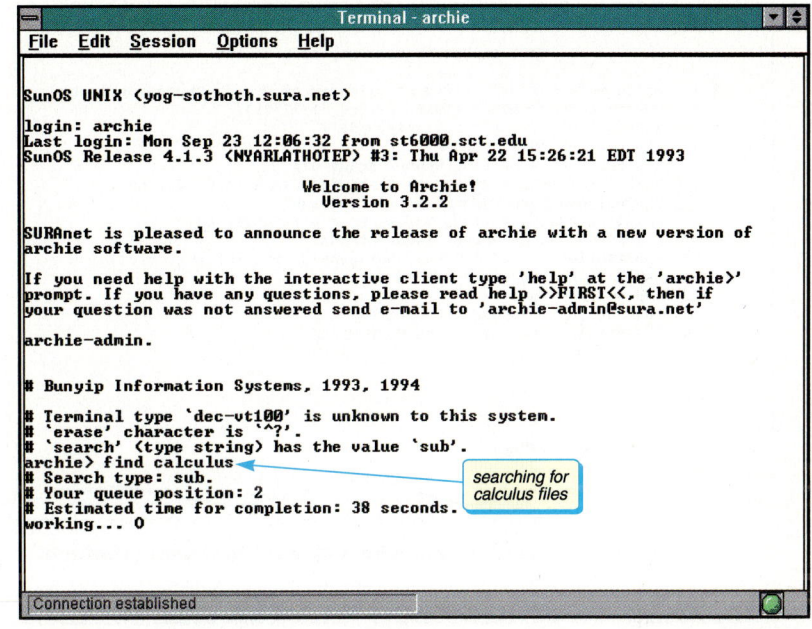

FIGURE 1-28 *Archie helps you find files when you do not know their location on the Internet.*

FIGURE 1-29 *Archie can display a brief description of files in its lists with the whatis command.*

Gopher

Initially developed by the University of Minnesota to help its users find answers to local computing questions, gopher has since developed into a world-wide service that helps organize the vast collection of information available on the Internet.

Gopher started out as a document retrieval system. Over time, it has been modified to serve as a user-friendly, menu-driven way of retrieving files over the Internet.

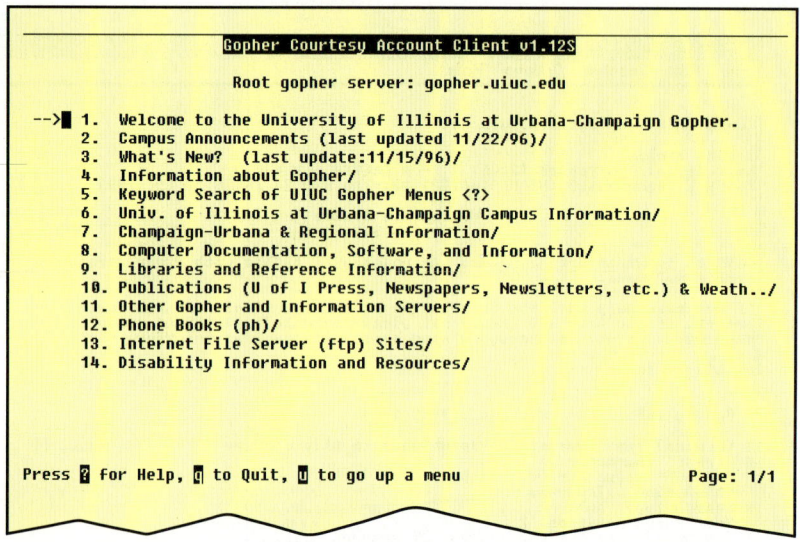

FIGURE 1-30 *Gopher presents you with a menu-driven user interface.*

Once connected to a gopher server, you will be presented with a hierarchy of menus through which you will page forward and backward to find what you are interested in. Figure 1-30 shows the main menu that displays when you start a gopher session. Just indicate the file you want by moving the arrow on the left side of the screen to your choice, press the ENTER key, and gopher will send it to you. Figure 1-31 illustrates using gopher to retrieve a file. You type in the electronic mail address where you want the file sent and gopher will mail it.

Any computer site on the Internet can run a gopher server. The collection of gopher servers has been referred to as **Gopher-Space**, and as the **Gopher Web**. This is because gophers can be linked together, so you can reach other gopher servers containing items that are not stored on the server to which you are currently connected. You will use gopher in Project 2 to retrieve files.

Veronica

Just as archie performs a search of its lists of files, veronica performs a search of GopherSpace. **Veronica** is used within gopher to allow you to quickly find files and retrieve them.

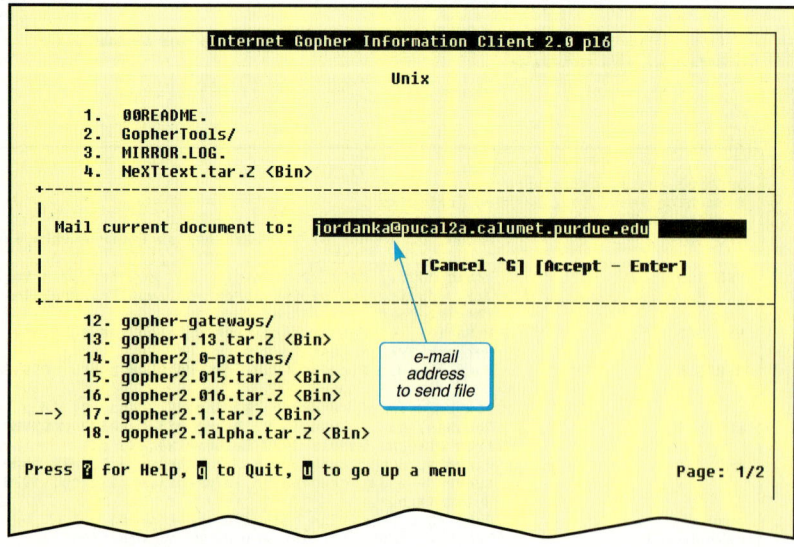

FIGURE 1-31 *Gopher can mail files to you.*

You type in a filename and veronica will return a list of menu items that point to those filenames. This lessens the time considerably to search through numerous gopher servers looking for files. Figure 1-32 illustrates setting up a veronica search for archie software. The filename ARCHIE was typed in and veronica will perform the search.

Most gopher servers have veronica search capabilities as one of their menu choices. You will use veronica in Project 2.

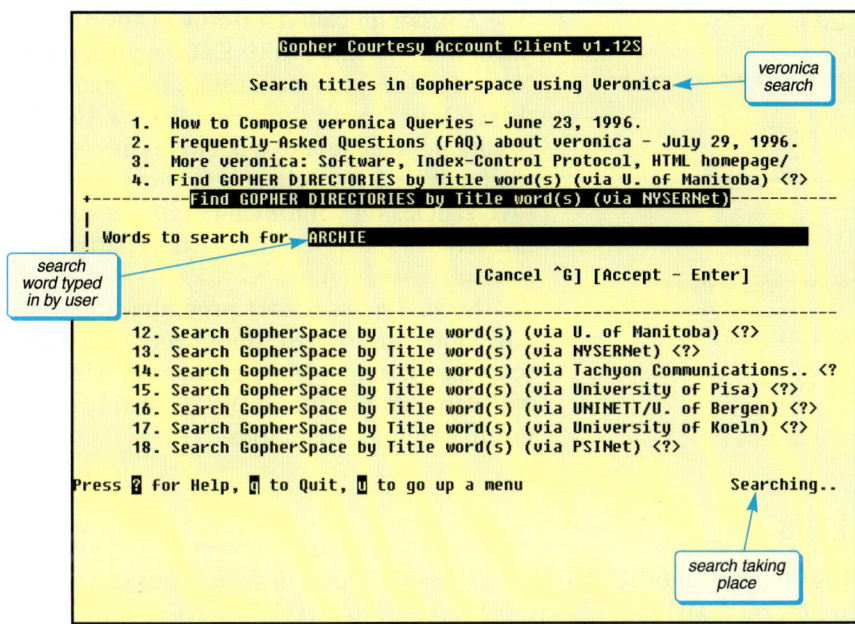

FIGURE 1-32 *Just like archie, veronica can perform a filename search.*

News Groups

It is human nature for people with similar interests to be drawn together to discuss and share their thoughts, information, opinions, and research. Sometimes, people form clubs or discussion groups where they can talk and exchange ideas about their mutual interests.

A very large number of electronic discussion groups called **news groups** are available on the Internet. You can post, or send to the news group your thoughts and opinions about a particular topic, and read what other people have to say. The articles that accumulate on a particular topic are called a **thread**.

There are news groups on vendor products such as Novell, Microsoft, IBM, and UNIX, on subjects such as recipes, gardening, punk rock, or on just about any topic you can think of. Figure 1-33 contains a small list of the thousands of news groups available on the Internet. The discussion topics are organized into broad categories, some of which are listed in Figure 1-34 on the next page.

A news group name will begin with one of these category names, followed by one or more words that narrow down the main topic of the group. The news group comp.lang.pascal in Figure 1-33, for example, is a group interested in computers. The group further limits discussions to programming languages, specifically, Pascal. You will find miscellaneous agricultural issues discussed in the alt.agriculture.misc news group.

comp.lang.c
comp.lang.c++
comp.lang.fortran
comp.lang.pascal
alt.3d
alt.abuse.recovery
alt.activism
alt.agriculture.misc
alt.alien.vistors
alt.hotrod
misc.forsale
rec.games.video
rec.sport.boxing
sci.space
sci.virtual-worlds

FIGURE 1-33
Thousands of news groups exist on the Internet. This is just a small sample.

FIGURE 1-34
News group prefixes.

NAME	DESCRIPTION
comp	Computer topics
alt	Alternative discussion groups
biz	Business groups
gnu	GNU software foundation groups
ieee	Electrical engineering groups
info	Information about topics
misc	Miscellaneous topics
news	Groups pertaining to news
rec	Recreational topics
sci	Scientific topics
talk	Discussion groups

USENET is the term used to describe the collection of computer sites that has agreed to share and forward the thousands of discussion groups. When an article is posted to a news group on one system, it will be duplicated throughout USENET, with each participating computer site eventually getting a copy of the article. Some news group computer sites may have groups of local interest, campus events, or course tutoring, for example.

A program called a **news reader** allows users to participate in USENET news groups. News readers provide a useful command-driven interface to the news groups. Using the program, you can move between news groups, read new articles, follow a particular thread, save articles on your local computer, and submit articles for other news group participants to read.

Several news reader programs are available. Some are rn, trn, tin, or nn on UNIX systems and Trumpet news reader for Windows. Netscape, an Internet browser, also has news group reading capabilities.

Mailing Lists

Mailing lists are another form of discussion group in which you can participate on the Internet. Mailing lists are very similar to USENET news groups, but instead of using a news reader program to access articles, mailing list messages are delivered and read using electronic mail. There are thousands of mailing lists maintained on computers all over the Internet. Project 2 describes procedures to obtain information on mailing lists.

Mailing lists work using a very simple technique. When sending mail, you can send electronic carbon copies to other people. Mailing lists take this concept and automate it. This is achieved by combining the concept of e-mail carbon copies with special software called a **listserv**. The listserv program is responsible for receiving new mailing list messages and automatically sending those messages to all the people who belong to the list.

The listserv program requires that you indicate your desire to join the mailing list. To join a mailing list, you send your request, along with your e-mail address to the special listserv account at the Internet address where the list is maintained. This is called **subscribing**.

This special listserv account is different from the list account where current participants send their messages. This is to prevent subscription requests from being sent to all the current list participants. The account that manages requests for participation in the list is called listserv. The name of the account where messages are submitted is usually some short, indicative name ending with -L. Several lists can be handled by a single listserv program. Figure 1-35 contains a sample of some mailing lists and their topics at the University of Stony Brook, one of the many computer centers on the Internet that manages mailing lists. Some of the mailing lists managed by the Stony Brook listserv program are ESE-L, which is a list interested in expert systems, PHIL285, which is a list about a philosophy course, and BSLN-L, which is a list for black student leaders.

Several reasons why you would want to subscribe to a mailing list are: (1) you want to see what other people are saying about a topic; (2) you are interested in what is currently state of the art concerning that topic; (3) you need help or want to find out about any problems concerning a topic; (4) you are doing research; and (5) you are just plain curious.

Use care when you subscribe to mailing lists. You should not subscribe to as many lists as you find interesting. Some lists generate large amounts of mail and your mailbox can quickly become overloaded with hundreds of messages if you subscribe to too many lists. Most of the messages would probably go unread because you would tire of spending most of your day going through them.

You should temporarily suspend participation in, or terminate the subscriptions to your lists when you go on vacation, or will not read your mail for a period of time. Terminate your subscription when your account will be deleted from the computer system. Otherwise, the listserv program will keep trying to deliver messages to your account. These messages take up disk space. The system administrator would have to delete your mail and request your removal from the list. It is your responsibility to do these things.

```
AFFNET     -Affirmative Action Officers mailing list
ALLIN1-L   ALL-IN-1 Managers and Users mailing list.
BSLN-L     Black Student Leadership Network
CLASS-L    Classification, clustering, and phylogeny estimation
COMPWYNY   Composition Classes in Wyoming and New York
CSSA-L     -University at Stony Brook Chinese Student Scholar Association
DECRDB-L   Oracle Rdb (formerly DEC Rdb) Mailing list.
ESE-L      Expert Systems Environment mailing list.
FISHNET    Fiber-based Island-wide Super High-speed NETwork
HIS393     Stony Brook HIS393 Discussion List
IEEETCPC   -IEEE Technical Committee on Personal Communications
I3ECON     Innovation in Instruction of Economics
MNYACW-L   Metropolitan New York Alliance for Computers and Writing
NPY-L      -NPY Discussion list
ORACLE-L   ORACLE database mailing list.
PHIL285    Philosophy 285 List
POLYSEM    Philosophy Seminar
PROFNET    PROFNET mailing list.
SBIEEE-L   SUNY/Stony Brook IEEE Local Chapter
SBPC-L     SUNY/Stony Brook PC Interest Group
SBSTAT-L   SUNY/Stony Brook Statistical Software Interest Group
SBSUPER    Stony Brook Supercomputer Mailing list
SBSWE-L    Society of Women Engineers - Student Section at SUNY Stony Brook
SBWISE     Stony Brook Women in Science and Engineering Program
SBWISEHS   Stony Brook Women in Science and Engineering High School Program
SOC303-L   SOC 303 Course
THR10101   Stony Brook THR101-01 Discussion List
THR10102   Stony Brook THR101-02 Discussion List
WIPSE      Stony Brook Women in Physical Science and Engineering Organization
WNS699     Stony Brook WNS699 Discussion List
```

[list name] [list topic]

FIGURE 1-35 *These are just a few of the many mailing lists available on the Internet.*

WAIS

If you wanted to know about bonsai, are doing research on the national debt, or need information on any other subject, how can you find information about it on the Internet?

Documents dealing with almost anything you can imagine are available on the Internet, but finding the ones that deal with your interests poses a problem. WAIS was developed to help solve this problem.

WAIS (Wide Area Information Service) is a search tool that helps to locate and retrieve documents on the Internet. Unlike gopher and archie, which search for the filename only, WAIS searches the contents of documents for search words that you type, and then it displays, ranked in order by a special score, any documents it finds. The score is based on whether the search words appear in the title of the document, their frequency in the document, and other criteria. WAIS can search multiple databases of documents simultaneously and have documents sent to you. WAIS will search only those documents that are available to it. This means that not every document on the Internet will be accessible.

Figure 1-36 shows the results of searching for the word Vietnam. The score column contains a value indicating the amount of certainty that the document contains what you are searching for, with 1000 being the highest possible score. Notice the highlighted line contains a score of 1000. This means that WAIS is confident this document contains something that would interest you. The document is displayed by pressing the SPACEBAR.

FIGURE 1-36 *WAIS search facilities help narrow down a topic.*

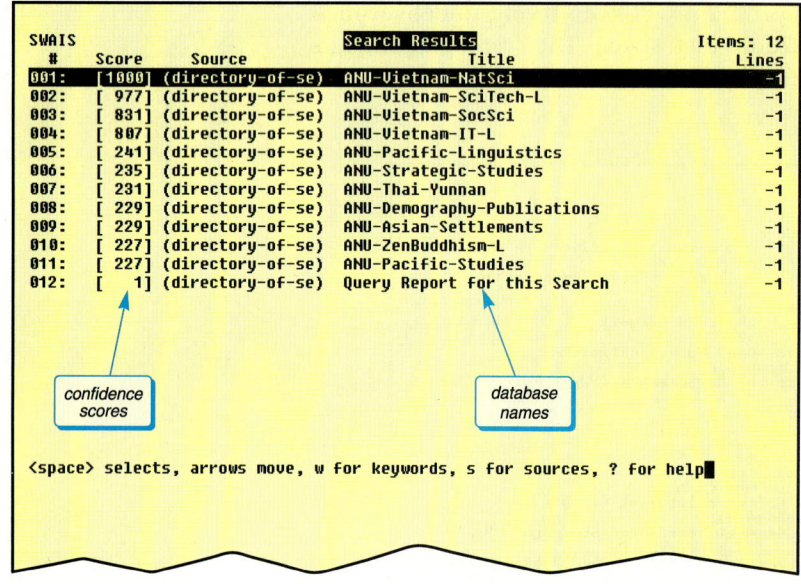

Internet Relay Chat

Although they provide a way to converse with people from around the world, the messages and articles from electronic mail and news groups are somewhat old when you read them. They take some time to arrive and stay in your mail box or in the news group repository until you issue commands to read them.

There is a way to talk live, directly online to people all over the world. It is called **Internet relay chat**, or **IRC**. Internet relay chat is like a computerized party-line, with everyone reading other people's comments, and typing their own comments for everyone else to see, all in the time it takes to transmit the packets over the Internet and display them on a participant's terminal screen.

Internet relay chat can have hundreds of people all trying to converse at the same time. Fortunately, just as USENET organizes topics into news groups, IRC organizes conversation topics into groups called **channels**. You can join existing channels and take part in the on-going conversation there, or create your own, new channel. Even with this attempt at organization, conversations can easily get disorganized as the number of people on a channel increases. Figure 1-37 shows a sample conversation occurring on an IRC channel called #chatzone.

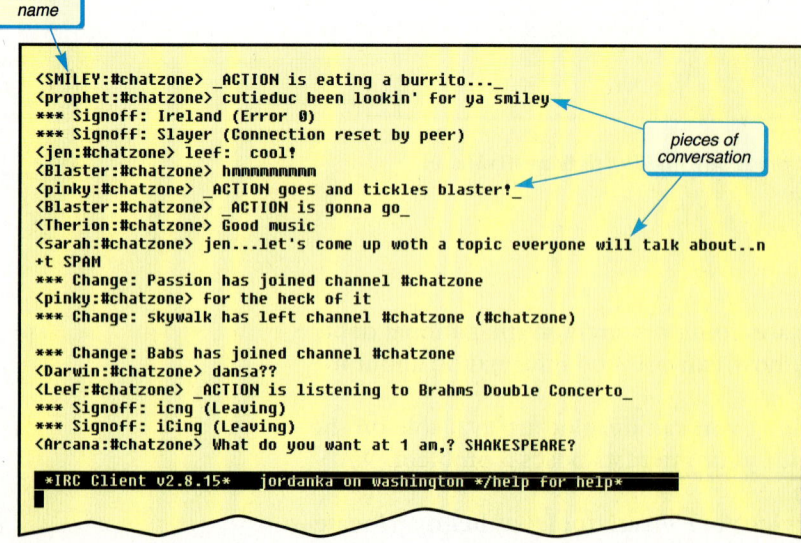

FIGURE 1-37 *Internet relay chat, or IRC, lets you carry on live conversations over the Internet.*

▶ WORLD WIDE WEB

Suppose you are reading *Great Expectations* by Charles Dickens and come upon a word you do not understand. You have to stop reading, get a dictionary, look up the word, then reread the sentence or paragraph in which it appears so you can understand the author's meaning. This takes time and is distracting, but necessary to understand the author's intentions.

If the Dickens novel were stored on a computer, however, you could possibly click the word with the mouse, and a little window would appear with the definition and perhaps a picture. The definition also may contain a word you do not know, so you can click that word and its definition will appear. Then, you click a special place in the definition window and it disappears, letting you return to your reading. This concept already exists. It is called **hypermedia** and is used extensively with CD-ROM technology.

Hypermedia works by specifying certain words or pictures as **anchors**. The anchors contain links to other text, pictures, or sound. These other text and pictures can, in turn, have anchors embedded in them. This hypermedia concept has been put to use on the Internet in the form of hypertext. **Hypertext** is a non-linear method of presenting and reading information. When you read a printed book, you usually start at the beginning and read it all the way through to the end. You went through the book in a straight line fashion. This is referred to as linear text. Hypertext allows you to jump around in a non-linear fashion. You can go straight to the section of the document in which you are most interested. Computers make hypertext easy to implement.

Special characters and commands, called **HTML**, or **hypertext markup language**, are interspersed with, and surround the text making up a hypertext document. HTML indicates how the text will be formatted. Special HTML anchors contain the locations of other resources that are to be accessed when clicked with the mouse. You can identify an anchor because the mouse pointer will change shapes when positioned over it. Figure 1-38 shows the mouse pointer shape when moved over an anchor.

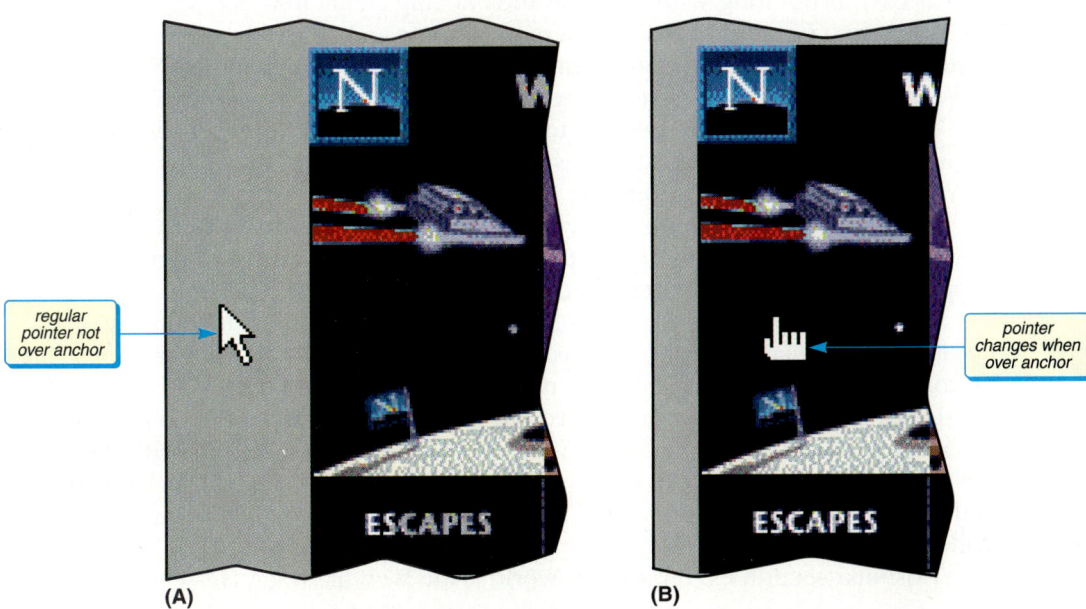

FIGURE 1-38 *The mouse pointer shape (A) changes to a little hand when moved over an anchor (B).*

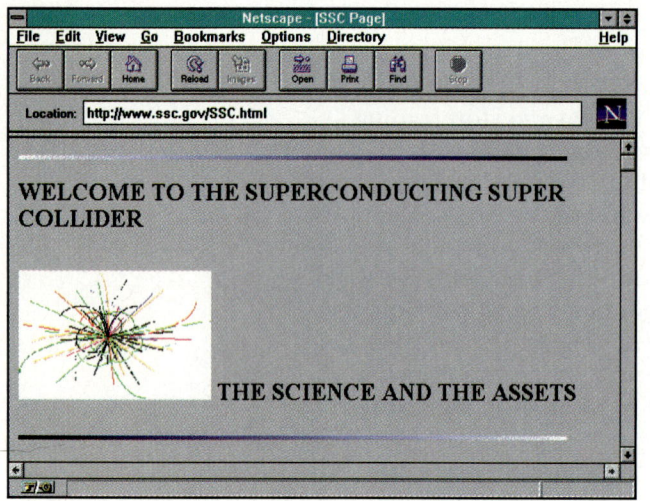

FIGURE 1-39 *Internet browsers such as Netscape are used to display hypertext documents.*

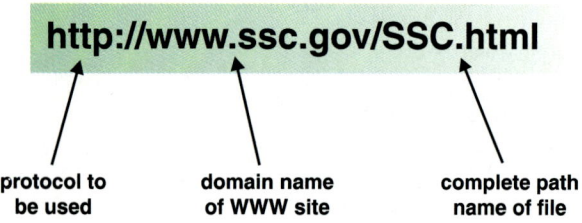

FIGURE 1-40 *The anatomy of a URL.*

These other resources can be text files, pictures, video clips, sound clips, or other HTML documents. The beauty of hypertext is that these resources do not have to be stored on the same computer. With a special program called an Internet **browser**, they can be retrieved from any computer on the Internet. Figure 1-39 shows how a hypertext document looks when displayed with Netscape, a popular Internet browser program. Netscape will be described later in the project.

The hypertext anchors contain **Universal Resource Locators (URL)**. Pronounced "you are ell," URLs contain information such as what protocol to use for handling a file, the host computer address, and the directory path of a filename. Figure 1-40 illustrates the URL for the hypertext document in Figure 1-39.

Recall that the resource associated with an anchor can be another hypertext document. In fact, most of the hypertext documents on the Internet contain links to other hypertext documents on other computer systems. These collections of hypertext links throughout the Internet create an interconnected network of links. This network of links is called the **World Wide Web (WWW)**. The World Wide Web is a great research tool. Using the hypertext links, related information is organized together for easy retrieval and viewing. You do not have to search blindly around several remote computer systems looking for information on a topic.

Internet browser programs were created to make accessing the World Wide Web as easy as pointing with a mouse and clicking an anchor. Figures 1-41 and 1-42 show two popular browser programs: Mosaic and Netscape. Mosaic was developed by the National Center for SuperComputing Applications (NCSA). Netscape was developed by Netscape Communications Corporation.

The browsers use client/server techniques, so you use Internet resources only if you click a hypertext link, and those resources are limited to the time necessary to transport the linked file from one computer to another.

There are no main menus or any particular starting points in the World Wide Web. You can jump in anywhere you wish by specifying a URL to open. Most people start with special hypertext documents called home pages.

A **home page** is typically the starting point for a World Wide Web site. Because of this, many sites try to make their home page as spectacular as possible by combining eye-catching graphics and specially formatted text.

Links from the home page take you to additional resources the computer site makes available over the World Wide Web. If you have a local World Wide Web server available, you can make your own home page using HTML language, graphics, sound, and text and make it available for others to view using a World Wide Web browser.

This next section examines one World Wide Web browser, Netscape.

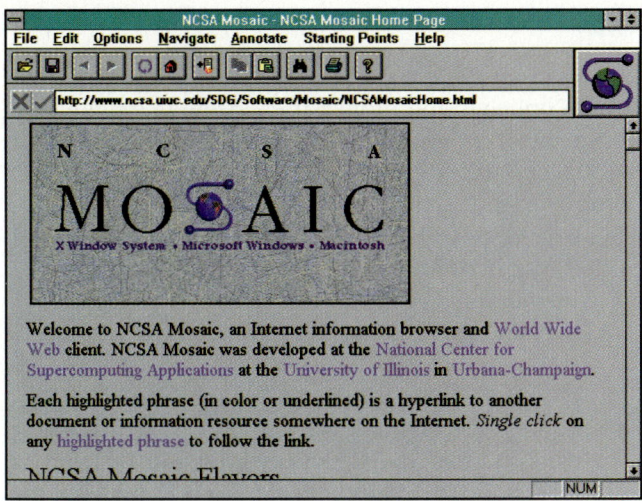

FIGURE 1-41 *Mosaic was one of the first Internet browser programs.*

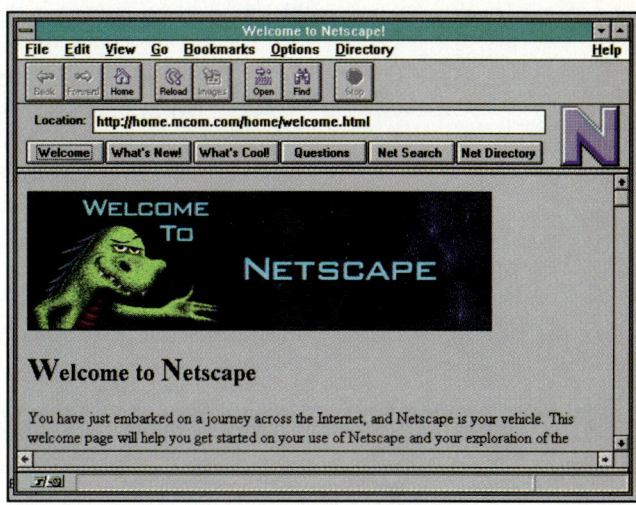

FIGURE 1-42 *Netscape utilized the best features of Mosaic and added more.*

Netscape

When you browse through a book, you glance through it looking for something of interest. Internet **browsers** allow you to use a graphical interface to look at the many hypertext documents on host computers around the world. One such browser is called Netscape.

Netscape is available from Netscape Communications Corporation. It provides graphical display of plain and formatted text, hypertext, in-line access to graphs, images, audio and video clips, and multimedia and hypermedia documents. It has hypertext, FTP, TELNET, WAIS, news reader, gopher, archie, and limited electronic mail support.

Documents and files retrieved with Netscape can be stored or printed. Cut and paste is supported. Navigation and history tracking facilities are available, and you can create and save hotlists of interesting documents. **Hotlists** allow you to retrieve your favorite documents without having to remember where they are located on the Internet. Figure 1-43 shows a drop-down menu containing choices of interesting and useful Internet sites.

Although Netscape does not, at least for now, provide two-way communication (you cannot receive electronic mail using Netscape), the Netscape Communications Corporation is still working on enhancing Netscape as new releases become available.

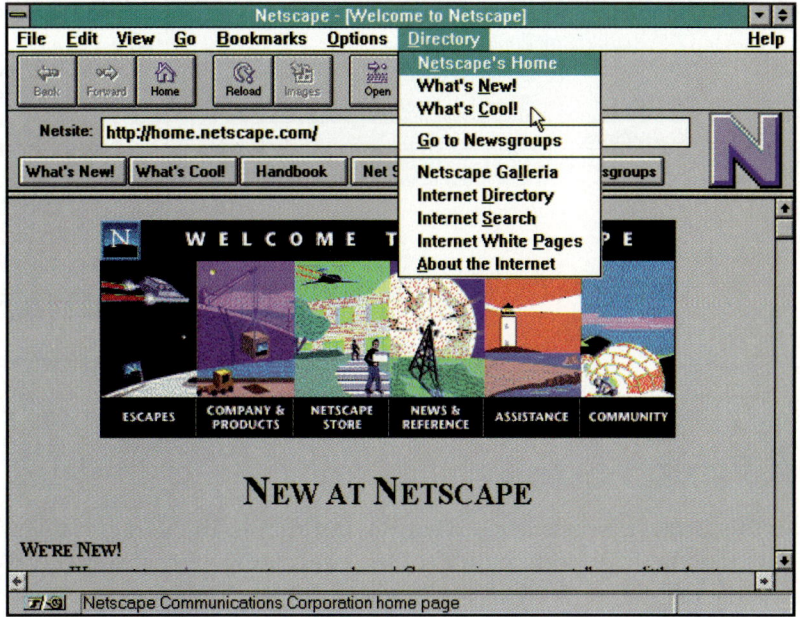

FIGURE 1-43 *Netscape features include interesting and useful Internet locations already built in.*

▸ Access to the Internet

Access to the Internet is becoming easier all the time. Most schools, from grade schools through colleges and universities, provide students with free access to the Internet. Some public libraries and local governments offer limited public Internet access during normal business hours. Computing service providers such as CompuServe, Prodigy, and America Online offer access to the Internet. Thus, using a modem and special communications software that can be purchased or is supplied by the online computing service provider, you can access the Internet from your personal computer at home. Figure 1-44 contains a list of online computing service providers and a sample screen from Prodigy.

The charges for having your own Internet connection at home vary greatly. Like credit card charges, there can be fixed and variable fees. Some providers have a slightly higher fixed monthly charge with a low hourly connect-time fee. Others have a lower fixed monthly charge along with a higher hourly connect-time fee. You have to estimate the length of time per month you will use the services, and comparison shop by calculating the charges you would accumulate. The growing number of providers is making it easier to get online everyday.

NAME	DESCRIPTION	PHONE
America Online	Fastest growing provider; news, weather, shopping, finance, travel, and more	800-827-6364
Prodigy	Largest online provider; news, weather, shopping, finance, travel, and more	800-776-3449
CompuServe	Most comprehensive of all services; business oriented	800-848-8199
Delphi	Internet access and services	800-695-4005
GEnie	News plus professional and technical databases	800-638-9636
Imagination	Games and entertainment	800-743-7721
eWorld	General-interest service started by Apple	800-775-4556
Dow Jones	Finance and business news	800-522-3567

FIGURE 1-44 *Online service providers offer connections to the Internet.*

▸ Project Summary

In this project, you learned what the Internet is and some of its history. Bridges, data lines, and different data line media used to connect host computers were discussed. You learned that TCP/IP is the communications technique used on the Internet. Internet addresses, domain naming, packet switching, and how computers route packets were described. The services offered on the Internet were listed. Tools that have been developed for use on the Internet were described. Different discussion techniques such as news groups and mailing lists were explained. You learned about hypertext, browsers, and the World Wide Web. Different techniques for accessing the Internet were discussed.

▶ Key Terms and Index

anchor *(I.25)*
archie server *(I.19)*
ARPANET (Advanced Research Projects Agency Network) *(I.3)*
bridge *(I.4)*
browser *(I.26, I.27)*
channels *(I.24)*
client/server computing *(I.12)*
coaxial cable *(I.7)*
commercial software *(I.17)*
copyright *(I.17)*
DARPA (Defense Advanced Research Projects Agency) *(I.3)*
data line *(I.5)*
demon *(I.12)*
domain naming *(I.9)*
dotted decimal format *(I.9)*
electronic mail *(I.11, I.12)*
e-mail *(I.11, I.12)*
e-mail address *(I.13)*
fiber-optic cable *(I.7)*
file transfer protocol (FTP) *(I.11, I.16)*
finger *(I.14)*
flaming *(I.14)*
freeware *(I.18)*

FTP *(I.11, I.16)*
gateway *(I.4)*
gopher *(I.20)*
GopherSpace *(I.20)*
Gopher Web *(I.20)*
home page *(I.26)*
host computer *(I.8)*
hotlist *(I.27)*
HTML (hypertext markup language) *(I.25)*
hypermedia *(I.25)*
hypertext *(I.25)*
Information Superhighway *(I.4)*
Internet relay chat (IRC) *(I.24)*
IP address *(I.9)*
IRC *(I.24)*
leased line *(I.5)*
license *(I.17)*
listserv *(I.22)*
mail box *(I.13)*
mailing list *(I.22)*
microwave *(I.7)*
modem *(I.6)*
Netscape *(I.27)*
network *(I.4)*
news groups *(I.21)*
news reader *(I.22)*
packet switching *(I.8)*

packets *(I.8)*
protocol *(I.3)*
provider *(I.6)*
public domain software *(I.18)*
route table *(I.9)*
satellite *(I.7)*
shareware *(I.18)*
sniffer *(I.14)*
subscribing *(I.22)*
switched line *(I.5)*
TCP/IP (Transmission Control Protocol/Internet Protocol) *(I.3)*
TELNET *(I.11, I.15)*
The Internet *(I.4)*
thread *(I.21)*
twisted pair wire *(I.7)*
unzip *(I.17)*
URL (Universal Resource Locator) *(I.26)*
USENET *(I.22)*
veronica *(I.20)*
WAIS (Wide Area Information Service) *(I.23)*
Web site *(I.3)*
World Wide Web (WWW) *(I.3, I.25, I.26)*

STUDENT ASSIGNMENTS

STUDENT ASSIGNMENT 1
True/False

Instructions: Circle T if the statement is true or F if the statement is false.

T F 1. TCP/IP (Transmission Control Protocol/Internet Protocol) was first used at universities and then the government started using it.
T F 2. TCP/IP allows different types of computers and operating systems to communicate.
T F 3. Two computers communicating over phone lines is called a protocol.
T F 4. The Internet is a collection of networks.
T F 5. Data sent using TCP/IP is divided up into pieces called packages.
T F 6. Internet addresses were developed because domain names are so hard to remember.
T F 7. Finger is a network testing tool.
T F 8. A demon is a virus that goes around the Internet erasing disk files.
T F 9. Services on the Internet rely heavily on client/server techniques.
T F 10. TELNET provides a terminal session on a remote computer.
T F 11. You can give FTP (file transfer protocol) a filename, and it will find the file and send it to you.

(continued)

PROJECT 1 INTRODUCTION TO THE INTERNET

STUDENT ASSIGNMENT 1 (continued)

T F 12. The four broad catagories of software are commercial, shareware, freeware, and public domain.
T F 13. Packaging is used to efficiently send groups of electronic mail messages over the Internet.
T F 14. You do not have to pay for any software you obtain from the Internet.
T F 15. You can give gopher a filename, and it will find the file and send it to you.
T F 16. Archie started as a way to answer people's computer questions.
T F 17. News groups allow access to electronic copies of the daily newspapers.
T F 18. There is no way to search the contents of text files on the Internet.
T F 19. Netscape is a type of browser that is used to access the Internet.
T F 20. Several mailing lists are managed by a single listserv program.

STUDENT ASSIGNMENT 2
Multiple Choice

Instructions: Circle the correct response.

1. TCP/IP is a set of _____ that describe how computers will talk to each other.
   a. books   b. modems   c. languages   d. protocols
2. Networks on the Internet are connected with high-, medium-, and low-speed _____ .
   a. protocols   b. typists   c. computers   d. data lines
3. TCP/IP software will look inside a _____ to see if it can deliver packets directly to their destination.
   a. protocol   b. route table   c. data line   d. bridge
4. An Internet address is composed of _____ .
   a. street, city, state and zip code
   b. characters unreadable by humans
   c. four sets of numbers separated by periods
   d. area code, phone number, and unique computer identifier
5. A demon is a(n) _____ .
   a. account name   b. computer virus c. program bug   d. service program
6. Packaging a number of programs into one file makes it easy to _____ .
   a. retrieve programs over the Internet with FTP
   b. run the programs
   c. search the contents of the programs for a character string
   d. organize the directories at an FTP site
7. A _____ gives you the right to use a purchased software program.
   a. GUI   b. computer   c. copy   d. license
8. Gopher was initially developed to help users _____ .
   a. get answers to computing questions
   b. display computer graphics
   c. learn touch typing
   d. get their mail messages
9. A mailing list receives mail from list participants and automatically sends it to _____ .
   a. a gopher server
   b. all other list participants
   c. a printer
   d. all computers on the Internet
10. In a hypertext display such as Netscape, you can identify an anchor because _____ .
    a. it is shaped like an anchor
    b. the mouse pointer will change shape when positioned over it
    c. the mouse pointer will cause the computer speaker to click when placed on it
    d. the mouse pointer will freeze, or be anchored, when placed on it and no longer move

STUDENT ASSIGNMENT 3
Short Answer

Instructions: Write the correct definition next to the key term.

1. thread _____

2. packet _____

3. domain name _____

4. URL _____

5. protocol _____

6. flaming _____

7. TCP/IP _____

8. home page _____

9. archie _____

10. TELNET _____

11. news group _____

12. client/server _____

13. IP address _____

14. demon _____

15. anchor _____

16. veronica _____

17. browser _____

18. World Wide Web _____

19. Web site _____

20. hypertext _____

STUDENT ASSIGNMENT 4
Internet Capabilities

Many services and resources are available on the Internet. Go to the library and obtain at least two recent articles on the Internet, addressing its many capabilities. Write a one-page summary of your findings.

STUDENT ASSIGNMENT 5
Internet Providers

Commercial Internet connection providers such as Prodigy or America Online offer connections to the Internet from your home. Find out if there are providers near your home that offer access through a local call or a toll-free 800 number. Obtain a membership packet from at lease two providers and compare the services offered and their fee structures.

STUDENT ASSIGNMENT 6
Accessing Government Information

Most government entities are going online on the Internet, making information available about what they do, and about current events. Find out the e-mail addresses of your local and national elected government representatives. Send them a message asking for information about a current event or piece of legislation you are interested in. Share any response with your class.

STUDENT ASSIGNMENT 7
Developing a Gopher System

Gopher was initially developed to automatically provide answers to requests for information. Assume you are in charge of developing a set of local gopher menus for all the student clubs and organizations at your school. How would you lay out the menus? What types of information would you include for each club?

STUDENT ASSIGNMENT 8
Searching a WAIS Database

Prepare a list of keywords that you would use for searching a WAIS database for each of the following topics: astronomy; Buddhism; disabilities; geology; politics; weather; zoology.

STUDENT ASSIGNMENT 9
Internet Browsers versus Internet Tools

What are some of the advantages and disadvantages of using an Internet browser program such as Netscape as opposed to using Internet tools such as FTP, archie, gopher, or WAIS? Prepare a table that illustrates these differences.

THE INTERNET
Introductory Concepts and Techniques

PROJECT TWO

ACCESSING INTERNET SERVICES FROM UNIX

OBJECTIVES You will have mastered the material in this project when you can:

- Login and logout of UNIX
- Send and read electronic mail messages
- Perform mail box management functions
- Display user account information on remote host computers
- Start and end a remote terminal session
- Send and receive computer files
- Search for files using archie
- Retrieve files using gopher
- Search for files using veronica
- Send and read articles in news groups
- Perform news group management functions
- Participate in a mailing list
- Search for, display, and retrieve documents using WAIS
- Engage in live conversations using Internet relay chat (IRC)

▶ INTRODUCTION

In the previous project, you learned what the Internet is and what services are available. Project 2 introduces you to using popular Internet service programs in a UNIX environment so you can start taking advantage of the many entertainment, business, and educational opportunities available on the Internet.

You will see how to carry out commonly performed activities such as using remote computing resources, doing research, transferring files, and communicating with people around the world. This project starts with the most popular service—electronic mail—but first, a little background on UNIX.

▶ GETTING STARTED IN UNIX

To use Internet services on a computer running the UNIX operating system, you must **login**, or identify yourself, to the UNIX system. Then, UNIX knows you are allowed to use computing resources. Your instructor will give you an **account**. That account will have a **password** that protects it from unauthorized use by others.

I.33

PROJECT 2 ACCESSING INTERNET SERVICES FROM UNIX

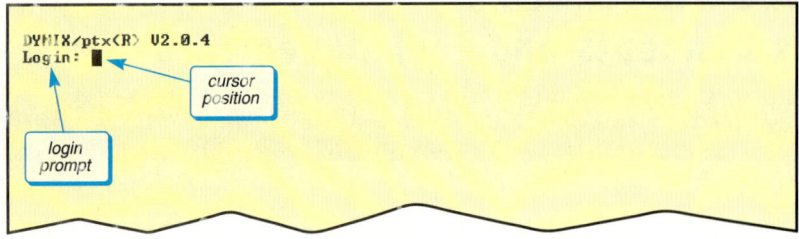

When first starting, UNIX displays a login prompt on the screen (Figure 2-1). A **prompt** is a message from the operating system that requests you to perform some function, such as typing certain information or inserting a diskette.

FIGURE 2-1

To illustrate how to login to a UNIX system, the account name, jordanka, with a password of dv4t53p will be used. If you are stepping through this project on a terminal, replace the account name and password with your own.

TO LOGIN TO A UNIX SYSTEM ▼

STEP 1 ▶

At the UNIX login prompt, type `jordanka` **and press the ENTER key.**

A prompt for the password for the account displays (Figure 2-2).

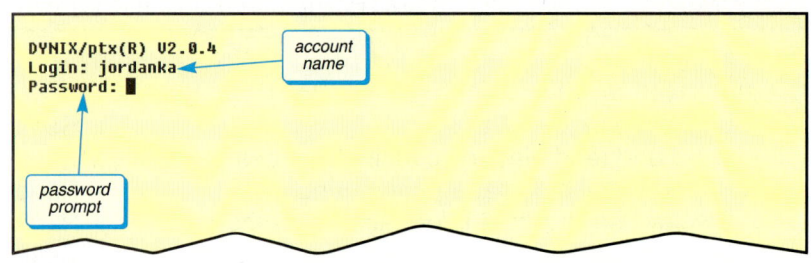

FIGURE 2-2

STEP 2 ▶

Type `dv4t53p` **and press the ENTER key (the password will not display on the screen as you type it).**

Session startup messages display, followed by a UNIX command prompt (Figure 2-3). A **command prompt** *is an indication that the operating system is waiting for you to enter a command. In this case, the command prompt is a % (percent sign).*

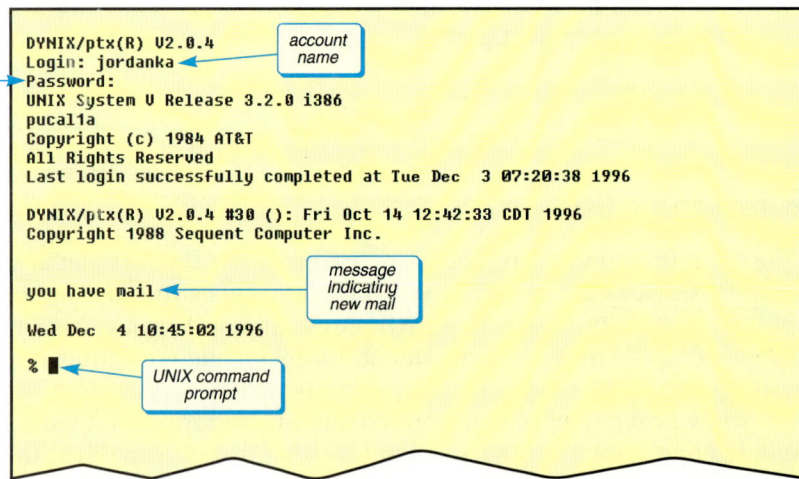

FIGURE 2-3

▲

During the login process, special files, called **login scripts** or login profiles, will execute. These special files contain settings and commands that tailor the UNIX terminal session. The login script may set the terminal type used, specify a default text editor, set disk search paths, customize the command prompt, and indicate if there is any unread mail in the mail box (see Figure 2-3 above). When the UNIX command prompt (%) appears, the terminal session has been established, and you are ready to start using UNIX.

UNIX operating systems are case-sensitive. **Case-sensitive** means that in filenames, as well as commands, a capital letter is not the same as a lowercase letter. For example, a file called Myfile is not the same as a file called myfile. Directory names and filenames have to be typed exactly as they appear in the directory list.

Getting Help in UNIX

All UNIX systems documentation is stored online. **Online** means the information is stored on the computer's disk drives. To see a documentation manual page for a particular UNIX command, you use the **man** command. You indicate to the man command the name of the program about which you wish more information. For example, the following steps show how to display information about the FTP program. FTP is a program used frequently on the Internet to transfer files.

TO VIEW UNIX MANUAL PAGES

STEP 1 ▶

At the UNIX command prompt (%) type `man ftp` **to view the documentation (Figure 2-4).**

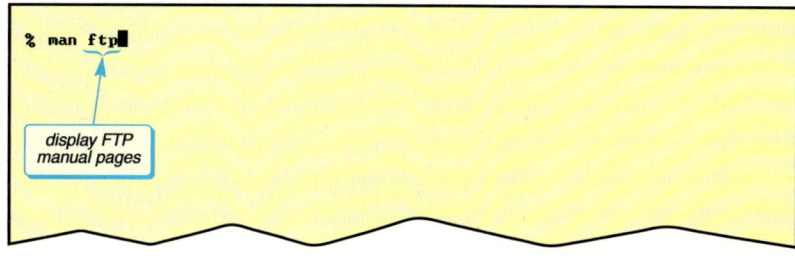

FIGURE 2-4

STEP 2 ▶

Press the ENTER key.

The first manual page for the FTP command displays (Figure 2-5). This manual page contains the parameters and options available for FTP. Notice the --More-- notation at the bottom of the screen, which indicates there is more help available on FTP.

STEP 3 ▶

Press the ENTER key until you reach the end of the help text, or type the letter q**, which stands for quit, if you wish to stop viewing the documentation.**

The UNIX command prompt (%) displays when you type q, indicating UNIX is ready for you to enter another command.

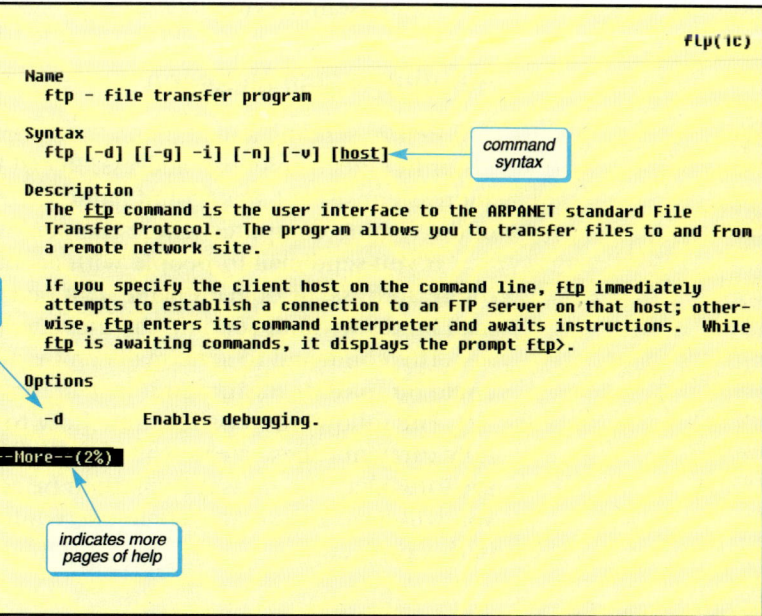

FIGURE 2-5

Using man, you can read the online documentation for all the basic TCP/IP service programs, such as FTP or TELNET, as well as any Internet service programs, such as gopher or a news reader, that your computer center may have available. See Figure 1-13 on page I.10 of Project 1 for a list of Internet services and Table 1-1 on page I.18 for a list of the Internet tools.

When you have finished using UNIX, you should **logout**. Logging out lets the UNIX operating system know you are finished using UNIX. The following shows how to logout of a UNIX system.

TO LOGOUT OF A UNIX SYSTEM

Step 1: At the UNIX command prompt, type `logout` and press the ENTER key.

The login prompt displays, as shown earlier in Figure 2-1 on page I.34.

Another way to logout is to type CTRL+D. That is, press and hold down the CTRL key, press the letter D, and then release both keys.

You learned how to login and logout of a UNIX system and display the documentation for Internet service programs and tools. The remainder of the project assumes you are always logged in to the UNIX system.

▶ Using Electronic Mail

Once **logged in** to a UNIX system, you can work with Internet services such as electronic mail. Corresponding with electronic mail consists of composing and sending messages to others and managing the messages that others send to you.

Sending a Mail Message

Before sending a mail message to someone over the Internet, you must know his or her electronic mail address. Recall from Project 1 that an individual's mail address consists of an account name followed by the IP address, or domain name, of the remote computer where the person's account is located.

If you send mail to people with accounts on the same computer you are using, the IP address, or domain name, can be omitted. The mail will be delivered to their mail boxes without sending the message out over the Internet.

The command to send mail can be different on different computer systems. It could be **mail** or **mailx**. Your instructor can tell you the proper command.

The following steps illustrate how to send a mail message. For you to successfully carry out these steps, you should substitute your account name wherever you see jordanka. The message will then be sent to your own account. This is to ensure you will have a mail message to use while continuing through the section on e-mail in this project.

TO SEND A MAIL MESSAGE

STEP 1 ▶

At the UNIX command prompt (%), type `mailx jordanka` **and press the ENTER key.**

A subject line prompt displays (Figure 2-6). The purpose of the **subject line** is to contain a brief description of the contents or purpose of the mail message.

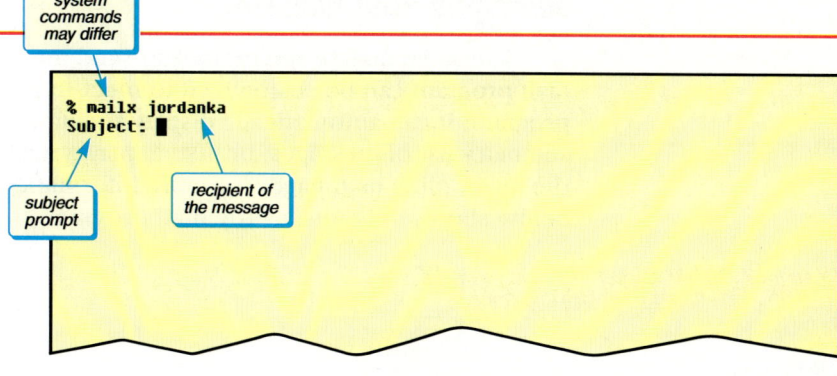

FIGURE 2-6

STEP 2 ▶

Type `Meeting of the Math Study group` **and press the ENTER key.**

The cursor moves down to the next blank line (Figure 2-7).

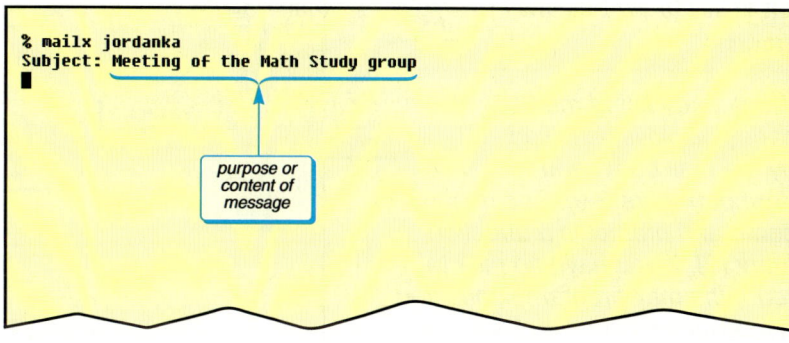

FIGURE 2-7

STEP 3 ▶

Type `The Math Study group will meet on Thursday in room C120 at 6:00pm.` **and press the ENTER key.**

STEP 4 ▶

At the beginning of a blank line, press CTRL+D.

The message EOT displays, followed by the UNIX command prompt (Figure 2-8). **EOT** stands for **end of text**. You have just sent a message to yourself. This was done to ensure that there would be at least one message in your mail box for use with the other electronic mail examples that follow.

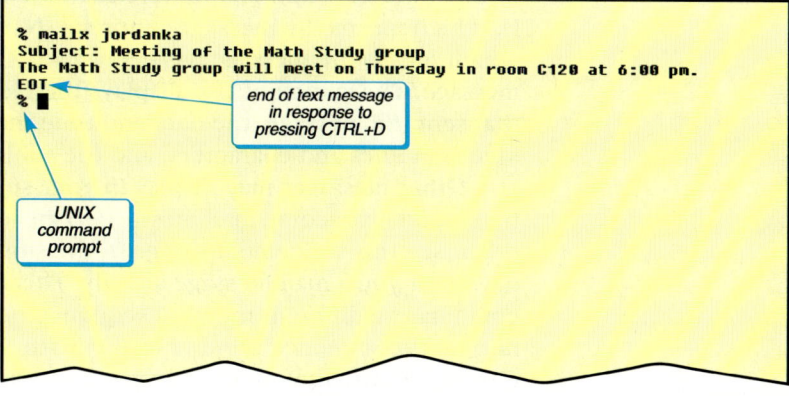

FIGURE 2-8

It is important to correctly indicate the content or purpose of the message, not only when using electronic mail, but also in other Internet service programs. This allows the recipient to categorize and screen mail without having to read each message. This screening process will be illustrated later in the project in the section on displaying a message summary list. If your subject is vague or missing, people will probably just delete the message without reading it.

Managing Your Mail Box

The same mail program used to send messages is used to read new mail. The mail program can be customized to meet individual preferences. When starting the program, it can automatically display the most recently received message, display a summary list of messages, or just display a mail command prompt. You can read the mail online man pages for more information about customizing mail. The step below shows how to start the mail program.

TO START THE MAIL PROGRAM

STEP 1 ▶

Type `mailx` and press the ENTER key to start the mail program.

A summary list of messages displays, followed by the mail command prompt (Figure 2-9). The mail command prompt is a question mark (?). If you have no mail to read, the mail program sends you a message saying you have no mail to read and returns you to the UNIX command prompt.

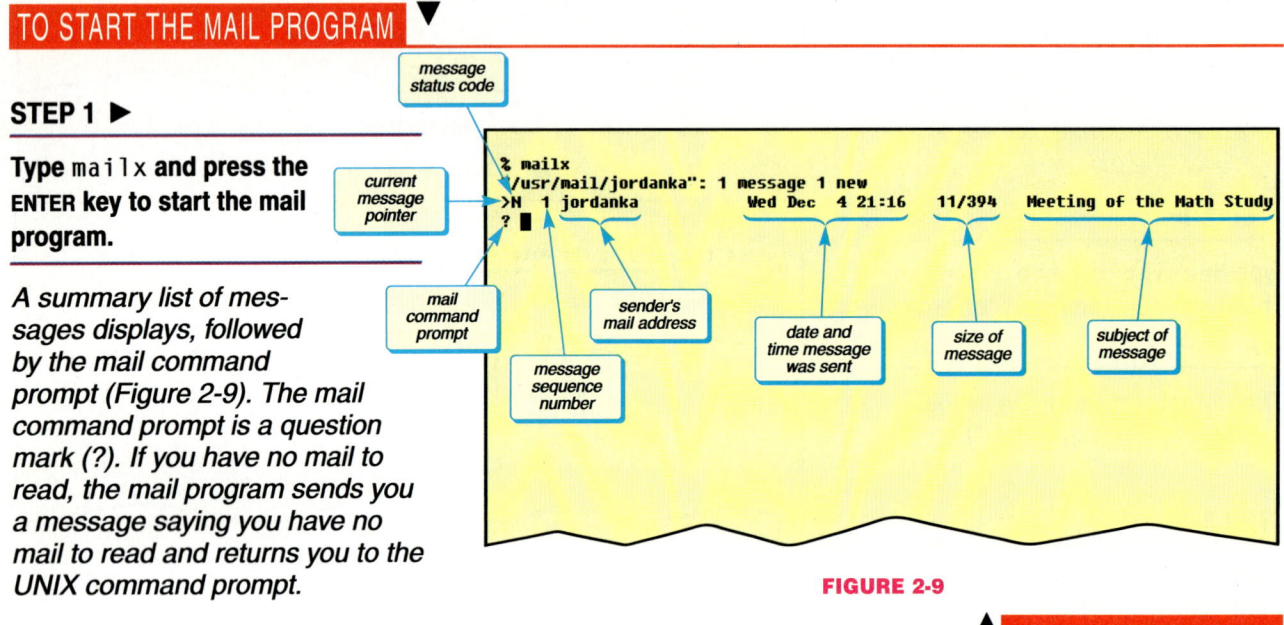

FIGURE 2-9

The summary list of messages contains several pieces of information. A **status code** indicates whether you have read the message yet. Possible status codes are U, which means the message is unread, N, which means new message, or blank, which means the message has been read. A **sequence number** identifies each message. The summary also displays the electronic mail address of the account that sent the message, the date and time the message was sent, how large the message is in lines and characters, and the subject of the message.

Other messages may display in your summary list. Some colleges and organizations send a welcome mail message to an account when it is first created. You might see this welcome message in the summary list. One of your friends could have sent you a mail message already. This means your Math Study group message could have a different message sequence number than shown in Figure 2-9. Make note of the sequence number of the Math Study group message in your summary display and use that number as you continue with the project.

At the mail command prompt, you enter commands that allow you to read, send, and save messages and manage your mail box.

Managing Mail Messages

Mail messages are managed by using mail commands along with the sequence number assigned to each message. Specifying the sequence number with mail commands is optional. When the sequence number is omitted, the command will operate on the message called the **current message**. Suppose a letter carrier left a bundle of letters in the mail box at your house. The current message would be equivalent to the letter on the top of the bundle.

When you start the mail program, the first message in the summary list is the current message, just like the letter on top of the bundle of letters left by the letter carrier. The current message is indicated by the greater than symbol (>) next to it in the summary list, as shown earlier in Figure 2-9. The easiest way to read mail is to start with the current message. The next step displays the current mail message.

TO READ THE CURRENT MESSAGE ▼

STEP 1 ▶

At the mail command prompt, press the ENTER key.

The current mail message displays (Figure 2-10).

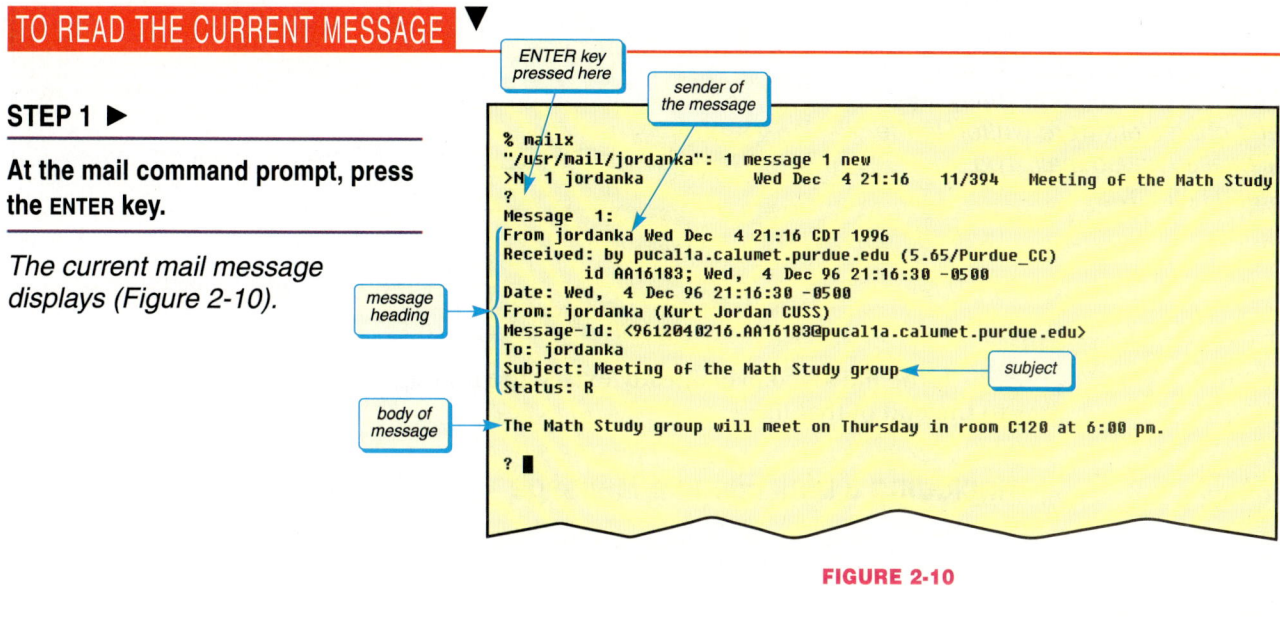

FIGURE 2-10

Notice that the message contains two parts. The first part consists of a message heading. The message heading contains message routing information included by the mail delivery program, the message sender, the message recipient, and the subject. The second part of the mail message is the body of the message. The body contains the actual text typed in by the message sender.

Saving Mail Messages

Some messages you receive may be so important that you will want to save them on disk. For example, a message may contain program source code or answers to a problem that you will want for future reference. Perhaps you just want to preserve a record, or **audit trail**, of your correspondence.

To illustrate saving a mail message, the step on the next page shows how to save message 1, Meeting of the Math Study group, in a disk file called saved.mail. Remember, you might have other messages, so substitute the proper message sequence number that corresponds to the Math Study group message.

TO SAVE A MESSAGE TO DISK

STEP 1 ▶

Type s 1 saved.mail to save the message, and press the ENTER key.

Mail displays "saved.mail" [New file] 11/394 (Figure 2-11). The numbers indicate how many lines and characters were written to the file called saved.mail. The s stands for save.

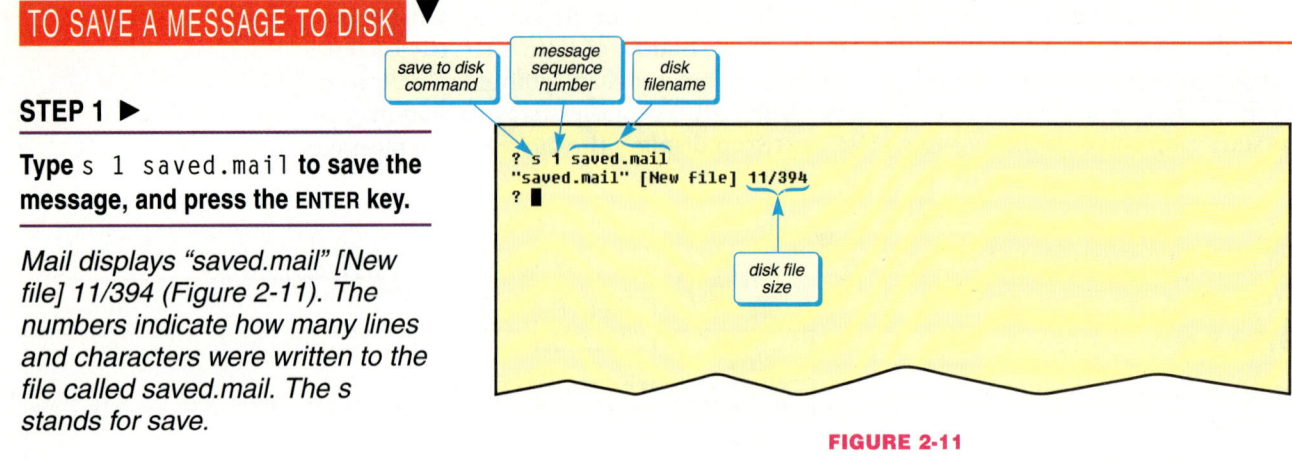

FIGURE 2-11

If the file saved.mail already exists, the message will be **appended**, or added, to the end of that file.

Including a Disk File in a Message

Just as you may want to save a message to disk, you may want to include a disk file in one of your mail messages. For example, you can include some research you are doing in a message to a colleague at another school or submit an assignment to your instructor for grading.

The initial steps for including a disk file in a message are much the same as for sending a mail message. The disk file will be included as part of the body of the message. To show how to include a disk file in a mail message, the saved.mail file created in the previous steps will be included in a new message, as shown in the following steps.

TO INCLUDE A DISK FILE IN A MESSAGE

STEP 1 ▶

Type m jordanka and press the ENTER key. Type Including a disk file and press the ENTER key. Type Here is an included disk file: and press the ENTER key.

The cursor moves down to the next blank line (Figure 2-12).

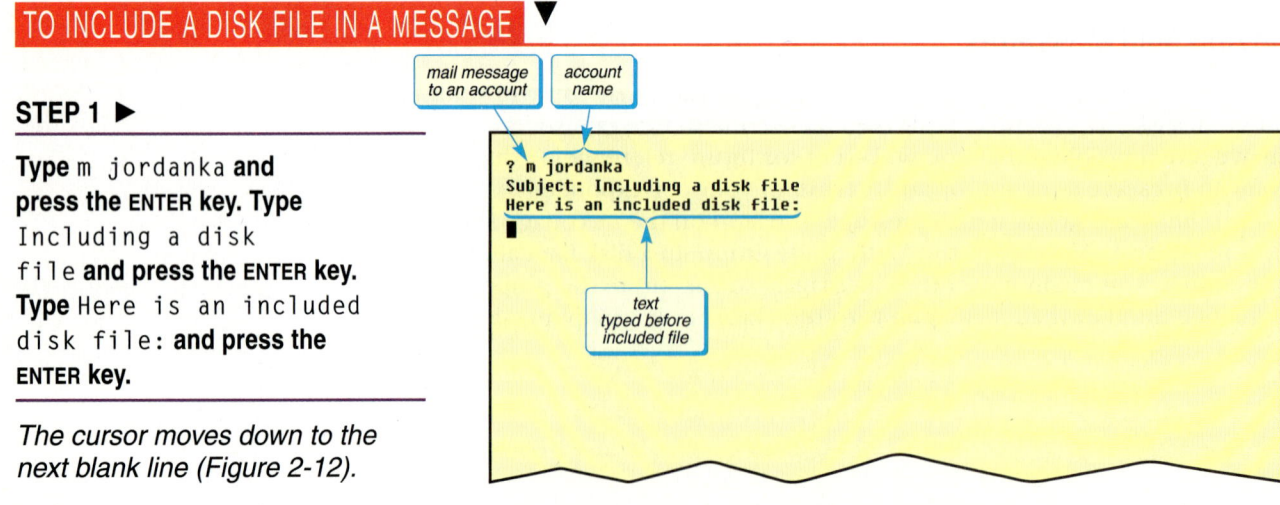

FIGURE 2-12

USING ELECTRONIC MAIL   I.41

STEP 2 ▶

Type ~r saved.mail to include the file and press the ENTER key.

A line containing "saved.mail" 12/404 displays (Figure 2-13). This confirms that the saved.mail file has been included, and that the file is 12 lines long with 404 characters in it.

STEP 3 ▶

Press CTRL+D.

An EOT message displays, followed by the mail command prompt. The message, again, has been sent to your mail account.

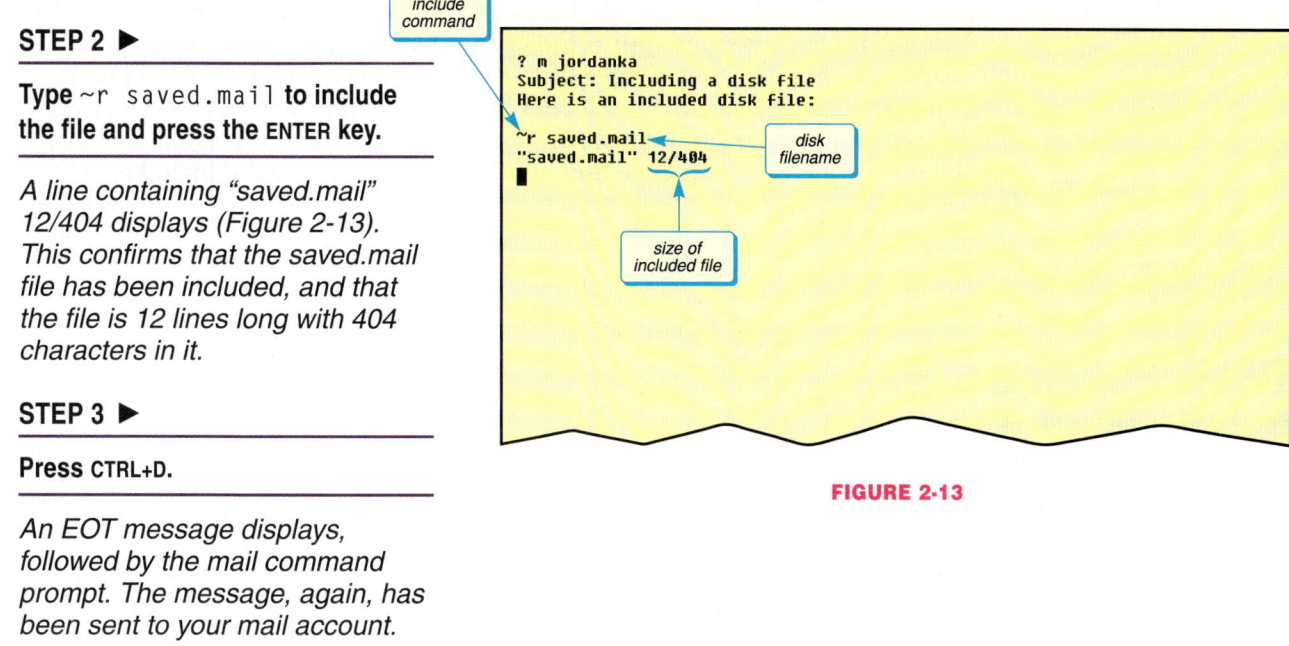

FIGURE 2-13

Text can be typed before and after the included file. The next section shows how to read other messages you might have.

Reading Other Messages

Mail messages appear in the message summary list in the order they are received. You do not have to read the messages in this order. Just as you might pull a letter that looks more interesting from the middle of the bundle of mail from the post office, you can select any message to read by making it the current message. The subject line of a message often gives an indication of its contents. Most people decide which messages to read and which to skip by scanning the subject lines. You can see it is important to provide a subject that correctly indicates the purpose or contents of your messages. Remember, the subject lines appear as part of the message **summary list**. The following step illustrates how to display a message summary list.

TO DISPLAY A MESSAGE SUMMARY LIST ▼

STEP 1 ▶

Type h to display the message summary list, and press the ENTER key.

A summary list of message headings displays (Figure 2-14).

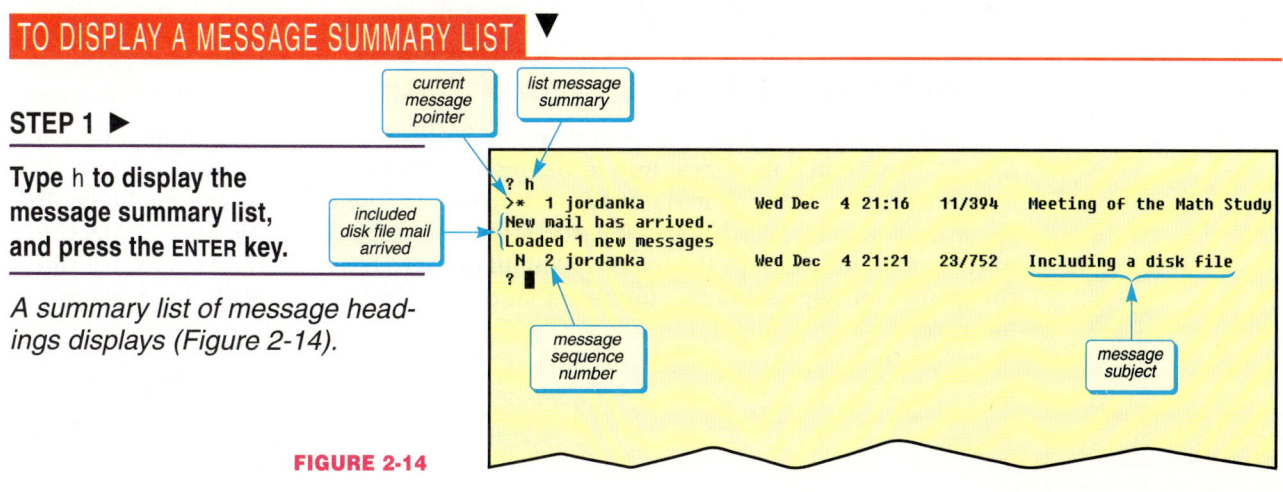

FIGURE 2-14

You will notice messages appear indicating that new mail has arrived. The new mail is the message containing a disk file that you created and sent in previous steps. Now message 2 can be selected by making it the current message, as shown in the following step. Remember, you might have other messages, so substitute the proper message sequence number that corresponds to the Including a disk file message.

TO MAKE A MESSAGE THE CURRENT MESSAGE

STEP 1 ▶

Type 2 and press the ENTER key to make message 2 the current message.

The contents of the mail message with sequence number 2 displays (Figure 2-15).

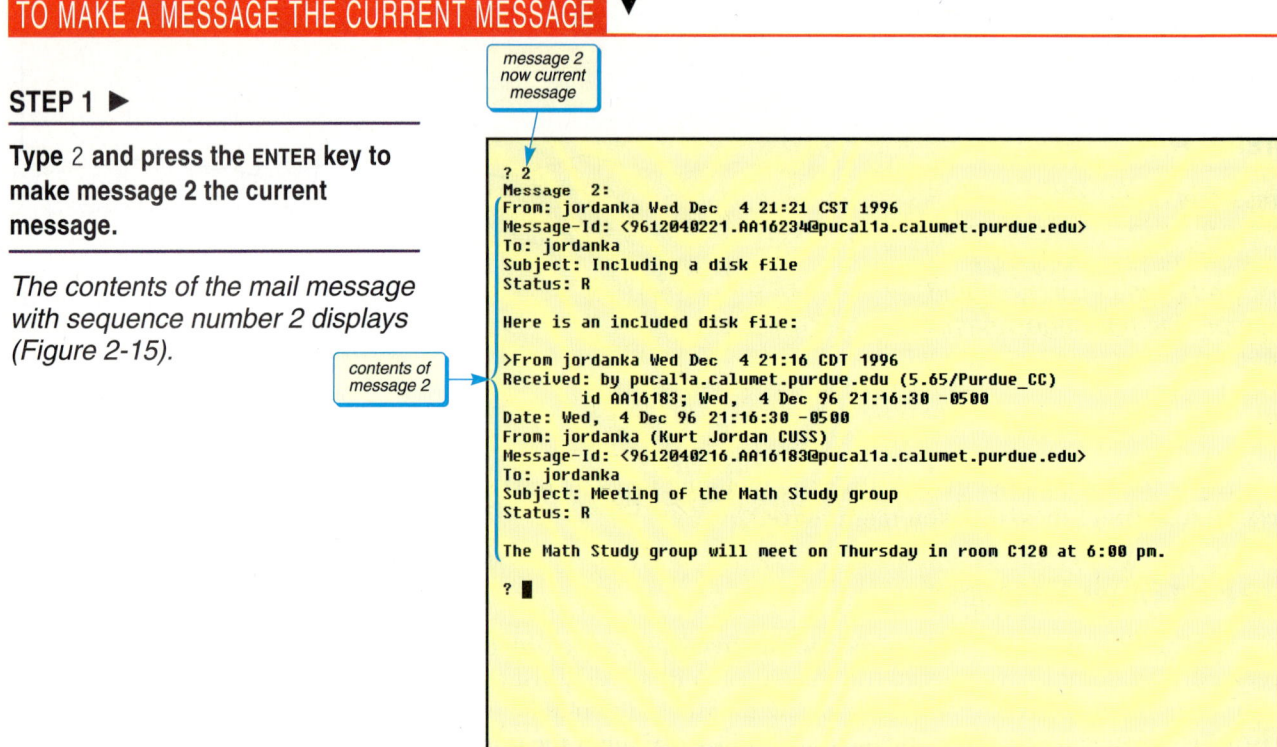

FIGURE 2-15

This technique can be used to redisplay the same message several times. Just enter the sequence number and the message will display.

Deleting a Mail Message

Having read your mail, you should remove unwanted messages from your mail box. With several dozen messages in the mail box, reading the summary list becomes cumbersome. The **d command** deletes messages from your mail box. To show how to delete a mail message, the following steps delete message 1, Meeting of the Math Study group. Remember, you might have other messages, so substitute the proper message sequence number that corresponds to the Math Study group message.

TO DELETE A MAIL MESSAGE

STEP 1 ▶

Type d 1 to delete the first mail message, and press the ENTER key.

The mail command prompt displays (Figure 2-16).

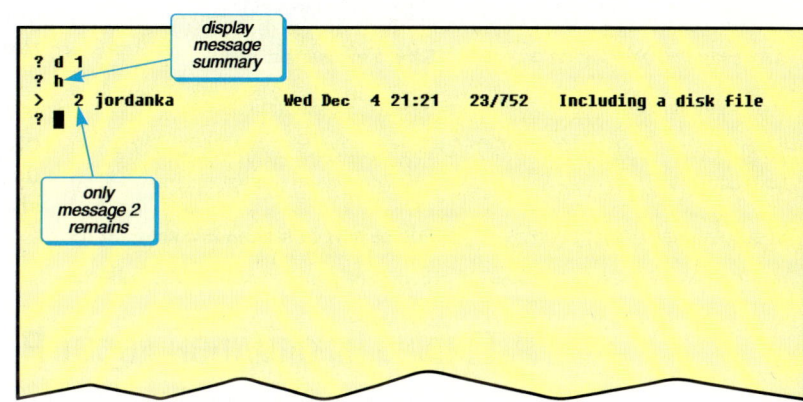

FIGURE 2-16

STEP 2 ▶

Type h to display the message summary list, and press the ENTER key.

The message summary list displays, allowing you to verify that message 1 is gone (Figure 2-17).

FIGURE 2-17

Be considerate in managing your mail box. Allowing old messages to accumulate in your mail box wastes disk space. Many computer systems have mail boxes stored on a different disk from where other personal files are stored. The system administrator responsible for mail may have a **policy** in place governing how much space a person's mail box can occupy and how long old messages are allowed to stay. You should remove unwanted messages or store them in disk files in your own personal directory.

In case you ever forget how a certain command works, the available mail commands and their parameters can be displayed by typing the ? command at the mail command prompt.

When you finish managing your mail, you can exit the mail program. The following step summarizes this procedure.

TO EXIT THE MAIL PROGRAM

Step 1: Type q to exit the mail program, and press the ENTER key.

A message displays indicating the number of messages in the mail box, followed by the UNIX command prompt (%). Messages you deleted with the d command are removed. The status of messages, whether they have been read or not, is preserved.

▶ TABLE 2-1

MAIL COMMAND	MAIL TASK
h	Access help
d message-number	Delete a message
h	Display a message summary list
CTRL+D	End a new message
q	Exit the mail program
~r file-name	Include a disk file in a message
mailx	Read new mail
r	Reply to a message
s message-number file-name	Save a message to disk
message-number	Select a message to read
mailx account-name@host-address	Send a new message from the UNIX command prompt
m account-name@host-address	Send a new message while in the mailx program

Another way to exit mail is with the **x command**. This command terminates the mail program ignoring any changes made to your mail box. For example, any deleted messages will not be removed, and the status of messages you read will be changed so they are still marked as unread. This allows you to recover messages you accidentally deleted.

Mail is a program with many features. You need only to master a few commands to be proficient. Table 2-1 summarizes the electronic mail commands described in this project and their functions.

You have learned how to send messages to and receive messages from other Internet users. The next section describes how to obtain information about these Internet users.

▶ FINDING INFORMATION ABOUT PEOPLE

ecause the Internet is used worldwide, finding information about people online can be overwhelming. Two Internet services that assist in this task are finger and whois.

To display information about an account on a remote host computer using finger, the account name and IP address (or domain name) of the host computer where the account is located must be supplied. This is the same address used in sending this person electronic mail. The IP address can be omitted if the account is on the local host computer. The following step shows how to display information about the jordank account at Nova University in Fort Lauderdale, Florida.

TO FIND ACCOUNT INFORMATION USING FINGER ▼

STEP 1 ▶

At the UNIX command prompt, type `finger jordank@alpha.acast.nova.edu` **and press the ENTER key.**

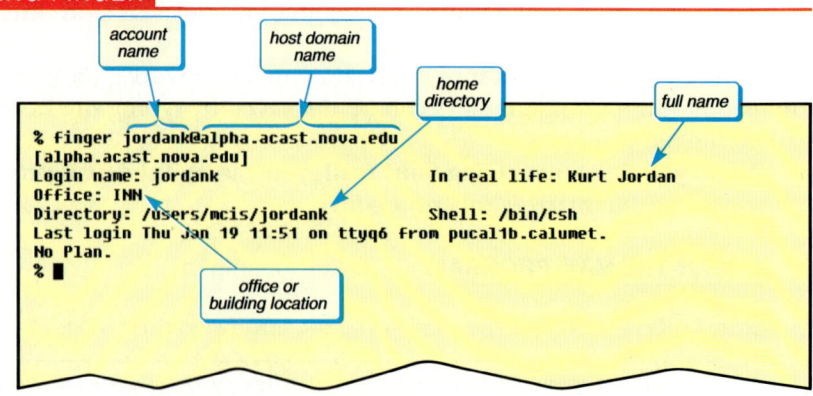

FIGURE 2-18

Several lines of information about the account display (Figure 2-18). The first line contains the domain name of the remote host. The second line contains the account name and full name of the account owner. The third line contains information indicating where Kurt Jordan's office is located. The fourth line contains the home directory used by the jordank account. The fifth line shows when the account was used last.

While finger needs an account name to work properly, whois can retrieve information even though the actual account name or host is not known, as shown in the following step.

TO FIND ACCOUNT INFORMATION USING WHOIS

STEP 1 ▶

At the UNIX command prompt, type `whois clinton` **and press the ENTER key.**

The results of the query for clinton display (Figure 2-19). Each line contains information about one entity. The first part of the line is the person's or organization's name. The next part of the line contains either the electronic mail address or the TCP/IP address of the entity. The last three lines contain information about using INTERNIC.

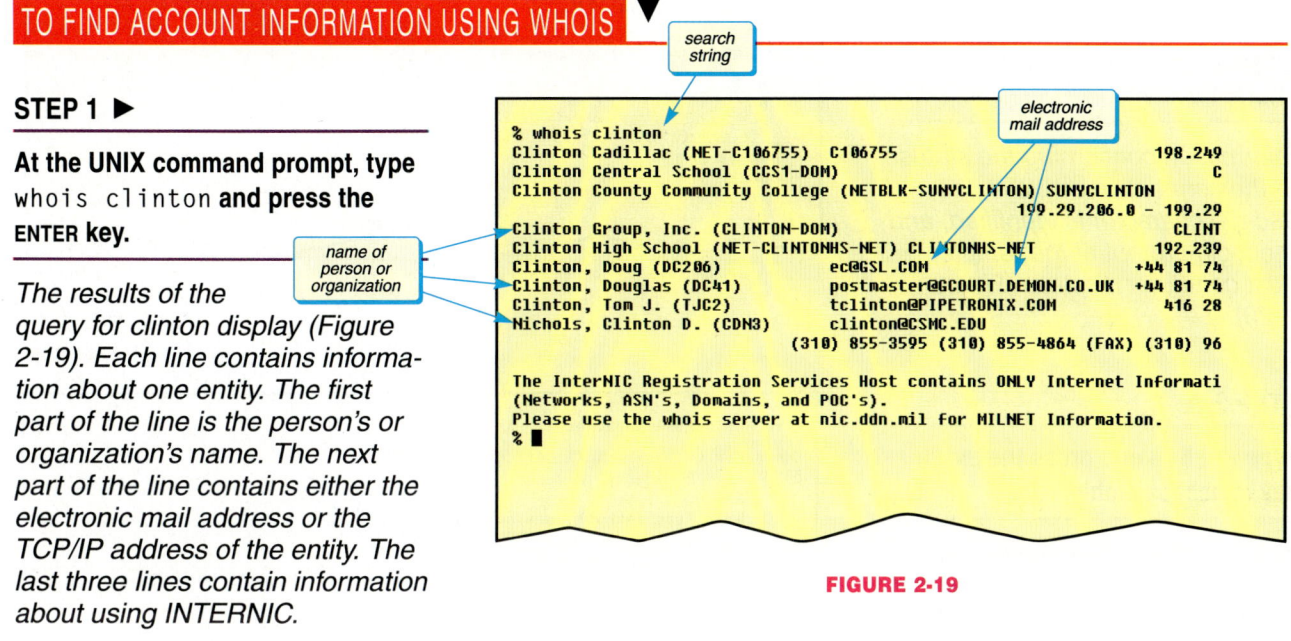

FIGURE 2-19

The whois command sends the request to the INTERNIC database of registered information. **INTERNIC** stands for **Internet Information Center**. Each database entry contains a unique identifier, a name, and other information about businesses, host computers, networks, and people who have registered with INTERNIC.

Using the steps and techniques just presented, you can access the information you need about people and organizations. The following sections of this project describe several Internet services that connect directly to a remote host computer.

▶ TERMINAL SESSIONS ON REMOTE HOST COMPUTERS

The Internet allows your local computer to connect to, and function as a terminal on remote host computer systems all over the world. You can then continue as if the terminal were physically connected to the remote host, running its programs and accessing its files. The Internet service that does this is called **TELNET**. The Appendix lists some TELNET public access sites.

Some remote hosts have special login accounts that provide services such as library catalog searching. These special accounts, some of which are discussed later in this project, display menus instead of a command prompt. The steps on the next page illustrate how to use TELNET to access an archie server at sura.net. Sura.net is a popular archie public access site.

TO START A TELNET SESSION

STEP 1 ▶

At the UNIX command prompt, type `telnet archie.sura.net` and press the ENTER key to start the TELNET session.

Information concerning the status of the connection displays, the escape character is identified, and the login prompt of the remote host computer displays (Figure 2-20).

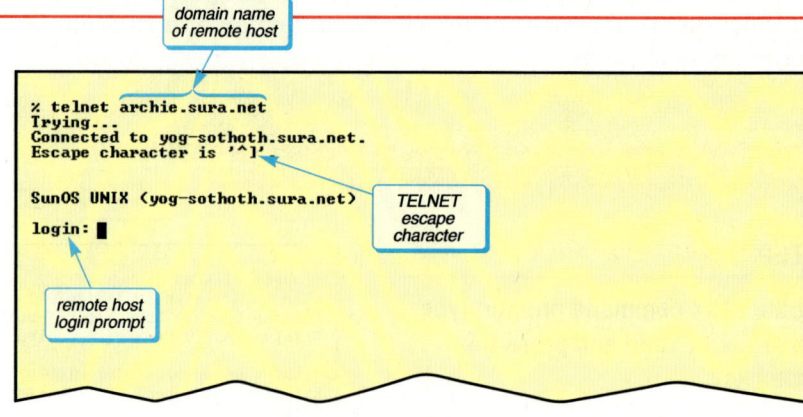

FIGURE 2-20

STEP 2 ▶

Type `archie` and press the ENTER key to access archie.

Several informative messages display and are followed by an archie command prompt (Figure 2-21). There is no password prompt because the archie service is available for public use. The TELNET session has been successfully established.

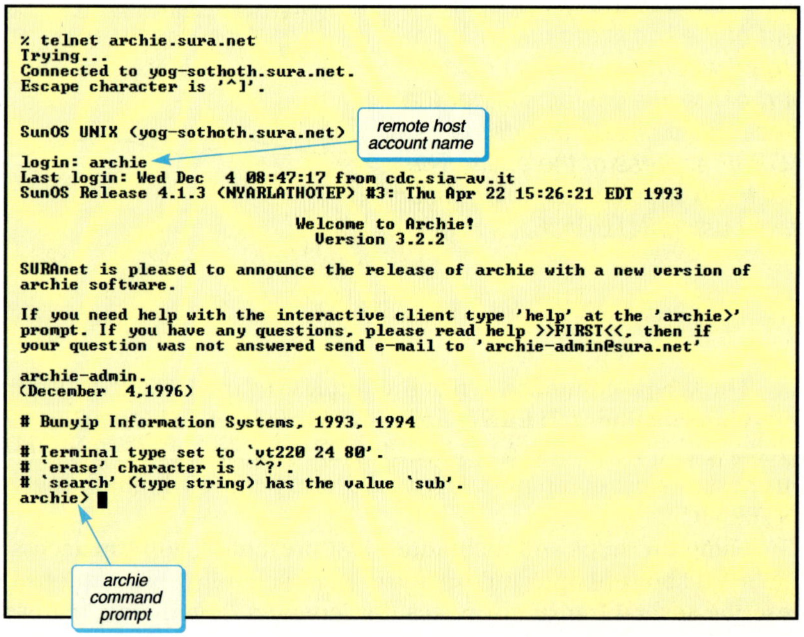

FIGURE 2-21

Managing TELNET

Figure 2-20 shows that one of the informational messages displayed by TELNET identifies the **escape character**, which allows direct communication with the TELNET program. In this case, it is ^], or CTRL+]. By pressing the escape character (CTRL+]), you can perform activities that control the TELNET session, as shown in the following step.

TO MANAGE THE TELNET SESSION ▼

STEP 1 ▶

Press CTRL+].

The communication session is suspended, and the TELNET command prompt displays (Figure 2-22).

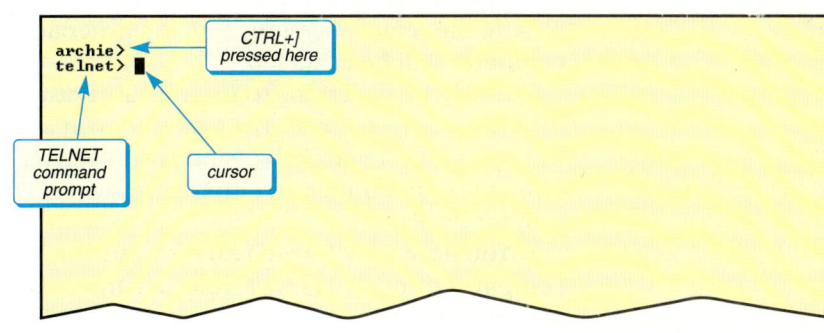

FIGURE 2-22

At the TELNET command prompt, commands are available to close the current connection, open a connection, display the status of the current connection, and set session parameters. A list of available TELNET commands can be displayed using the help command.

After issuing some TELNET commands, control can be returned to the remote session.

TO RETURN TO THE REMOTE SESSION

Step 1: Press the ENTER key twice.

The archie command prompt displays.

At this point, you can continue working with the remote computer. In this case, it is the archie server. When you have finished using the remote computer resources, you should terminate the TELNET session.

TO END THE TELNET SESSION ▼

STEP 1 ▶

Type bye to indicate you wish to end the TELNET session, and press the ENTER key.

A message displays indicating connection is closed by the foreign host. This is followed by the UNIX command prompt (Figure 2-23).

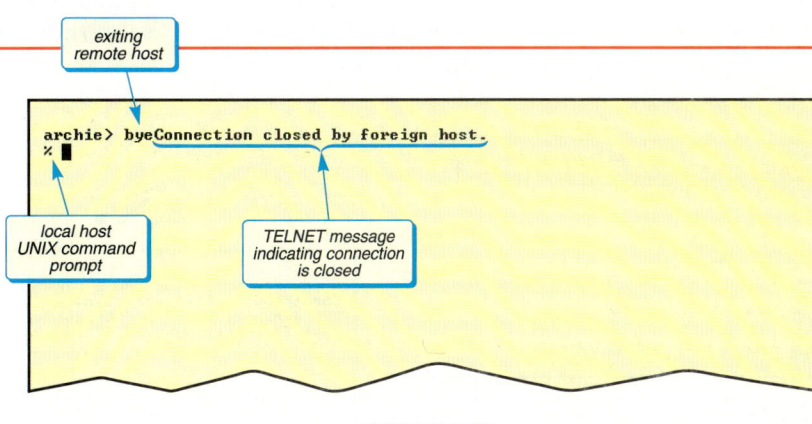

FIGURE 2-23

An alternative way of exiting TELNET is to press CTRL+]. When the TELNET command prompt displays, type `close`, and then type `quit`.

This second technique is less desirable because TELNET is ended by abruptly closing the remote session, and any programs running on the remote host computer will be canceled.

It may be necessary to use this abrupt technique, however, because of problems that can arise. For example, you are no longer receiving responses from the remote host and the session is still active, or you opened a connection to the wrong host computer. In either case, when TELNET finishes, the UNIX command prompt displays.

You have now learned how to use computing resources on a remote computer through TELNET. Another Internet service that uses remote computing resources is FTP.

▶ TRANSFERRING FILES WITH FTP

On the Internet, hundreds of thousands of documents, programs, images and sound recordings are available as shareware, freeware, and public domain. You can find helpful items such as income tax and budgeting programs, graphics viewers, complete operating systems, games, and educational programs. The FTP program allows these files to be transferred between computer systems so you can evaluate and, perhaps, keep them. The Appendix lists a number of popular FTP sites.

Before sending or retrieving files using FTP, you must have access to an account on both computers involved with enough authority on the remote host to read (if retrieving) or create (if sending) files.

Some remote sites have an anonymous account set up for public use that may or may not require a password. If an anonymous FTP site requests a password, it is usually for your electronic mail address.

Starting an FTP Session

To illustrate how to retrieve files from a remote computer, the following steps will show how to connect to the National Center for Supercomputing Applications FTP archives at the University of Illinois and retrieve the latest version of Mosaic. Recall from Project 1, Mosaic is an Internet browser program that runs under Microsoft Windows.

TO START AN FTP SESSION ▼

STEP 1 ▶

Type `ftp ftp.ncsa.uiuc.edu` **and press the ENTER key.**

Several lines of connection information display and are followed by a prompt for an account name (Figure 2-24).

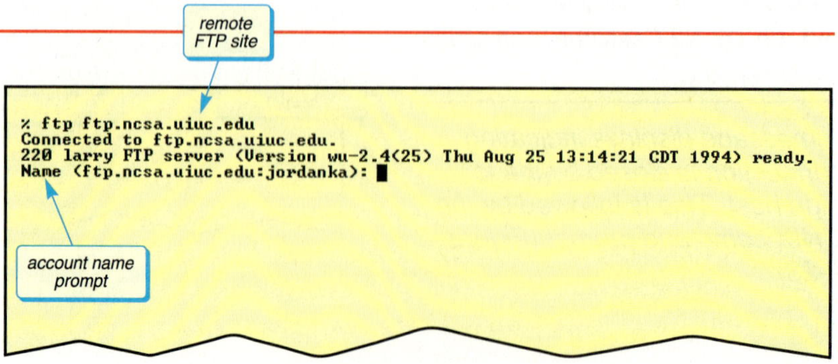

```
% ftp ftp.ncsa.uiuc.edu
Connected to ftp.ncsa.uiuc.edu.
220 larry FTP server (Version wu-2.4(25) Thu Aug 25 13:14:21 CDT 1994) ready.
Name (ftp.ncsa.uiuc.edu:jordanka): █
```

(remote FTP site; account name prompt)

FIGURE 2-24

STEP 2 ▶

Type anonymous **(Figure 2-25).**

The name anonymous is for public use.

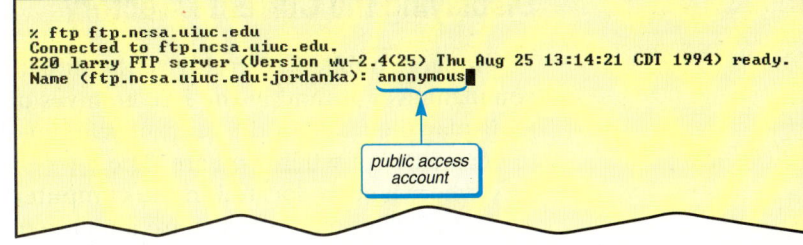

FIGURE 2-25

STEP 3 ▶

Press the ENTER key.

A prompt for a password displays (Figure 2-26). Most public access FTP sites request that you enter your electronic mail address as the password. This allows the site administrator to keep track of who is accessing the files.

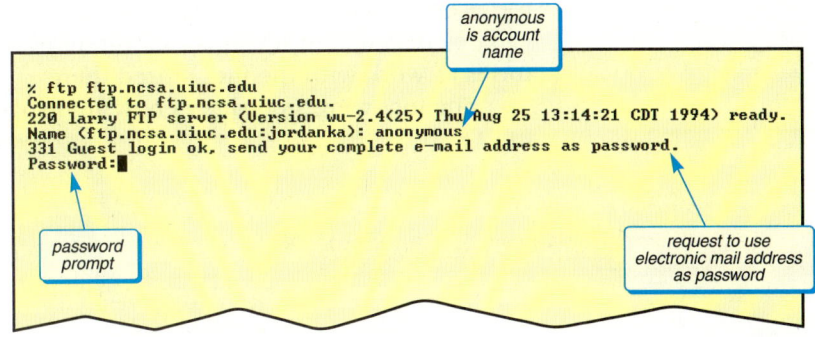

FIGURE 2-26

STEP 4 ▶

Type your e-mail address and press the ENTER key (the password will not display on the screen).

Several lines of information display and are followed by an FTP command line prompt (Figure 2-27).

```
230-Welcome to NCSA's new anonymous FTP server! I hope you find what you are
230-   looking for. If you have any technical problems with the server,
230-   please e-mail to ftpadmin@ncsa.uiuc.edu. For other questions regarding
230-   NCSA software tools, please e-mail softdev@ncsa.uiuc.edu.
230-
230-The mail archive-server is no longer supported. Of course, if
230-   you can read this, you don't need it anyway.
230-
230-Note to HyperFTP users: If you log in, and cannot list directories
230-   other than the top-level ones, enter a - as the first character of your
230-   password (e-mail address).
230-
230-If your ftp client has problems with receiving files from this server, send
230-   a - as the first character of your password (e-mail address).
230-
230-If you're ftp'ing from Delphi, please remember that the Delphi FTP client
230-   requires you to enclose case-sensitive directory and file names in double
230-   quote (") characters.
230-
230-You are user # 118 of an allowed 130 users.
230-
230-Please read the file README
230-   it was last modified on Fri Nov 22 18:54:35 1996 - 12 days ago
230-Please read the file README.FIRST
230-   it was last modified on Mon Dec  2 17:53:58 1996 - 2 days ago
230 Guest login ok, access restrictions apply.
ftp>
```

FIGURE 2-27

Notice the informational lines in Figure 2-27. The FTP site administrator has included instructions for several different groups of users, which indicate how to use the site successfully. There are e-mail addresses where suggestions and reports of problems can be sent. There is a message indicating how many simultaneous users are allowed in the site. You are directed to read special files named README, which contain other pertinent information about the FTP site. You have successfully established an FTP connection.

Displaying the Current Directory

In large public FTP archives, the directory structure can be very complex. As you maneuver around in the FTP archives directory structure, it may be necessary to display the name of the current working directory on the remote host computer to keep track of where you are. The **current working directory** is the subdirectory where you are located in the computer's directory structure.

UNIX computer systems use a hierarchical structure for organizing directories and files. User accounts have a default directory assigned as a **home directory**. This is the directory where the user is placed when first logging in. New subdirectories can be created under this home directory. New files and other directories can be created beneath those subdirectories. Users can change to these subdirectories to work with the files stored there.

The following step shows how to display the current working directory while in FTP.

TO DISPLAY THE CURRENT DIRECTORY

STEP 1 ▶

Type pwd **and press the** ENTER **key to display the current working directory.**

The name of the current directory on the remote host computer displays (Figure 2-28). pwd stands for print working directory. Figure 2-28 shows that / is the current working directory. This is because / is the home directory of the anonymous account.

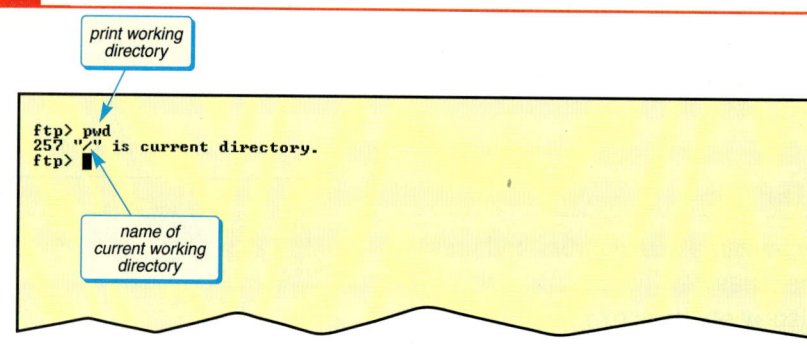

FIGURE 2-28

FTP allows you to transfer files between computers. To do this, you must know the names of the files you want to send or receive. The following step illustrates how to display a list of the files in the current working directory.

TRANSFERRING FILES WITH FTP

TO DISPLAY A LIST OF FILES ▼

STEP 1 ▶

Type `dir` and press the ENTER key.

A list of files in the current working directory displays (Figure 2-29).

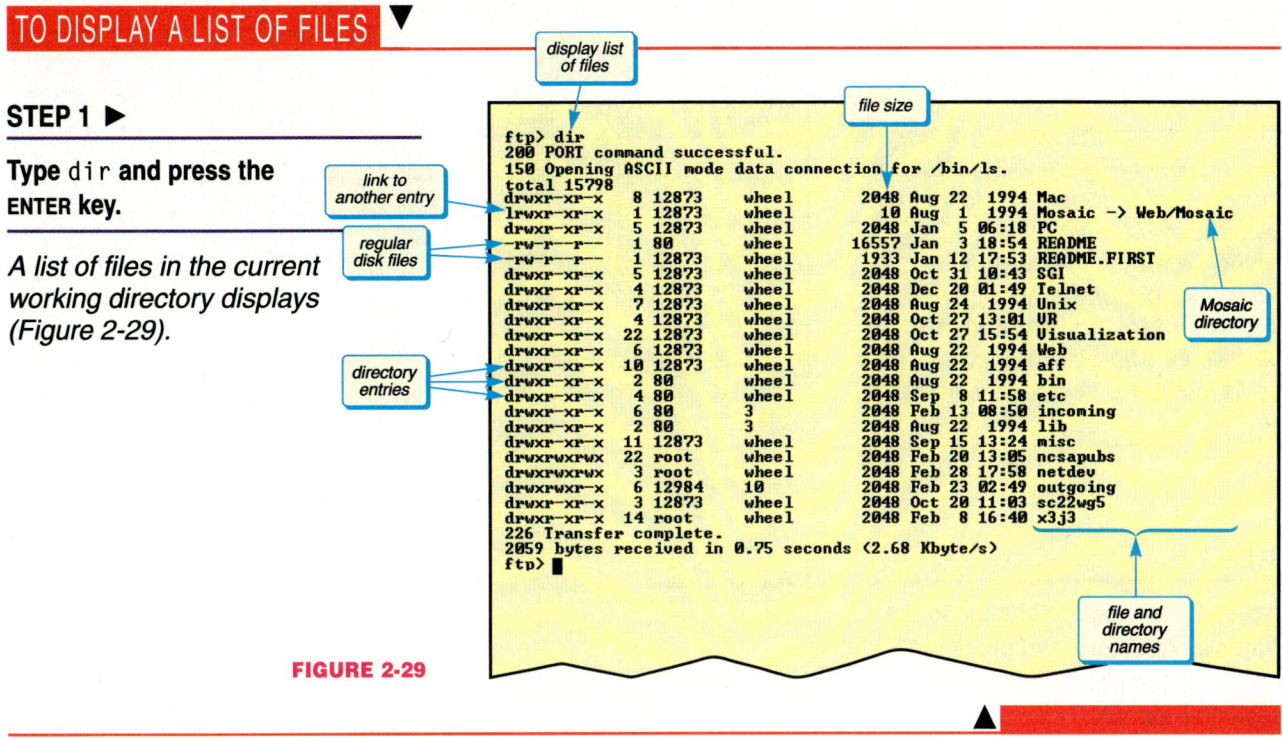

FIGURE 2-29

Figure 2-29 shows that, along with the README files, there are several directories. Each of these directories deals with different categories and interests. Entries that have the letter d in column one are directories. Entries with a hyphen (-) in column one are files.

One of the entries is called Mosaic. This is a special type of entry called a link. A **link** is a pointer to another file or directory. Links are identified by the letter l in column one. The link is illustrated in Figure 2-29 by the characters -> Web/Mosaic. The entry Mosaic actually points to the Web/Mosaic directory. You can be positioned in that directory by either changing to the Mosaic directory or by changing to the Web/Mosaic directory. The FTP site administrator may have added the link to make it easier for people to find Mosaic, thus reducing the time they spend logged in. Because you are looking for Mosaic, you should change to the Mosaic directory as illustrated in the following steps.

TO CHANGE DIRECTORIES AND DISPLAY THE CONTENTS OF VARIOUS DIRECTORIES ▼

STEP 1 ▶

Type `cd Mosaic` to change to the Mosaic directory, and press the ENTER key.

A message displays indicating the command was successful (Figure 2-30). Notice that the Mosaic entry has a capital M in it. Remember that UNIX systems are case-sensitive, so you must type the M as an uppercase letter. The contents of the Mosaic directory can be displayed with the dir command.

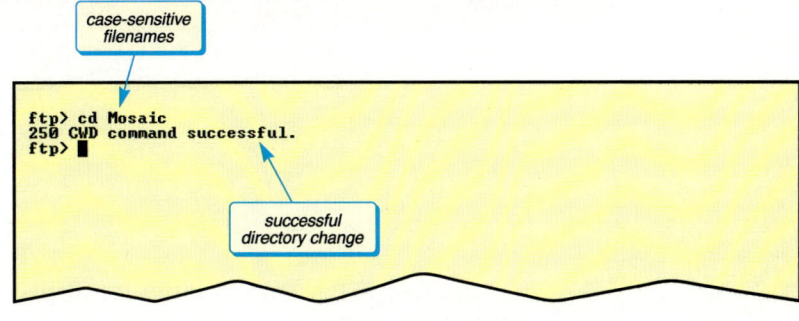

FIGURE 2-30

STEP 2 ▶

Type `dir` **and press the ENTER key.**

A list of files in the Mosaic directory displays (Figure 2-31). Notice there are directories for Mosaic for Macintosh, Mosaic for UNIX, Mosaic for Microsoft Windows, documentation, and other Mosaic information. Mosaic for Microsoft Windows can be found in the Windows directory.

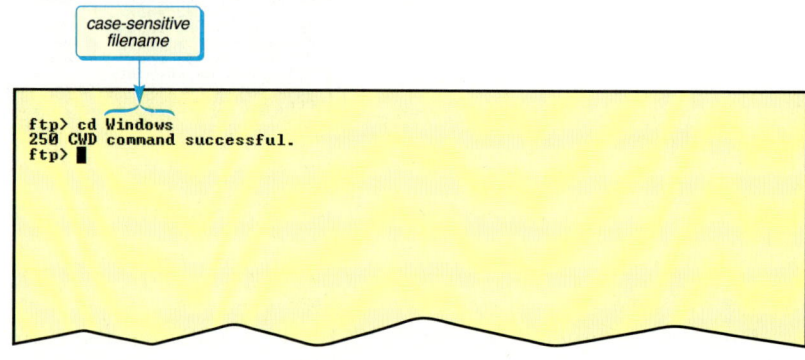

FIGURE 2-31

STEP 3 ▶

Type `cd Windows` **to change to the Windows directory, and press the ENTER key (do not forget to capitalize the W).**

A message displays indicating the command was successful (Figure 2-32).

FIGURE 2-32

STEP 4 ▶

Type `dir` **and press the ENTER key.**

A list of files in the Windows directory displays (Figure 2-33). Notice there are several versions of Mosaic, as indicated by the files ending with exe. There are also two files that contain readme in their names. One of these may indicate the differences between the Mosaic exe files.

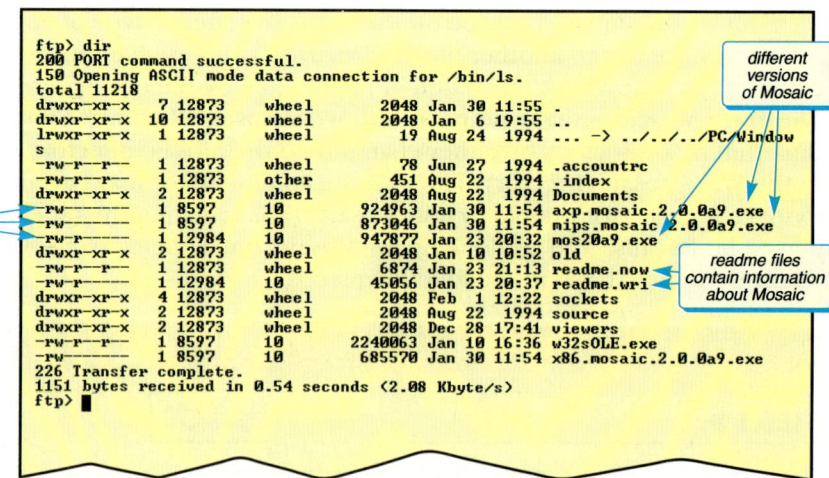

FIGURE 2-33

Because FTP has no facilities for displaying the contents of files, you must retrieve the readme.now file, and then use the file display commands available with UNIX on your local computer to read it as illustrated in the following steps.

TO RETRIEVE A TEXT FILE ▼

STEP 1 ▶

At the FTP prompt, type `get readme.now` to indicate you want to retrieve the readme.now text file, and press the ENTER key.

Informative messages display verifying the request (Figure 2-34). The transfer is now taking place. You must wait for the file transfer to complete. When the transfer is complete, messages appear indicating the number of bytes transferred and the elapsed time.

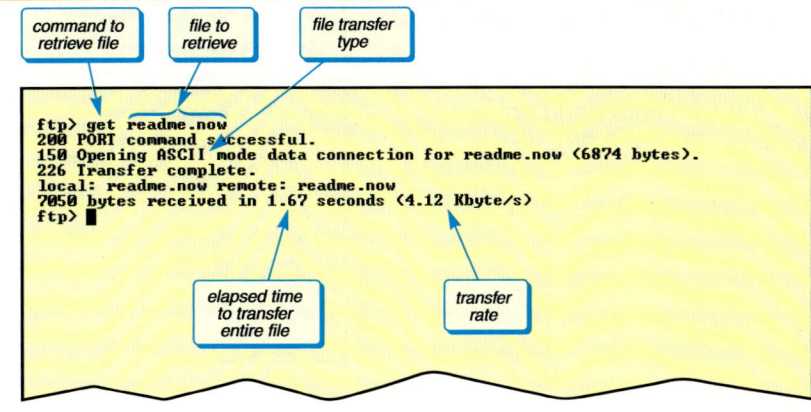

FIGURE 2-34

Large files take several minutes to transfer. The transfer speed depends on how many computers through which the packets have to travel, the traffic load, and the line speeds over which the packets travel. The readme.now file is now located in the current working directory of the local host computer. UNIX file commands can be used to display the file.

An FTP feature allows UNIX operating system commands to be executed without terminating the FTP connection. UNIX commands can be executed from within FTP by prefacing them with an exclamation point. The UNIX command that displays a text file one page at a time is called **more**. Follow these steps to execute the more command from the FTP prompt.

TO DISPLAY TEXT FILES IN FTP ▼

STEP 1 ▶

Type `!more readme.now` and press the ENTER key.

The contents of the readme.now file display (Figure 2-35). The file is displayed one screen at a time. The --More-- at the bottom of the screen means there are more pages of the readme.now file to be displayed.

FIGURE 2-35

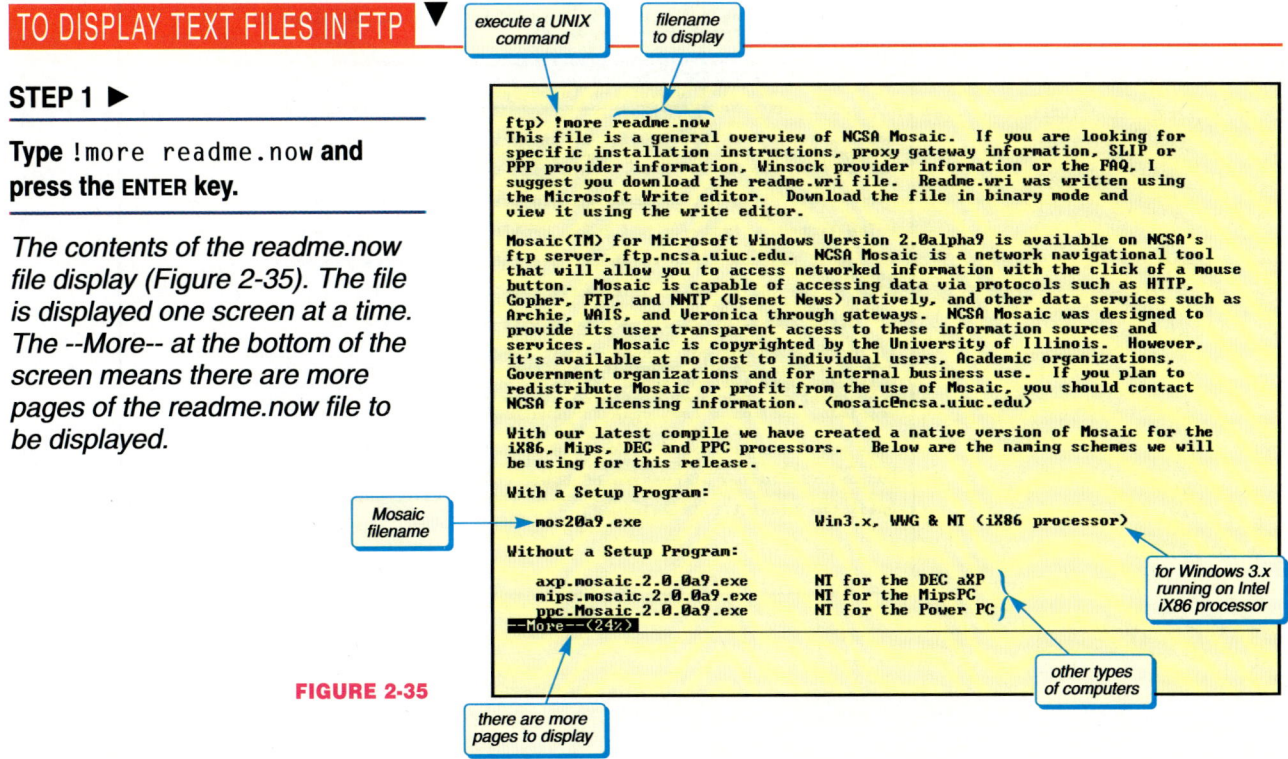

STEP 2 ▶

Type q **to end the more program.**

The readme.now display ends, and the FTP command prompt displays (Figure 2-36).

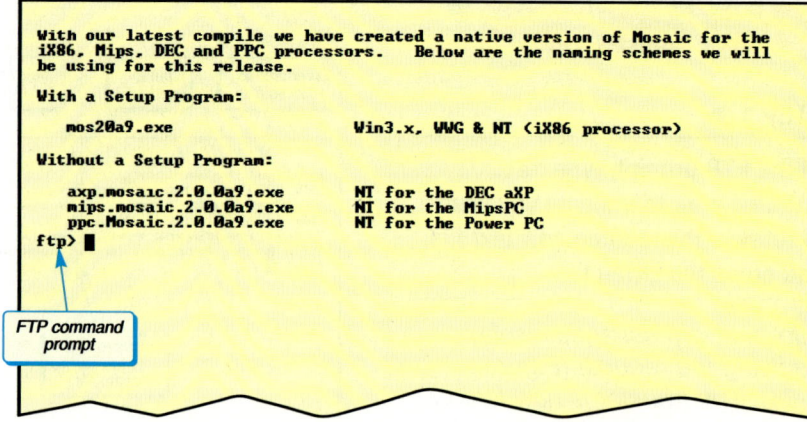

FIGURE 2-36

The readme.now file indicates that for Microsoft Windows, the proper Mosaic file is called mos20a9.exe. The .exe extension on the filename indicates it is a DOS-executable file. This type of file requires special handling from FTP.

Binary and Text Files

Characters are represented on both UNIX and MS/DOS computers using **ASCII**, which stands for American Standard Code for Information Interchange. The ASCII character set can be divided into characters that are visible and other characters that provide control information. These control characters help arrange the visible characters on a CRT screen or printer to make it easy to read. The files that contain this mixture of visible and control characters are called text, or ASCII files. They contain text that can be read. Figure 2-37 shows an example of a text file.

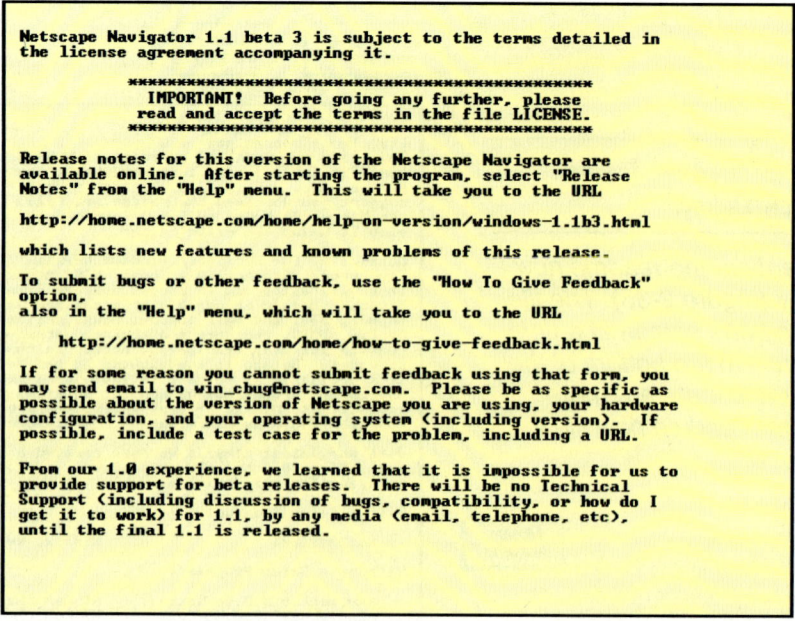

FIGURE 2-37

Another type of file, called a **binary file**, refers to files that contain executable programs or packages of programs. Binary files are not in a format that is readable by the human eye. Executable programs contain codes that control the computer while the program is running. Packaged files contain codes and other overhead information that have meaning to the packaging programs. They also change the text portions of the file using special encoding processes in order to conserve space. Figure 2-38 shows the contents of a binary file.

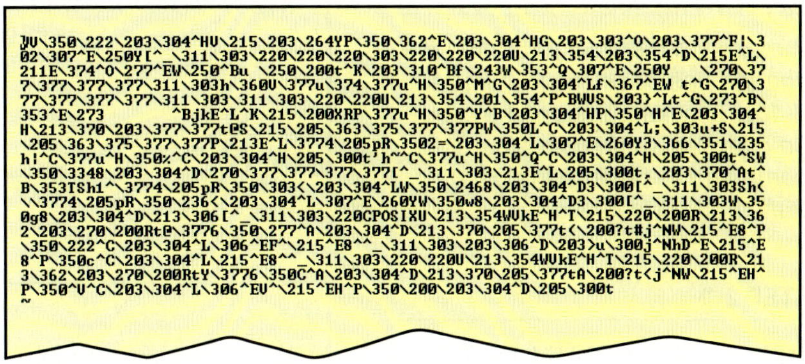

It is important to know which type of file you are working with because FTP handles the files differently. Transferring files from a UNIX system to MS/DOS or Microsoft Windows requires special processing because you are using two different operating systems. The FTP program may add extra control characters to text files so they display correctly.

You do not want FTP to add extra characters to an executable or packaged file during the transfer, however. This would make the file unusable. Therefore, you must indicate to FTP whether the file is text or binary format. You do this by setting a special switch to either ascii or binary. This switch setting is called the **transfer type**. The binary transfer type should be used to transfer mos20a9.exe because an executable file is also a binary file.

FIGURE 2-38

Changing File Transfer Types

The proper file transfer type must be set in order to transfer files without corruption. The current transfer type can be displayed, and changed if necessary, as shown in the step below.

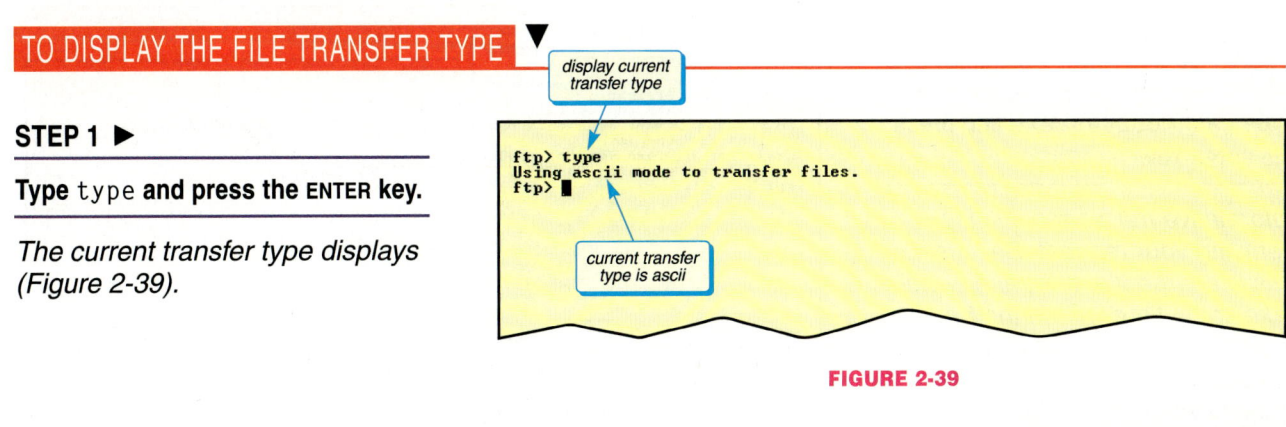

TO DISPLAY THE FILE TRANSFER TYPE

STEP 1 ▶

Type `type` **and press the ENTER key.**

The current transfer type displays (Figure 2-39).

FIGURE 2-39

The current transfer type is ascii. If the file were a text file, such as the readme.now file, you could proceed with the transfer. Because mos20a9.exe is a binary file, however, binary transfer is necessary. You must change the current transfer type from ascii to binary as shown in the steps on the next page.

TO CHANGE THE FILE TRANSFER TYPE ▼

STEP 1 ▶

Type `binary` to change from ascii to binary transfer type, and press the ENTER key.

A message displays indicating the change has been made (Figure 2-40). The file transfer type can be checked again using the type command to be sure the binary transfer type is active.

FIGURE 2-40

STEP 2 ▶

Type `type` and press the ENTER key.

The current transfer type displays (Figure 2-41).

FIGURE 2-41

Now that you are positioned in the proper directory and the correct transfer type is set, you can initiate the transfer as illustrated in the following step.

TO RETRIEVE A BINARY FILE ▼

STEP 1 ▶

Type `get mos20a9.exe` and press the ENTER key.

Informative messages display verifying your request. Because this is a large file, the transfer will take some time. When the transfer is complete, messages appear indicating the number of bytes transferred and the elapsed time (Figure 2-42).

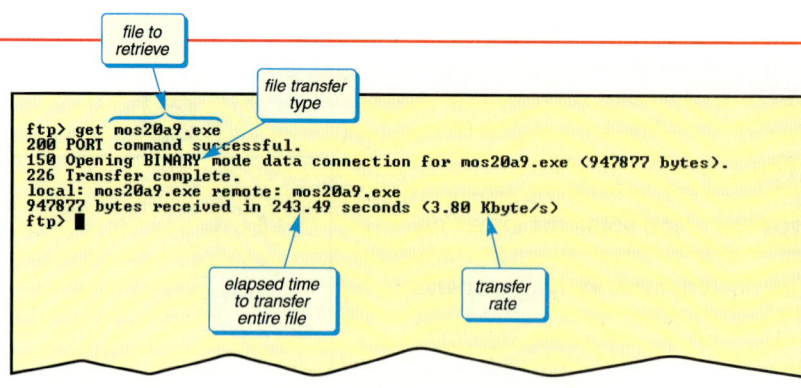

FIGURE 2-42

Public FTP sites are very popular, and many people access them every day. These sites are limited resources, so be considerate, and exit as soon as you finish transferring your files.

TO EXIT FROM THE FTP PROGRAM

Step 1: Type `bye` and press the ENTER key.

A termination message followed by the UNIX command prompt displays.

In this section, you learned how to retrieve files from a remote host computer. But retrieving files is only half of what FTP can do for you. The next section describes how to send files to a remote host.

Sending a File with FTP

Before you can send a file using FTP, you must have access to an account on a remote computer with authority to create files.

The following steps show how to transfer a text file called saved.mail to the jordank account at Nova University in Fort Lauderdale. You should substitute a different host address for Nova's and a different account name for jordank.

TO SEND A FILE USING FTP ▼

STEP 1 ▶

At the UNIX command prompt, type `ftp alpha.acast.nova.edu` and press the ENTER key. At the account prompt, type `jordank` and press the ENTER key. At the password prompt, type `ly2607` as the password and press the ENTER key.

Messages display indicating that jordank is logged in and are followed by an FTP command prompt (Figure 2-43).

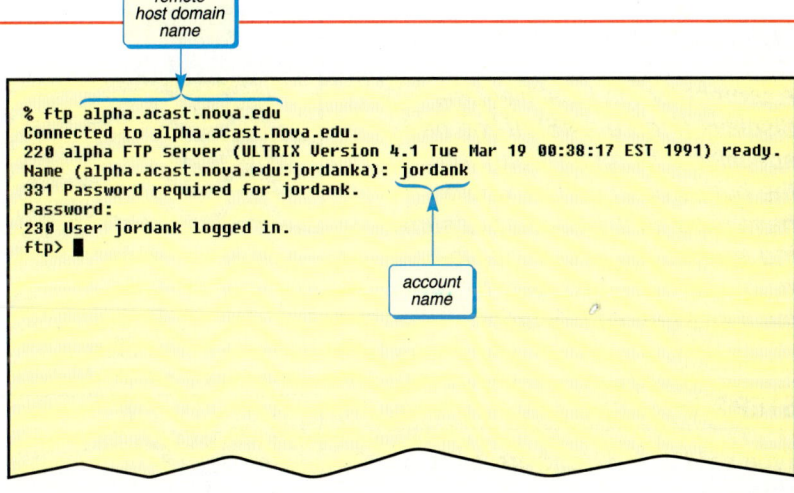

FIGURE 2-43

STEP 2 ▶

Type `put saved.mail` and press the ENTER key.

Informational messages display indicating the transfer is taking place. When the transfer is complete, messages display indicating the number of bytes transferred and the elapsed time (Figure 2-44).

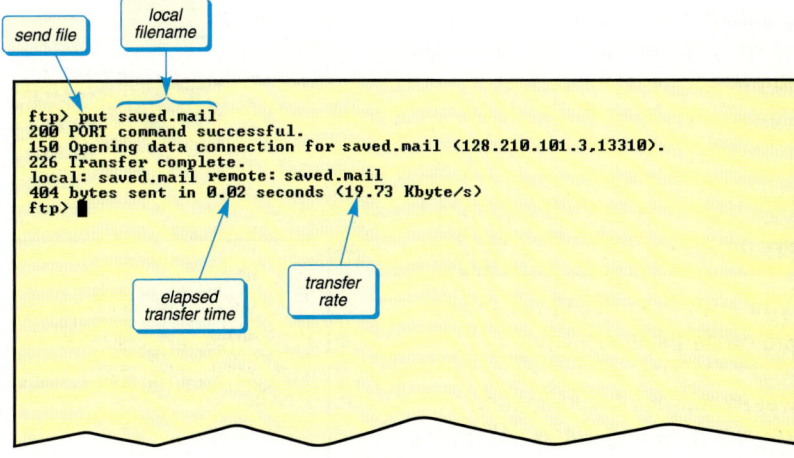

FIGURE 2-44

Transferring a File with a New Name

Several reasons exist why you may want to change the name of a file during a transfer. The Internet has many computers running many different operating systems. The rules for filenames on one computer may not be acceptable on another. For example, some UNIX systems allow up to 255 characters in a filename. MS/DOS systems, however, allow a maximum of only eight characters with an optional three-character extension in filenames. Another reason you may wish to change the filename is that a file with the same name may already exist on the remote computer, and you want to keep that file.

Fortunately, you can specify a different name to be used for the new file for both the get and put functions in FTP. Although an example of sending a file with a new name using the put command is shown in the following steps, the same technique applies to retrieving files using the get command.

TO SEND A FILE AND GIVE IT A NEW NAME ▼

STEP 1 ▶

Type `put` **and press the ENTER key.**

A prompt for the local filename displays (Figure 2-45). If you had specified a filename along with the put command, FTP would have initiated the transfer, assuming you wanted to use the filename you specified as both the local and remote filenames.

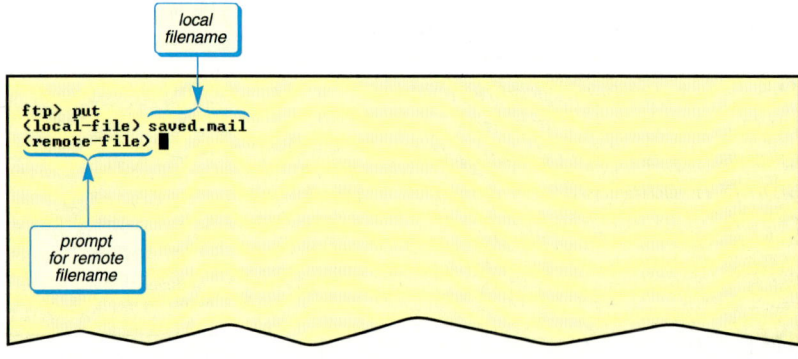

FIGURE 2-45

STEP 2 ▶

Type `saved.mail` **and press the ENTER key.**

A prompt for the remote filename displays (Figure 2-46). This is where you can give the file a new name.

FIGURE 2-46

STEP 3 ▶

Type `my.first.mail.message` **and press the ENTER key.**

Messages display indicating the transfer is taking place. When the transfer is complete, the number of bytes and elapsed time displays, along with an FTP command prompt (Figure 2-47).

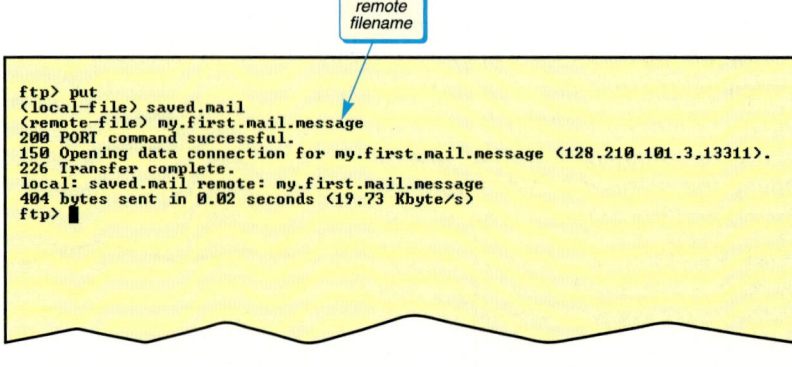

FIGURE 2-47

STEP 4 ▶

Type `dir` **and press the ENTER key.**

The directory list on the remote computer displays, verifying the file has a new name (Figure 2-48). After transferring the files, the FTP session can be ended with the bye command.

STEP 5

Type `bye` **and press the ENTER key.**

A termination message displays and is followed by the UNIX command prompt.

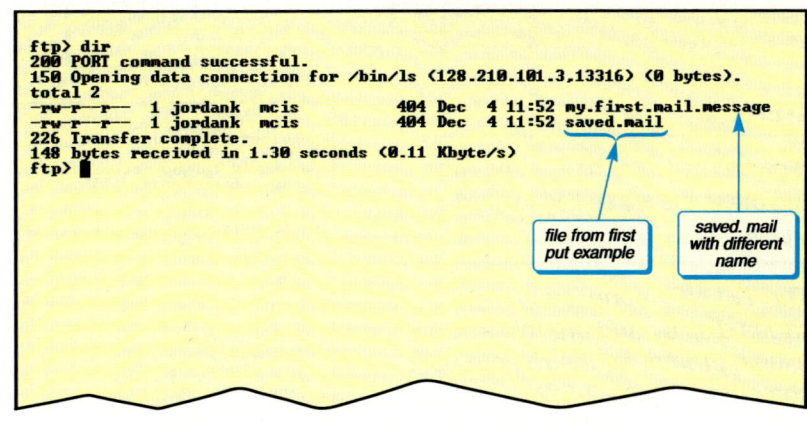

FIGURE 2-48

Table 2-2 summarizes the FTP commands used in this project.

The preceding section of the project demonstrated how to send files to a remote host computer using FTP. Transferring files requires that you know the names of those files. With thousands of computers on the Internet containing thousands of files each, how do you determine which one contains the program in which you are interested? Finding files on the Internet is easy using archie to perform a search.

▶ FINDING FILES WITH ARCHIE

Archie is an Internet service that will search a special database for filenames and display the host address and directory path where the file is located. This information can then be used with FTP to retrieve the file. Using TELNET or an archie client, you can contact an archie server.

Figure 2-49 illustrates archie servers available for use. The following steps show how to use TELNET to establish a session with the archie server at archie.sura.net and search for unzip, a UNIX file decompression utility.

▶ **TABLE 2-2**

FTP COMMAND	FTP TASK
cd	Change to another directory
?	Display a list of commands
pwd	Display the current working directory
dir	Display the filenames
type	Display the file transfer type
!command-name parameters	Execute a UNIX command
bye	Exit the FTP program
get file-name	Retrieve a file
put file-name	Send a file
ascii	Set the file transfer type to ascii
binary	Set the file transfer type to binary

```
archie.au                139.130.4.6        Australia
archie.uni-linz.ac.at    140.78.3.8         Austria
archie.univie.ac.at      131.130.1.23       Austria
archie.cs.mcgill.ca      132.206.51.250     Canada
archie.uqam.ca           132.208.250.10     Canada
archie.funet.fi          128.214.6.102      Finland
archie.univ-rennes1.fr   129.20.128.38      France
archie.th-darmstadt.de   130.83.128.118     Germany
archie.ac.il             132.65.16.18       Israel
archie.unipi.it          131.114.21.10      Italy
archie.wide.ad.jp        133.4.3.6          Japan
archie.hana.nm.kr        128.134.1.1        Korea
archie.sogang.ac.kr      163.239.1.11       Korea
archie.uninett.no        128.39.2.20        Norway
archie.rediris.es        130.206.1.2        Spain
archie.luth.se           130.240.12.30      Sweden
archie.switch.ch         130.59.1.40        Switzerland
archie.twnic.net         192.83.166.10      Taiwan
archie.ncu.edu.tw        192.83.166.12      Taiwan
archie.doc.ic.ac.uk      146.169.11.3       United Kingdom
archie.hensa.ac.uk       129.12.21.25       United Kingdom
archie.unl.edu           129.93.1.14        USA (NE)
archie.internic.net      198.49.45.10       USA (NJ)
archie.rutgers.edu       128.6.18.15        USA (NJ)
archie.ans.net           147.225.1.10       USA (NY)
archie.sura.net          128.167.254.179    USA (MD)   ◀ archie server searched in next section
```

FIGURE 2-49 — domain name — Internet address — location of archie server

TO START AN ARCHIE SESSION ▼

STEP 1 ▶

Type `telnet archie.sura.net` **and press the** ENTER **key to start archie.**

The TELNET connection messages display and are followed by a login prompt for the remote host computer (Figure 2-50).

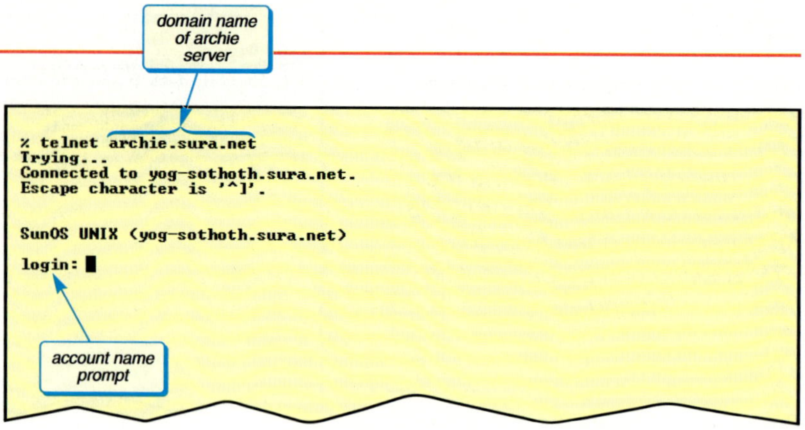

```
% telnet archie.sura.net
Trying...
Connected to yog-sothoth.sura.net.
Escape character is '^]'.

SunOS UNIX (yog-sothoth.sura.net)
login:
```
domain name of archie server → `archie.sura.net`
account name prompt → `login:`

FIGURE 2-50

STEP 2 ▶

Type `archie` **and press the** ENTER **key.**

Messages display indicating how to access help and declaring the default search type is sub. These messages are followed by the archie command prompt archie> (Figure 2-51). Default search type means this is the search type that will be used if you do not specify another type. Setting the search type will be explained later in this section. This archie server will not prompt for a password because the archie service is available for public use.

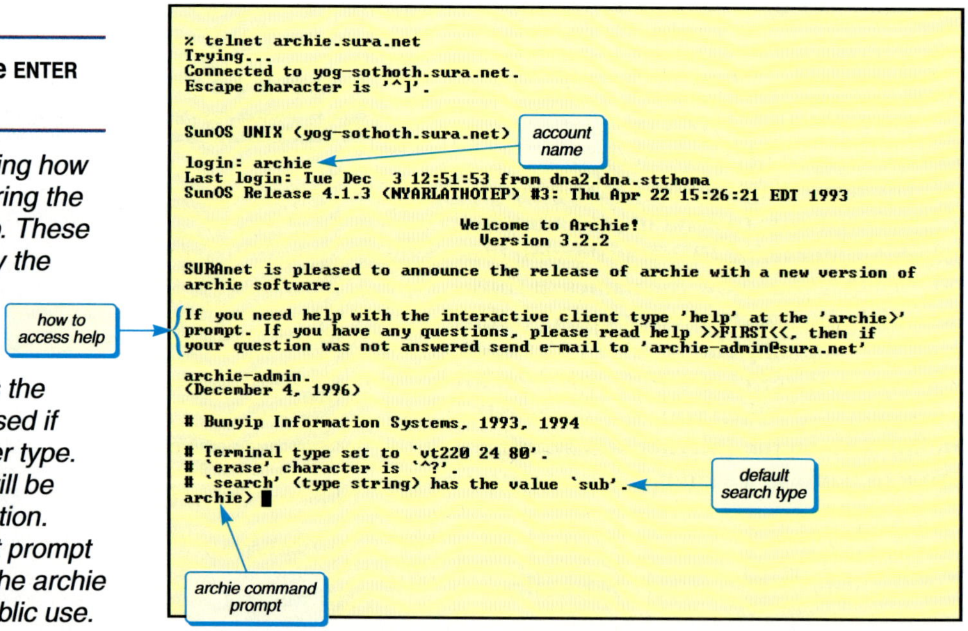

```
% telnet archie.sura.net
Trying...
Connected to yog-sothoth.sura.net.
Escape character is '^]'.

SunOS UNIX (yog-sothoth.sura.net)
login: archie
Last login: Tue Dec  3 12:51:53 from dna2.dna.stthoma
SunOS Release 4.1.3 (NYARLATHOTEP) #3: Thu Apr 22 15:26:21 EDT 1993
                    Welcome to Archie!
                       Version 3.2.2
SURAnet is pleased to announce the release of archie with a new version of
archie software.
If you need help with the interactive client type 'help' at the 'archie>'
prompt. If you have any questions, please read help >>FIRST<<, then if
your question was not answered send e-mail to 'archie-admin@sura.net'
archie-admin.
(December 4, 1996)
# Bunyip Information Systems, 1993, 1994

# Terminal type set to 'vt220 24 80'.
# 'erase' character is '^?'.
# 'search' (type string) has the value 'sub'.
archie>
```
account name → `archie`
how to access help
default search type → `'sub'`
archie command prompt → `archie>`

FIGURE 2-51

The archie service is now ready to perform searches. Information about archie commands is available with the help command.

Displaying Information about a File

Sometimes, you may not know quite what filename to give archie to use for searching. You will find that files on the Internet are not always named what you might expect. Archie keeps another database containing filenames and a brief description of the file. You can query this database with the whatis command to discover the names of files that include the word zip, as shown in the following step.

TO DISPLAY INFORMATION ABOUT A FILE

STEP 1 ▶

Type `whatis zip` **and press the ENTER key.**

The filenames that match zip, along with a brief description of each file, display (Figure 2-52).

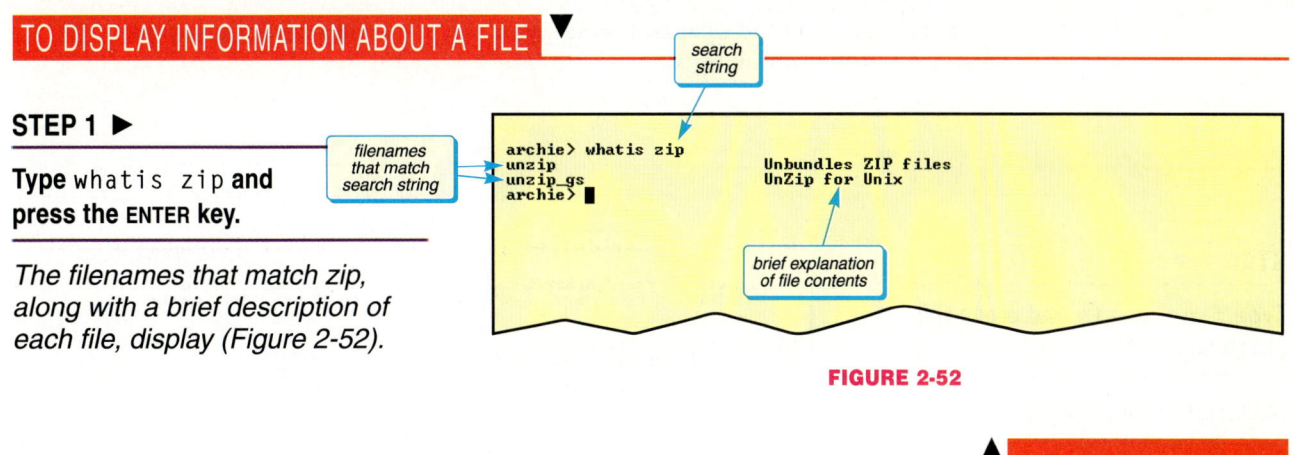

FIGURE 2-52

This archie server returned two entries for zip. These filenames now can be used for searching.

Setting the Search Type

The set search command controls the type of search that archie performs. Setting the type of search that archie performs affects the number of hits returned. You want to set a search type that returns just enough locations for you to successfully find the file, but not so many that there are many dozens of pages of locations returned.

The available search types are: **exact**, which searches for an exact filename match; **sub**, which searches for a noncase-sensitive match of any set of characters of the filename; **regex**, which uses a regular expression to match filenames; and **subcase**, which searches for a case-sensitive match of any set of characters of the filename. The best way to ensure that the minimum number of locations is returned is to use an exact search. This means archie must match your search word exactly.

Recall, in Figure 2-51, the default search type was sub. The following step shows how to set the type of search to exact.

TO SET THE ARCHIE SEARCH TYPE

STEP 1 ▶

Type `set search exact` **and press the ENTER key.**

An archie command prompt displays (Figure 2-53). The search type is now exact.

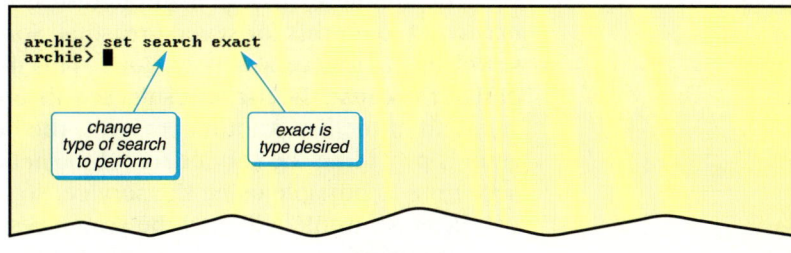

FIGURE 2-53

Now that the type of search is set, you can start a search for unzip as illustrated in the following step.

TO SEARCH FOR A FILENAME ▼

STEP 1 ▶

Type `find unzip` **and press the ENTER key.**

Information detailing the type of search being performed, the number of people ahead of you waiting to perform a search, and an estimated length of time to completion will appear briefly on the terminal screen. Eventually, the results of the search display (Figure 2-54).

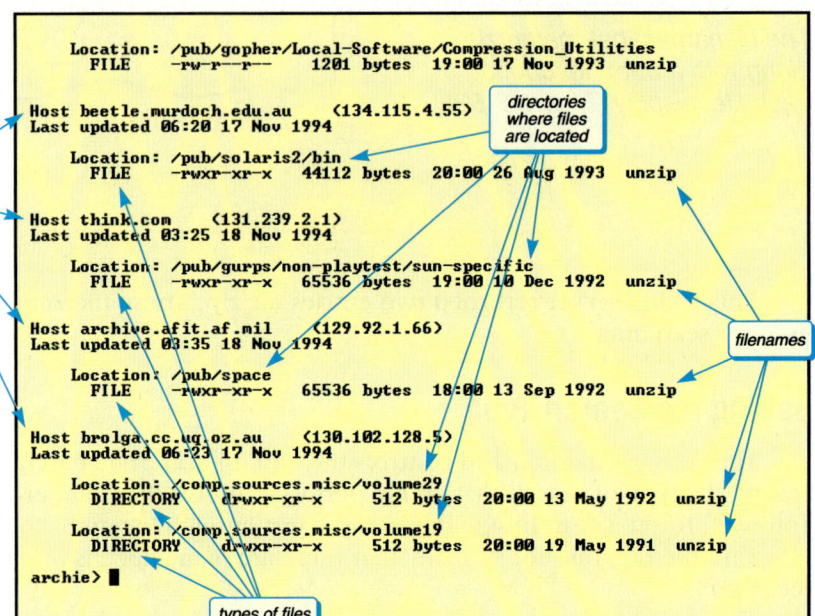

FIGURE 2-54

The results contain four pieces of information about each match: the host computer IP address (or domain name), the directory path or location of the file, the file type, which can be DIRECTORY or FILE, and the filename. The host name, directory path and filename are needed when using FTP to retrieve the file.

Mailing the Search Results

The archie server can mail the results of the search (Figure 2-54) to you. You may want to do this for several reasons. Sometimes the list of sites containing your search string is several screens long. This makes finding the closest site somewhat difficult because the list of results scrolls up on the screen, and you see only the very end of the list. Another reason is the host site running the archie server program is providing the service free. Internet courtesy requires that you spend as little time as possible using the service, so it will be available for others to use.

Because archie will mail the search results, you can exit the archie server immediately after the search is over. When the search results arrive in your mail box, you can take your time browsing through them. The following steps show how to instruct archie to mail the search results. You should substitute your own e-mail address for jordank@alpha.acast.nova.edu.

FINDING FILES WITH ARCHIE   **I.63**

TO HAVE ARCHIE MAIL THE SEARCH RESULTS ▼

STEP 1 ▶

Type `mail jordank@alpha.acast.nova.edu` **and press the ENTER key.**

An archie command prompt displays (Figure 2-55).

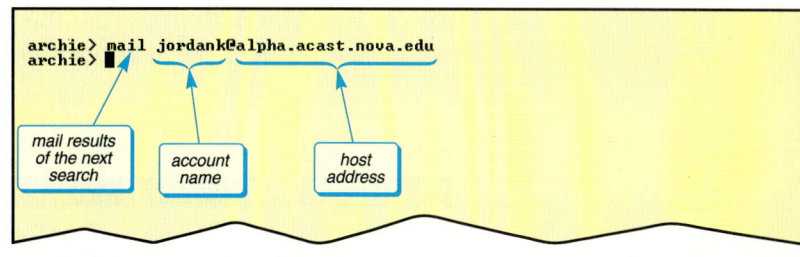

FIGURE 2-55

STEP 2 ▶

Type `find unzip` **and press the ENTER key.**

The search results display again (Figure 2-56). More importantly, the listing shown in Figure 2-56 is sent to your electronic mail account.

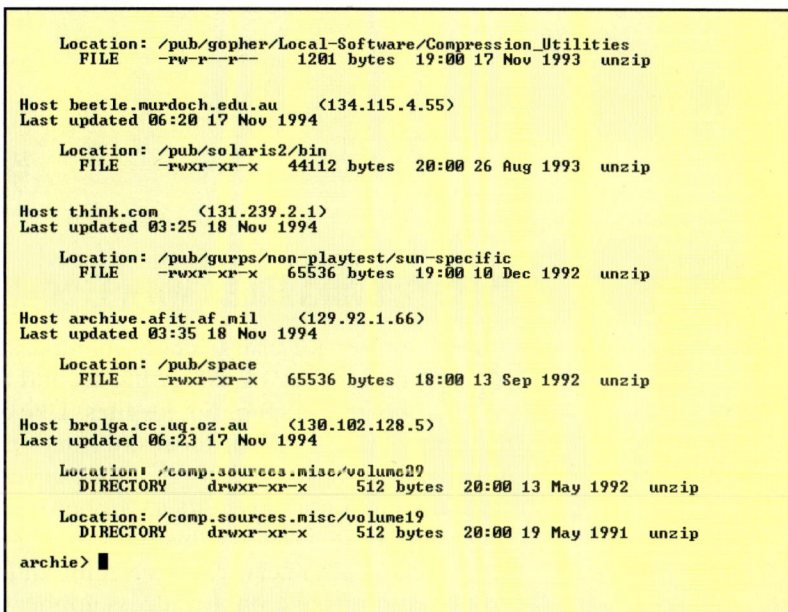

FIGURE 2-56

You now can exit archie and read the results using electronic mail (see pages I.41 and I.42).

TO EXIT AN ARCHIE SESSION ▼

STEP 1 ▶

Type `bye` **and press the ENTER key.**

A message indicating the TELNET connection has been closed followed by the UNIX command prompt (%) displays (Figure 2-57).

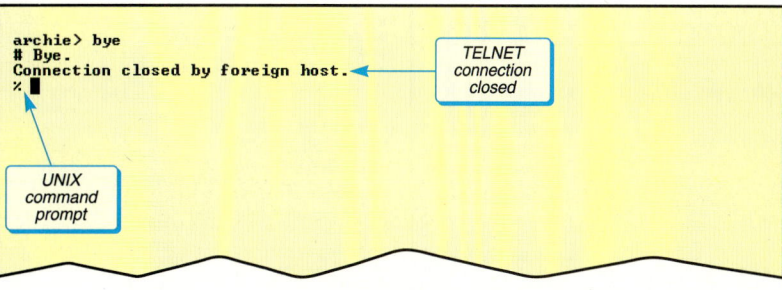

FIGURE 2-57

You have learned how to search for files using archie. Table 2-3 summarizes archie commands and their functions.

While archie will help you find the location of files on the Internet, it will not send them to you. You have to use another program, FTP, to retrieve them. Another Internet service, called gopher, not only will help you find files but also will retrieve them for you.

▶ **TABLE 2-3**

ARCHIE COMMAND	ARCHIE TASK
whatis file-name	Display a brief summary of a file's contents
help	Display help
bye	Exit the archie program
set search search-type	Indicate what type of search to perform
mail account-name@host-address	Mail the search results
find file-name	Start searching

▶ RETRIEVING FILES WITH GOPHER

Gopher is a user-friendly, menu-based tool for retrieving files. It hides the complexity of navigating around the Internet searching several host computers looking for files. Like archie, a gopher server can be reached by using TELNET. If your local site runs a gopher server, you can access gopher directly. Figure 2-58 lists some public access gopher sites that accept TELNET sessions if you do not have a local gopher server available. The Appendix lists several other gopher servers. To illustrate using gopher, the following steps show how to use a local gopher server to search for and retrieve a copy of the Emancipation Proclamation from a public access gopher site at wiretap.spies.com.

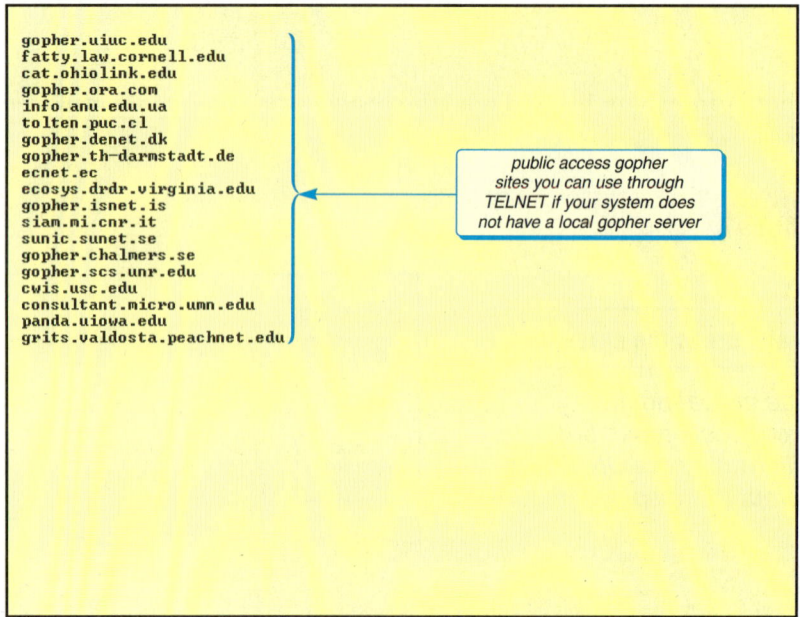

FIGURE 2-58

TO START A GOPHER SESSION

STEP 1 ▶

At the UNIX prompt (%), type `gopher wiretap.spies.com` **and press the ENTER key to start the gopher session.**

The main Gopher menu displays (Figure 2-59).

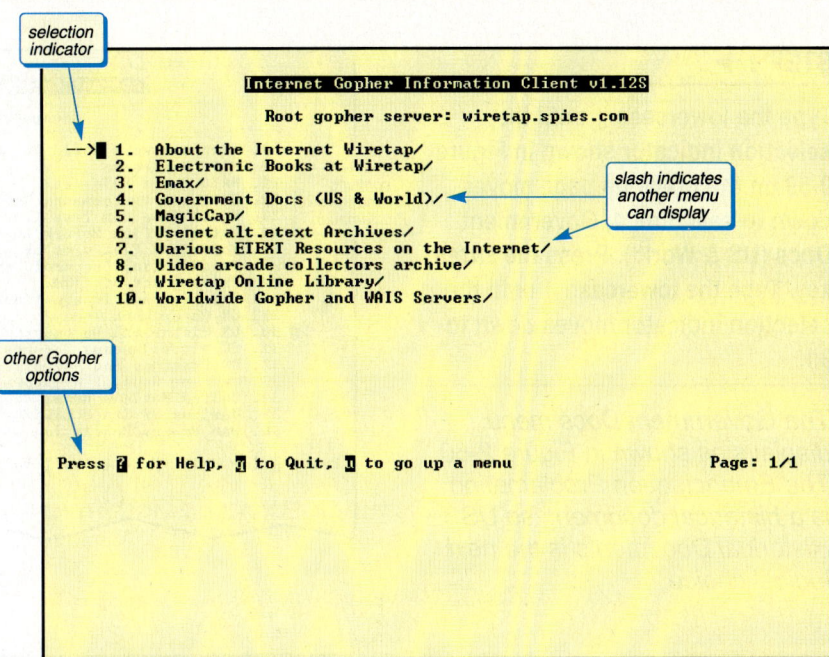

FIGURE 2-59

The Gopher menu contains a **selection indicator** (-->), which indicates the current selection to be made. The slash (/) at the end of each choice indicates that another menu will be displayed by making this selection. The line at the bottom of the screen indicates additional Gopher menu choices.

Navigating Gopher Menus

Gopher is a menu-driven service. Selections are made by moving the menu selection indicator up or down to point to your choice and then pressing the ENTER key. To move the selection indicator down, press the lowercase letter j. To move the selection indicator up, press the lowercase letter k. To remember the functions of these keys, think *jump down* (j = down) and *klimb up* (k = up). To move down or up a full screen at a time, press the uppercase letter J for down or the uppercase letter K for up.

By looking at the choices shown in the Gopher menu in Figure 2-59, you can see the likely location for an important document in the history of the United States, such as the Emancipation Proclamation document, would be Government Docs. The steps on the next page illustrate how to maneuver through the Gopher menus to find the document.

TO NAVIGATE GOPHER MENUS

STEP 1 ▶

Type the lowercase j until the selection indicator shown in Figure 2-59 on the previous page moves down to selection 4, Government Docs (US & World). Press the ENTER key. Type the lowercase j until the selection indicator moves down to 30.

The Government Docs menu displays as shown in Figure 2-60. The Emancipation Proclamation is a historical document, so US Historical Documents is the next logical choice.

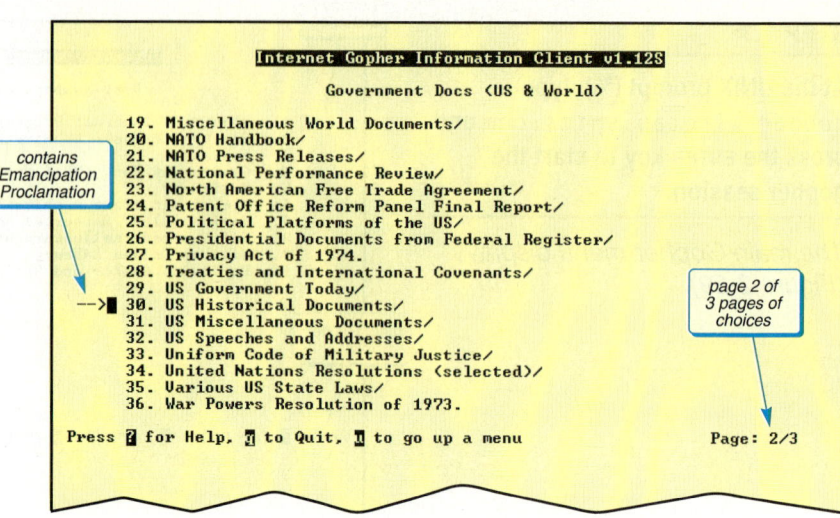

FIGURE 2-60

STEP 2 ▶

Press the ENTER key.

The US Historical Documents menu displays (Figure 2-61). The Emancipation Proclamation is number 3 on the list.

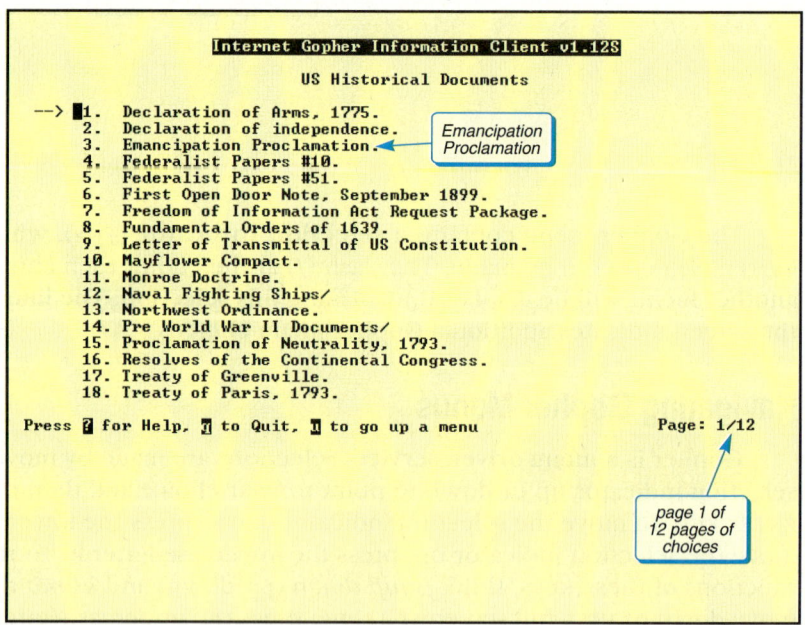

FIGURE 2-61

To retrieve the Emancipation Proclamation document, perform the following steps.

TO RETRIEVE THE DOCUMENT

STEP 1 ▶

With the selection indicator pointing to Emancipation Proclamation, press the ENTER key.

The contents of the document display, followed by prompts at the bottom of the screen indicating several options (Figure 2-62). Pressing the SPACEBAR displays the rest of the document. Typing q ends the display.

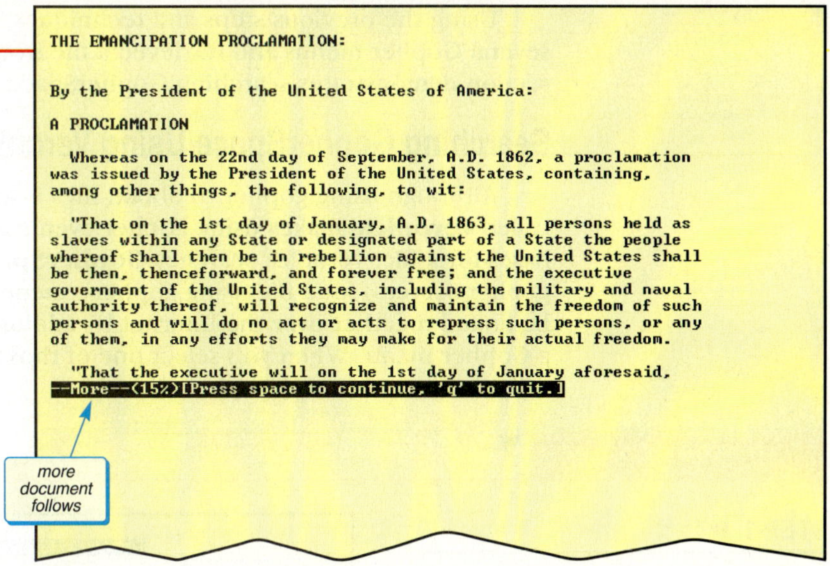

FIGURE 2-62

STEP 2 ▶

Press the SPACEBAR.

The next page of the document displays. At the end of the document, several new choices display at the bottom of the screen (Figure 2-63). The choices are to have the document mailed to you <m>, printed on the local host's printer <p>, or saved to a disk file <s>.

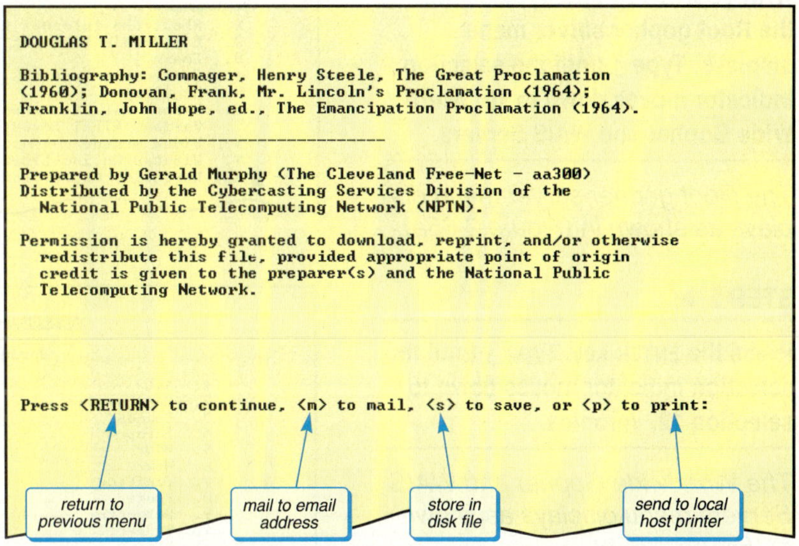

FIGURE 2-63

STEP 3 ▶

Type s to save the document to a disk file.

A box displays containing a prompt with the default name of the file to store the document.

STEP 4 ▶

Press the ENTER key to accept the default name.

A message displays in the lower right-hand corner of the screen indicating the transfer is taking place (Figure 2-64). The box disappears when the transfer is complete, indicating a copy of the Emancipation Proclamation is now in the current working directory on the local host computer.

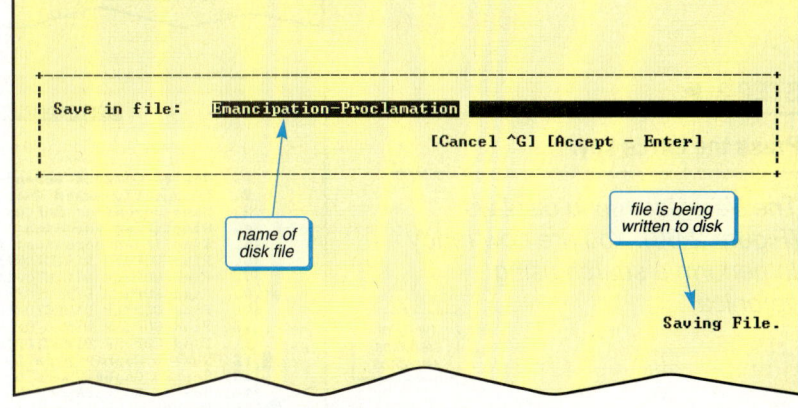

FIGURE 2-64

Using the previous steps and techniques, you have successfully navigated several Gopher menus and retrieved a file from a remote host computer. The next section demonstrates searching GopherSpace.

Searching GopherSpace Using Veronica

Although using gopher to obtain files is an easy process, a feature of gopher, called **veronica**, makes using gopher even easier. Just as archie searches its databases for a file, veronica searches **GopherSpace** (the interconnected collection of gopher servers) for a file using gopher's menu-driven interface. Gopher servers can be linked together over the Internet by adding entries for those gopher servers to a Gopher menu. When you select one of those menu choices, you are automatically connected to that gopher server.

TO ACCESS VERONICA

STEP 1 ▶

With gopher running, type u until the Root gopher server menu displays. Type j until the selection indicator moves down to 10, World Wide Gopher and WAIS Servers.

The Root gopher server menu displays as shown in (Figure 2-65a).

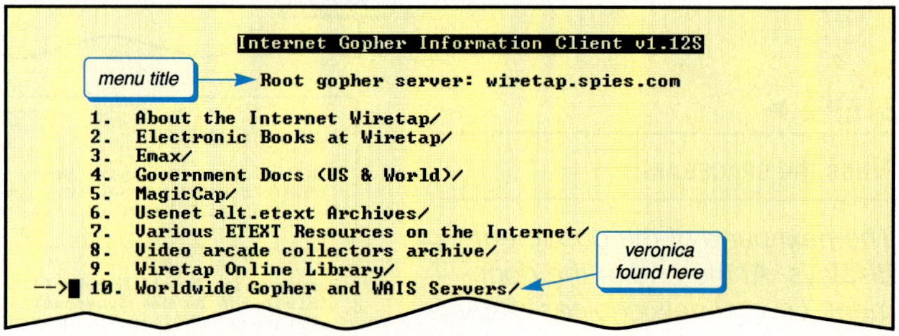

FIGURE 2-65a

STEP 2 ▶

Press the ENTER key. Type j until the selection indicator moves down to selection 12, Veronica.

The Worldwide Gopher and WAIS Servers menu displays as shown in (Figure 2-65b).

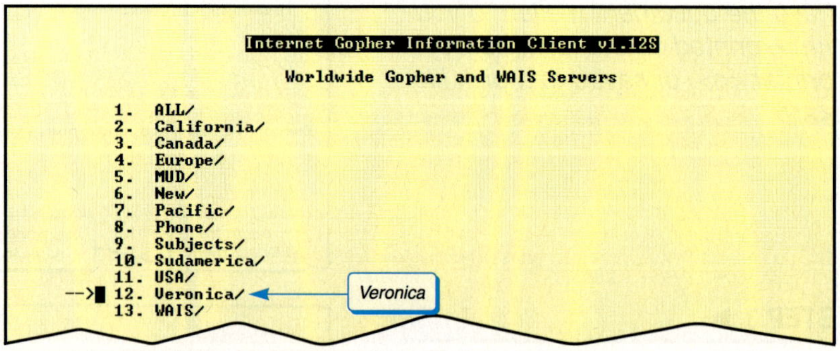

FIGURE 2-65b

STEP 3 ▶

Press the ENTER key.

The Veronica menu displays (Figure 2-66). You are now ready to perform a search using veronica.

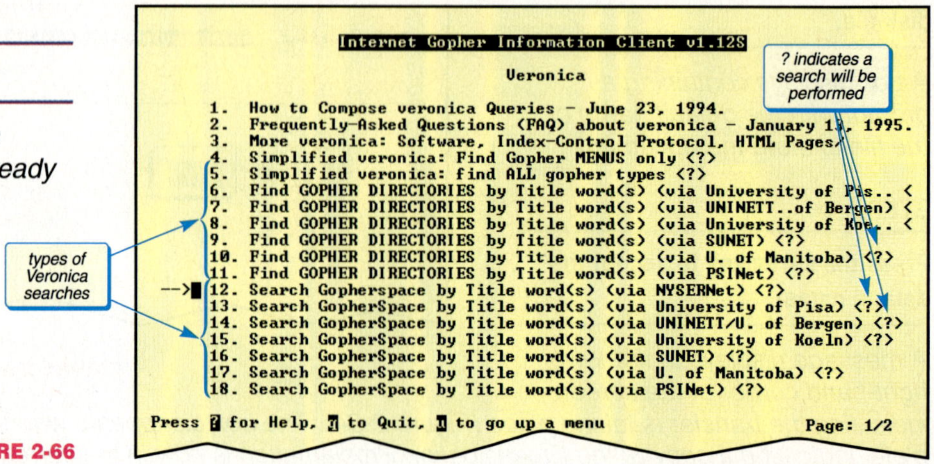

FIGURE 2-66

Searching with Veronica

Figure 2-66 shows several ways to search with veronica and several hosts from which to begin the search. Veronica can search for gopher directories only or search for the actual file. Several host computers are available as starting points. You can choose the one with the least amount of traffic, the one physically closest to you, or the one that you know contains the files for which you are looking. For this example, you should search all available gopher sites for pkzip, so the menu choices that indicate they search GopherSpace are the place to start. The following steps illustrate searching the NYSERNet gopher server for pkzip, a file compression utility for personal computers.

TO START A VERONICA SEARCH

STEP 1 ▶

With the selection indicator on 12 (Figure 2-66), press the ENTER key. Type `pkzip` in the box.

A box displays in which the filename pkzip is entered (Figure 2-67).

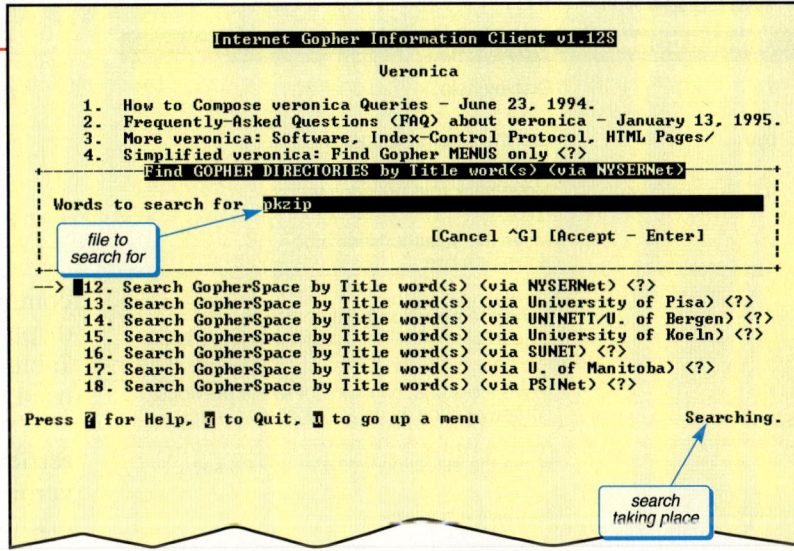

FIGURE 2-67

STEP 2 ▶

Press the ENTER key.

A message displays in the lower right-hand corner of the screen that indicates the search is taking place. When the search is completed, a Gopher menu displays with entries containing your search string (Figure 2-68). Notice there are 12 pages of menu choices. If you want to obtain a version of pkzip to run on your personal computer, items numbered 14 through 18 look promising. You retrieve the file the same way you retrieved the Emancipation Proclamation document.

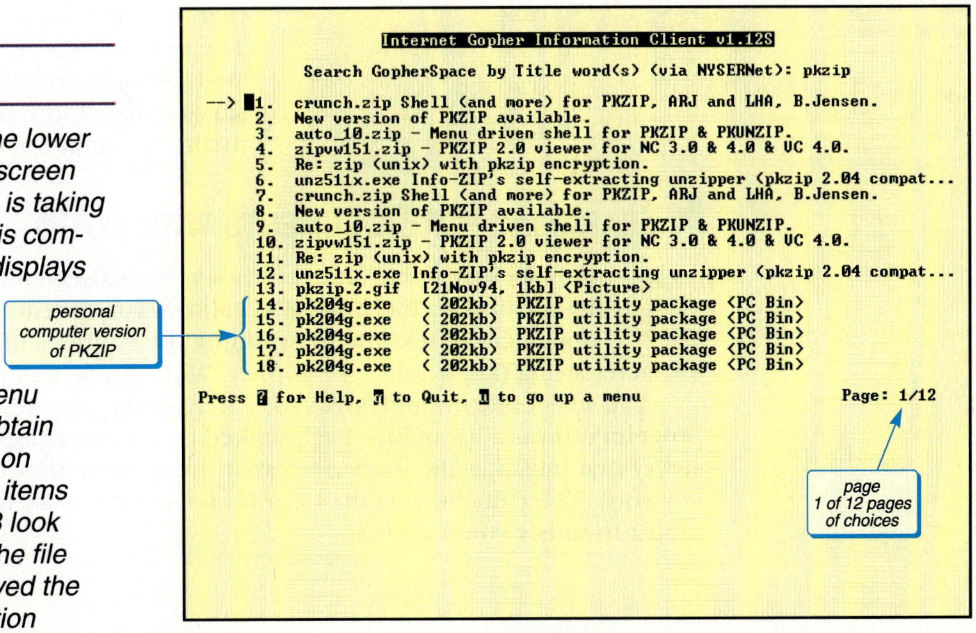

FIGURE 2-68

Moving the selection indicator to one of the files on lines 14 through 18 labeled PC bin and pressing the ENTER key displays a box in which a default filename appears. Pressing the ENTER key will indicate your desire to accept the default filename and gopher will start transferring the file. When the box disappears, the pkzip program will be in the current working directory of the local host computer.

Public access gopher servers, like public access archie servers, are limited resources. You should exit from the gopher server as soon as possible after obtaining your files. The following steps summarize this procedure.

TO END A GOPHER SESSION

Step 1: Type q and press the ENTER key.

A prompt displays asking if you want to quit.

Step 2: Type y and press the ENTER key.

The UNIX command prompt (%) displays.

Gopher has many other features and commands not illustrated in this project. To display help in gopher, type the ? command. Table 2-4 summarizes the gopher commands used in Project 2.

You have learned how to search for and retrieve files by name using gopher and veronica. But what if you want to find information about artificial intelligence and do not know the name of any documents? Fortunately, an Internet service is available that finds files by searching their contents. The next section shows how to use WAIS, or Wide Area Information Servers, the Internet service that stores and makes available documents on a multitude of different topics.

▶ **TABLE 2-4**

GOPHER COMMAND	GOPHER TASK
?	Display help
bye	Exit the Gopher program
u	Move back to a previous menu
j	Move the selection indicator down one line
J	Move the selection indicator to the next screen of choices on a multiscreen menu
K	Move the selection indicator to the previous screen of choices on a multiscreen menu
k	Move the selection indicator up one line
ENTER	Retrieve a document
ENTER	Select a menu item
s	Save a document to disk

▶ **SEARCHING FOR DOCUMENTS WITH WAIS**

Tools such as archie and gopher's veronica search for documents and files by the title, or filename. WAIS allows you to search for and retrieve a document or text file by scanning the contents of that document for a character string (keyword). Like gopher, WAIS is a menu-driven service.

You select one or more areas to search, enter your keyword, and the WAIS program returns a list of hits, each ranked by a score computed by the WAIS server that indicates the probability that the document or text file contains your keyword. These documents then can be retrieved for use in homework, research, or just to satisfy your curiosity.

Connecting to a WAIS Server

WAIS services are available from most of the popular gopher sites under the menu choice Worldwide Gopher and WAIS Servers (see item 10 in Figure 2-59 on page I.65). You can also use TELNET to connect to a remote host computer that provides public access to WAIS. Two popular public access WAIS server sites are quake.think.com, and sunsite.unc.edu.

In the following steps, TELNET is used to connect to the WAIS server at quake.think.com to obtain information about artificial intelligence.

TO CONNECT TO A WAIS SERVER USING TELNET ▼

STEP 1 ▶

Type `telnet quake.think.com` and press the ENTER key to connect to the WAIS server.

A login prompt from the remote host computer displays.

STEP 2 ▶

Type `wais` and press the ENTER key.

Informational startup messages display along with a prompt for your electronic mail address.

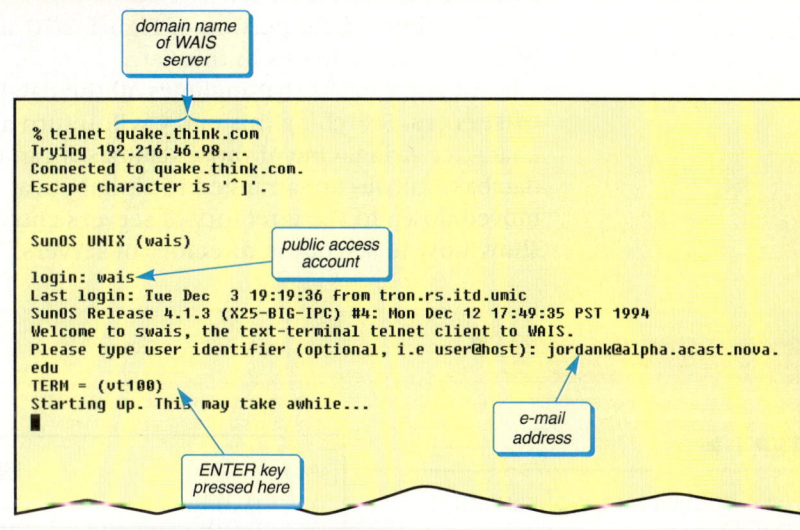

FIGURE 2-69

STEP 3 ▶

Type your e-mail address and press the ENTER key.

A prompt for a terminal type followed by the default type, vt100 displays (Figure 2-69).

STEP 4 ▶

Press the ENTER key to accept vt100.

A message displays asking you to wait while your session is being set up. After a short time, the WAIS Source Selection menu displays (Figure 2-70).

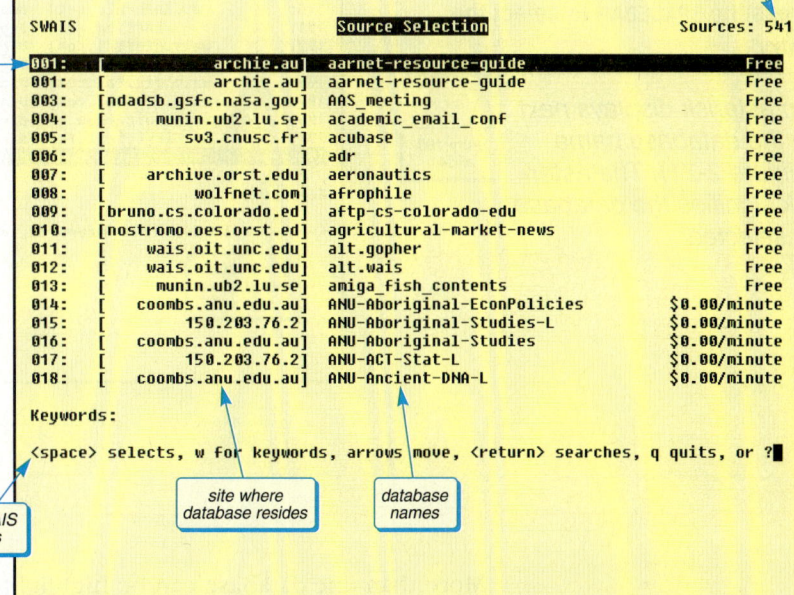

FIGURE 2-70

Selecting a Database

The entries on the Source Selection menu (Figure 2-70 on the previous page) represent WAIS databases. Before you can initiate a search, you must identify, or select, those databases you want to search. A **database** is a collection of data organized in a manner that allows access, retrieval, and use of that data. In this case, the data is documents.

Notice the dark **highlight bar** over the first database at the top of the screen in Figure 2-70. This highlight bar is used to select a database to search. The highlight bar is moved to other databases by pressing the lowercase letter j key for moving down, or the lowercase letter k key to move up. Recall, you can move down a full screen by pressing the uppercase letter J key or up a full screen by pressing the uppercase letter K key.

The upper right portion of Figure 2-70 shows a number indicating there are 541 available databases in this list.

An entry exists that includes all the databases in the list. It is called **directory-of-servers**. Searching this entry will return a list of databases containing your character string. One of those databases can then be selected for searching. The database entries are arranged in alphabetical order, so the highlight bar must be moved down to the directory-of-servers entry using J or j. The following steps show how to select the directory-of-servers.

TO SELECT A DATABASE ▼

STEP 1 ▶

Type j until directory-of-servers is highlighted.

STEP 2 ▶

Press the SPACEBAR to select the entry.

An asterisk displays next to the database name (Figure 2-71). The asterisk signifies the database is selected.

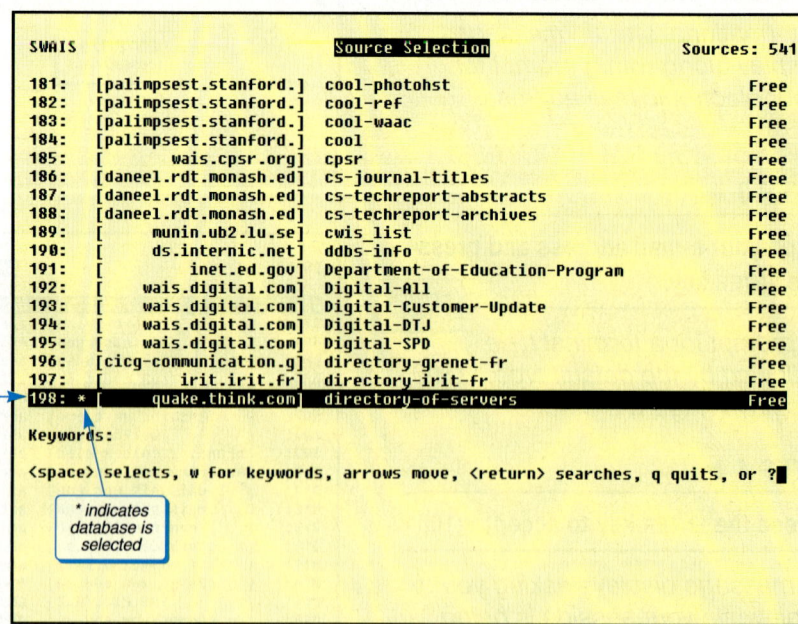

FIGURE 2-71

More than one database can be highlighted at the same time, so multiple databases can be searched simultaneously. In this case, because you have selected the directory-of-servers, it is not necessary to highlight additional databases. After the database is selected, you can start the search as shown in the following steps.

TO START THE SEARCH

STEP 1 ▶

Type w to move to the keywords area.

STEP 2 ▶

Type artificial intelligence and press the ENTER key.

A message displays indicating the search is taking place. After a short time, the search results will display (Figure 2-72). The results screen has two entries, the first and last, that contain information about the database you just searched and the search itself. You cannot search these entries because they do not point to actual databases. The entries that are left are databases that contain the character string artificial intelligence. The score column contains a number reflecting the probability that the entry contains the keyword, with 1000 meaning the character string is definitely there. The number in the score column is often referred to as the **confidence score**. You can now return to the Source Selection menu to select and search one or more of the databases listed in the search results.

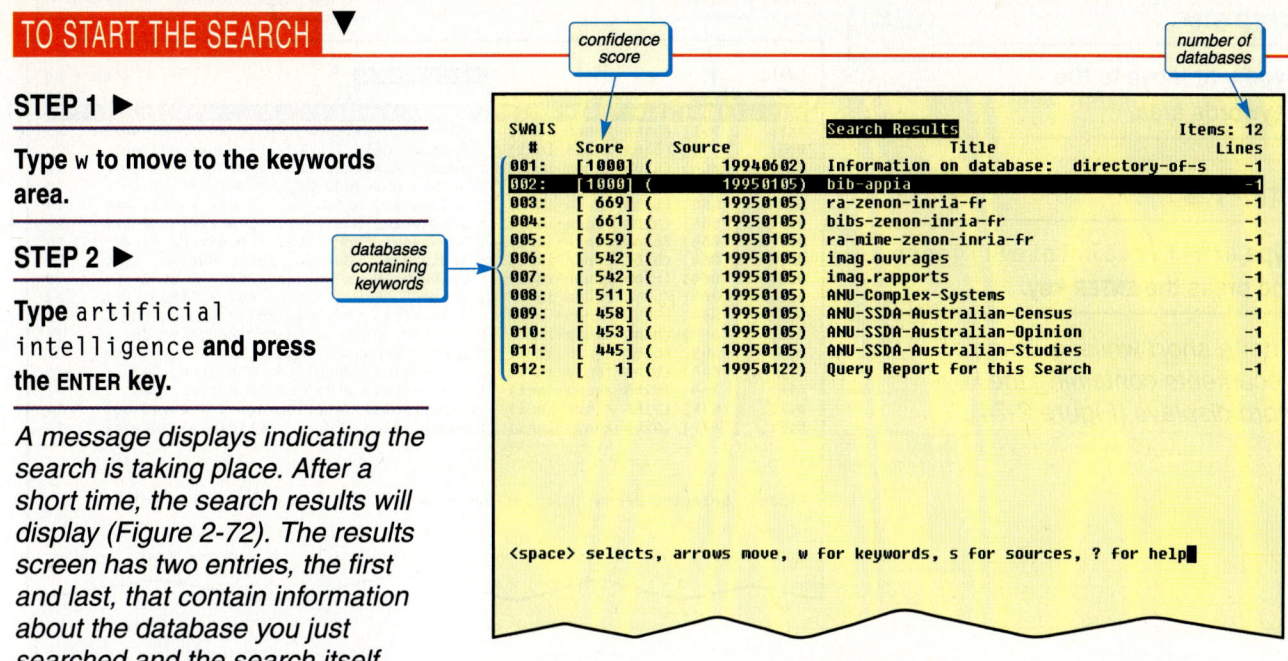

FIGURE 2-72

STEP 3 ▶

Type s to indicate you wish to select another source.

The Source Selection menu displays as shown in Figure 2-70 on page I.71.

STEP 4 ▶

Type j until the highlight bar is over the bibs-zenon-inria-fr database.

The bibs-zenon-inria-fr database is highlighted (Figure 2-73). The suffix of the domain name (fr) indicates this database is located in France.

STEP 5 ▶

Press the SPACEBAR.

An asterisk displays next to the database name as shown in Figure 2-73 to indicate the database is selected.

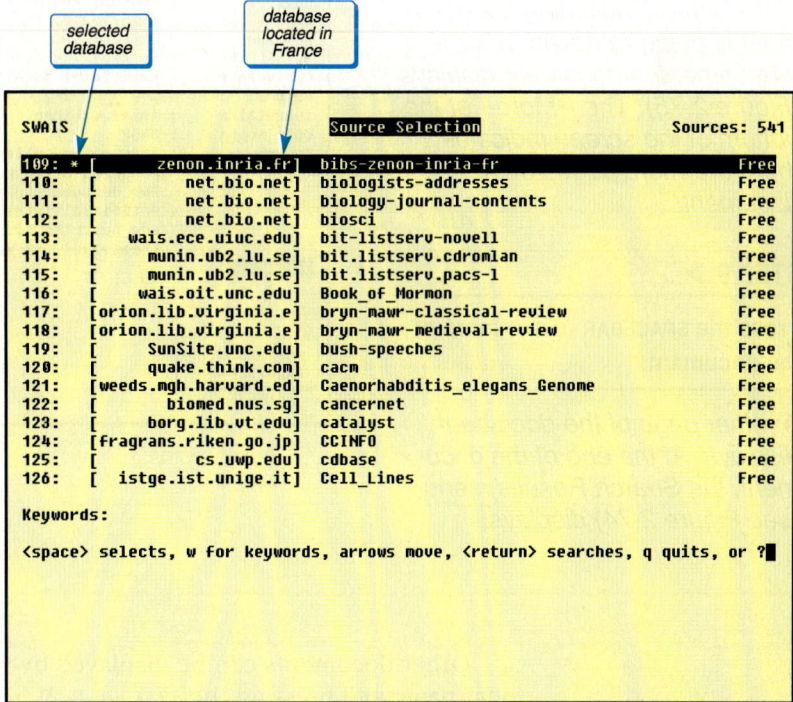

FIGURE 2-73

STEP 6 ▶

Type w to move to the keywords area.

STEP 7 ▶

Type artificial intelligence and press the ENTER key.

After a short while, a listing of documents containing the keyword displays (Figure 2-74).

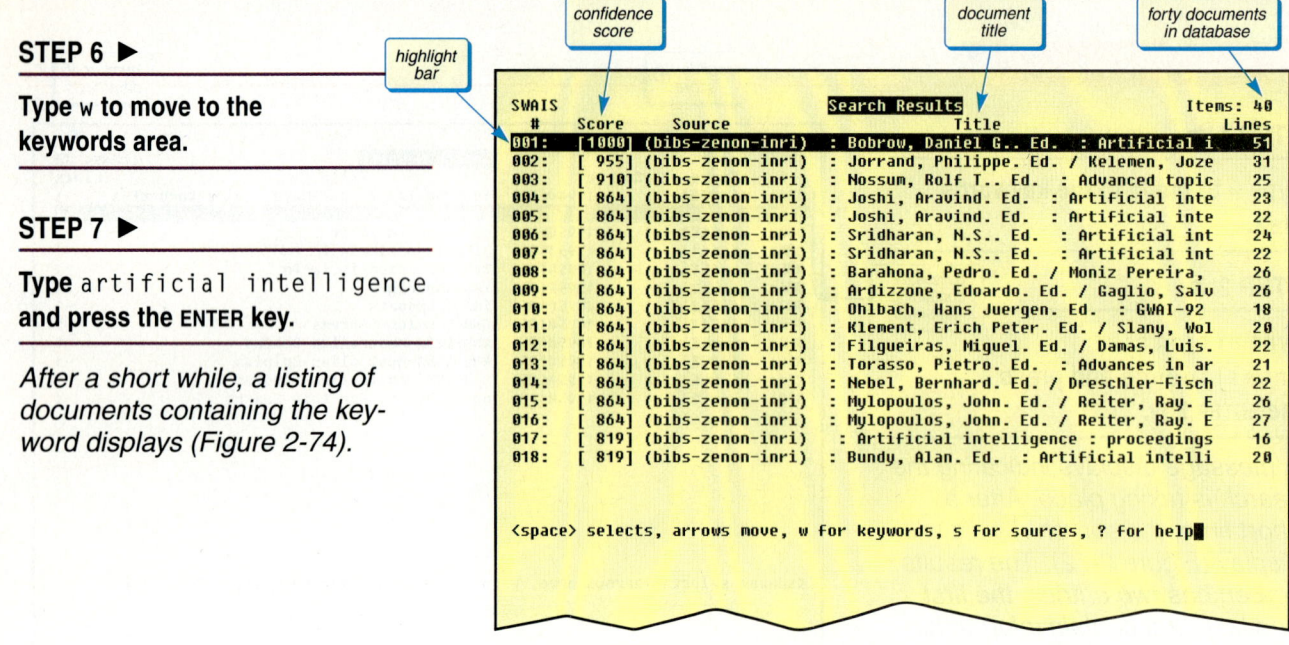

FIGURE 2-74

STEP 8 ▶

Press the SPACEBAR to choose the document.

A message displays at the bottom of the screen indicating the document is being retrieved. After a short time, the document displays (Figure 2-75). The --More-- at the bottom of the screen indicates there are more pages of the document.

STEP 9 ▶

Press the SPACEBAR to see more of the document.

Another page of the document displays. At the end of the document, the Search Results menu (see Figure 2-74) displays.

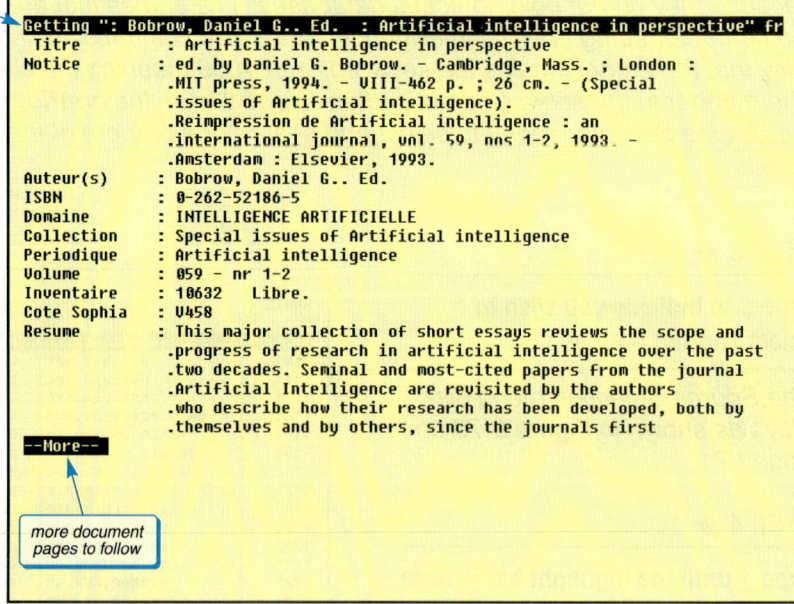

FIGURE 2-75

Other documents can be displayed by moving the highlight bar over the document name and pressing the SPACEBAR. When you find an interesting document, you can have it mailed to you so you can print it or use it in homework or research. The following steps illustrate how the Daniel G. Bobrow document can be mailed to you.

TO HAVE WAIS MAIL THE SEARCH RESULTS

STEP 1 ▶

Type m to have WAIS mail the result.

A prompt for an electronic mail address appears (Figure 2-76).

STEP 2 ▶

Type your e-mail address and press the ENTER key.

The WAIS command prompt displays. You must retrieve the document again to have it mailed.

STEP 3 ▶

Press the SPACEBAR to retrieve the document.

The document displays again and is mailed to the e-mail address specified in Step 2.

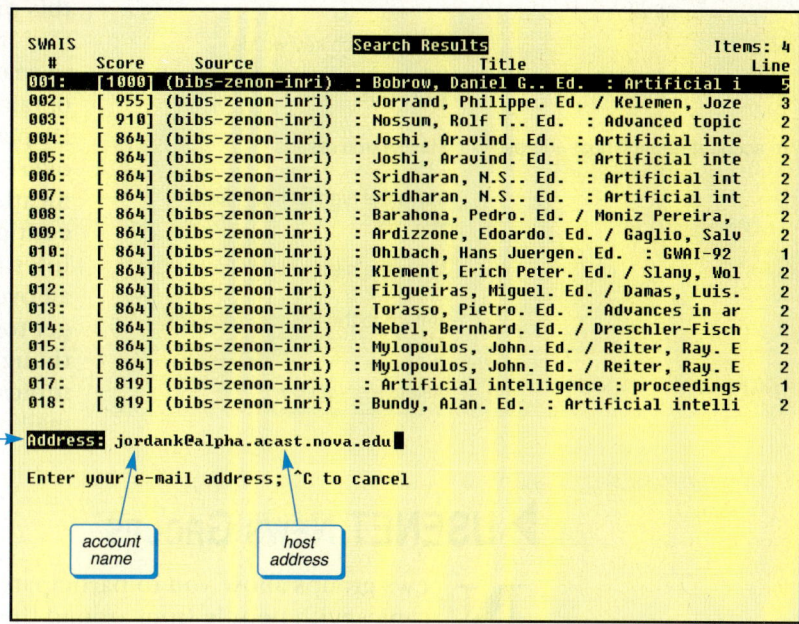

FIGURE 2-76

To obtain a list of available WAIS commands and their purposes, type h or ?.
When you have finished retrieving WAIS documents, you should exit the WAIS server. The following steps show how to exit WAIS.

TO EXIT THE WAIS SERVER

Step 1: Type q to end the document display.

The Search Results menu displays.

Step 2: Type q to exit the WAIS server.

The UNIX command prompt (%) displays.

▶ TABLE 2-5

WAIS COMMAND	WAIS TASK
?	Display help
w	Enter search key words
q	Exit WAIS
m account-name@host-address	Mail search results
j	Move the highlight bar down one line
k	Move the highlight bar up one line
s	Return to the Source Selection menu
SPACEBAR	Select a database

Table 2-5 summarizes the WAIS commands and their functions covered in this project.

In this section, you have learned how to search WAIS databases and display and obtain the documents that are stored there. Displaying documents and transferring files over the Internet is only part of the communication capabilities available. Project 2 continues with a discussion of three Internet services that allow people from all over the world with similar interests to get together electronically and share their thoughts and opinions on thousands of topics. The three services are news groups, mailing lists, and Internet relay chat.

▶ USENET NEWS GROUPS

News groups allow you to participate in conversations on thousands of topics with people from around the world. You must have access to a host computer running a news group server program and having the news group article repository. The **repository** is where all the articles are stored for all the news groups.

A **news reader** program is used to access news groups. Several are available: rn, trn, and nn are a few. The rn news reader program is illustrated in this project.

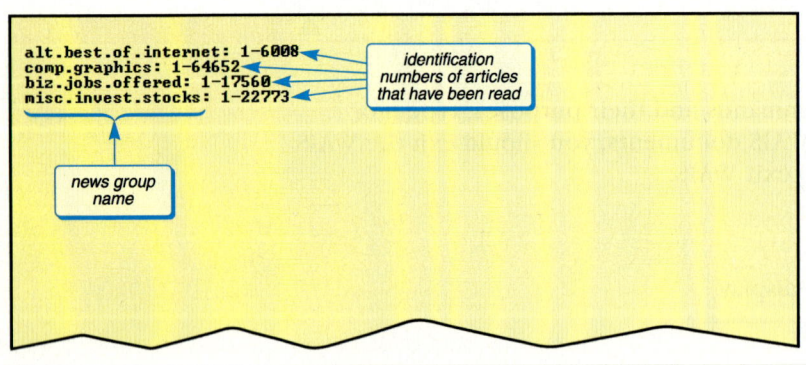

FIGURE 2-77

The news reader program uses a data file to store information about the news groups in which you are participating, including which article was the last one read. This data file is called **.newsrc**. It is stored in your home directory. Figure 2-77 shows the contents of a sample .newsrc file. You can edit this file by adding or removing news groups or changing the article numbers. Any changes made will take effect the next time the news reader is started.

News reader programs operate at several levels. Each level has a different vocabulary of commands with different types of actions.

When starting the news reader program, you will be at the news group level. You can enter a group to read its articles, skip around among the groups, **subscribe** to new groups, or **unsubscribe** to groups that no longer interest you. **Subscribe** means making a request to participate in the news group discussion. The news group level is indicated by the news reader prompt read now?.

Once you choose a news group to read, you descend a level into that particular news group. You can now read the articles in the order they arrived, skip around among the articles, mark unread articles as if they were read, and submit new articles for posting to the group. This level is indicated by a news reader prompt containing the words what next?.

When an article is chosen for reading, you descend another level into that particular article. You can page forward and backward through the article, save the article to disk, reply to the article, and display subsequent articles. Figure 2-78 summarizes the levels and corresponding activities within a news reader program.

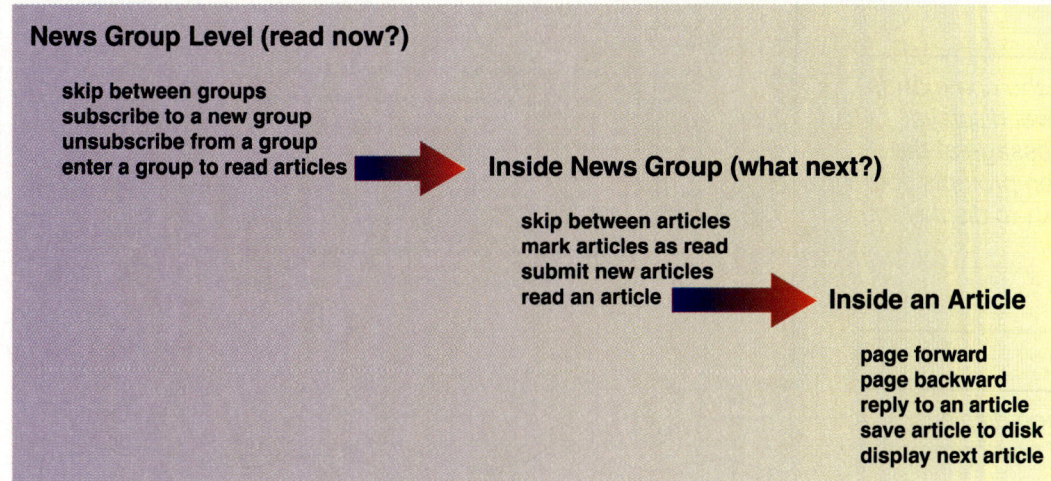

FIGURE 2-78 *The levels and corresponding activities within a news reader program.*

The following step shows how to start the rn news reader program.

TO START THE RN NEWS READER PROGRAM ▼

STEP 1 ▶

Type `rn -q` **and press the ENTER key.**

The computer displays one message for each subscribed news group indicating the name of the group and how many unread messages are available. This is followed by a read now? prompt (Figure 2-79).

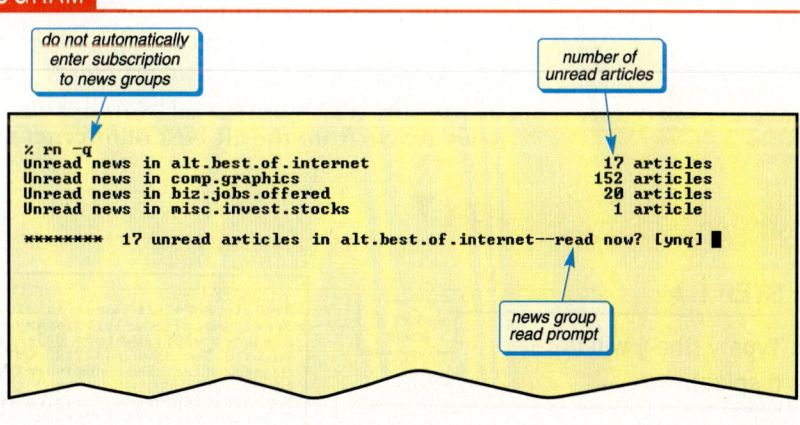

FIGURE 2-79

The -q tells the news reader program not to automatically enter your subscription to any new news groups that have appeared since you last read news. Subscribing can be a lengthy process and can subscribe you to thousands of news groups when you use the news reader for the first time. Then you would have to either edit the .newsrc file to remove unwanted groups or unsubscribe to them one at a time in the news reader program.

At this point, you are at the news group level. You can get a brief explanation of the commands for a particular level by typing the h command, as shown in the steps on the next page.

TO ACCESS HELP IN RN ▼

STEP 1 ▶

Type h **(the h will not display).**

A help screen with the commands available for that level displays (Figure 2-80). A message at the bottom of the screen prompts you to use the SPACEBAR to display the next help screen.

STEP 2 ▶

Press the SPACEBAR.

The next help screen displays, followed by a read now? prompt.

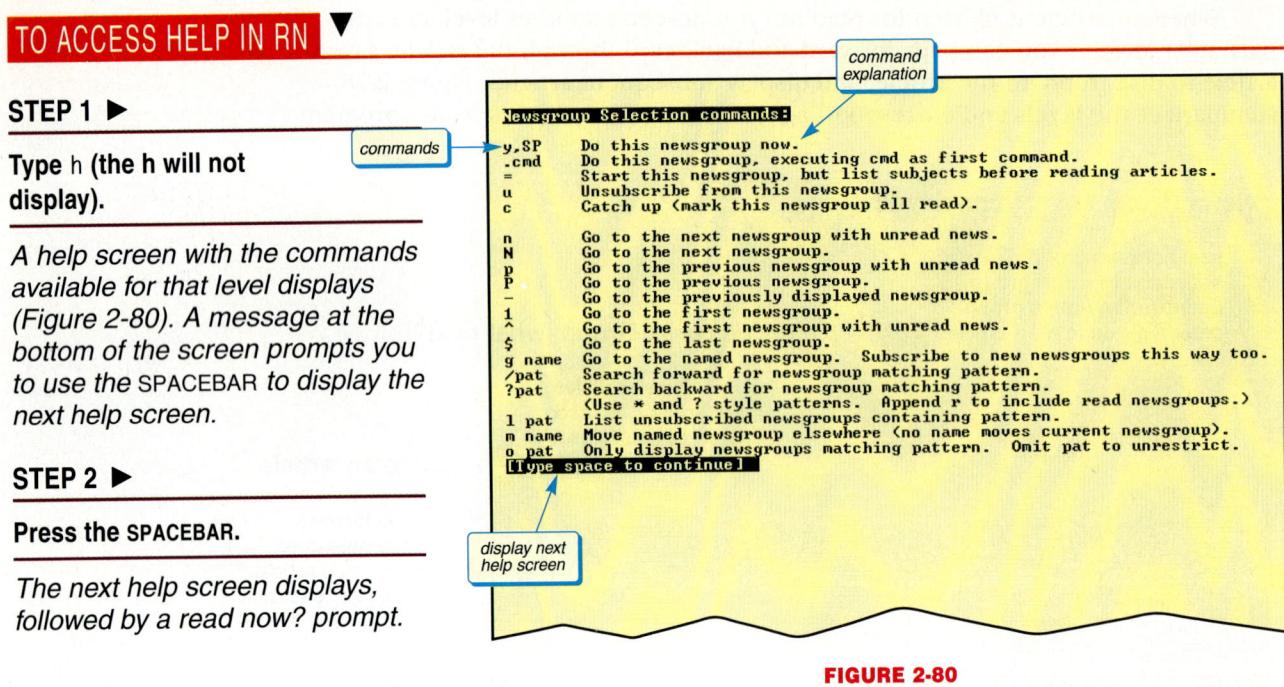

FIGURE 2-80

Reading News Group Articles

The easiest way to read articles is to start with the first group, read its articles, and then go on to the next group and repeat the process. The news reader starts by asking if you want to read articles from the first group, as illustrated in Figure 2-79 on the previous page. The following steps show how to read the first unread news article from the alt.best.of.internet news group.

TO READ NEWS ARTICLES ▼

STEP 1 ▶

Type y **(the y will not display).**

The first page of the first article displays (Figure 2-81), followed by either a --MORE-- message if the article spans more than one screen, or a message indicating the end of the article if the article can display in its entirety on only one screen. The article has several items of interest, including who sent the article, a brief description of the article contents, when it was sent, and the location from which it was sent. If the article spans more than one screen, the SPACEBAR is used to display the rest of the article.

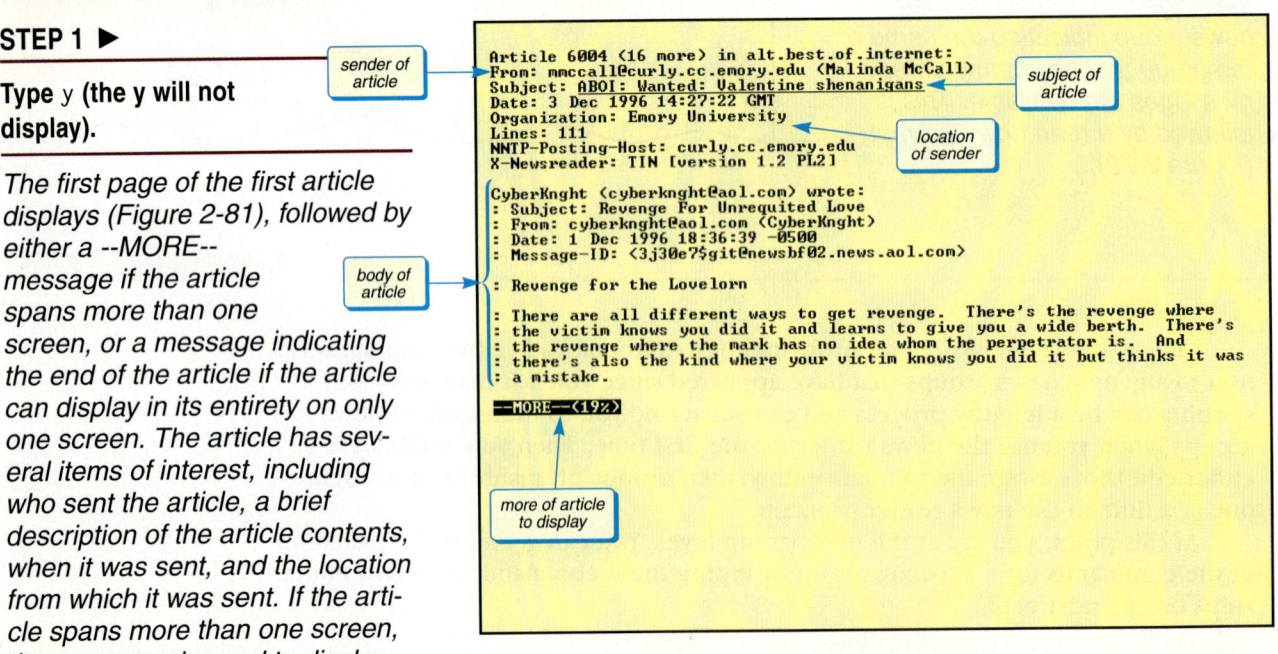

FIGURE 2-81

STEP 2 ▶

Press the SPACEBAR.

Another page of the article displays (Figure 2-82). At the end of the article, a message indicating the end of the article displays along with a what next? prompt. The next article is displayed by pressing the SPACEBAR.

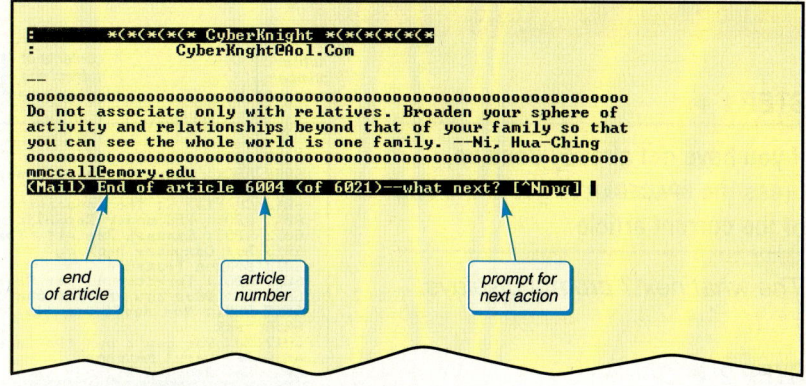

FIGURE 2-82

STEP 3 ▶

Press the SPACEBAR.

The next article displays (Figure 2-83). As explained in Step 2, the SPACEBAR is used to browse through this article until the end of the article is reached.

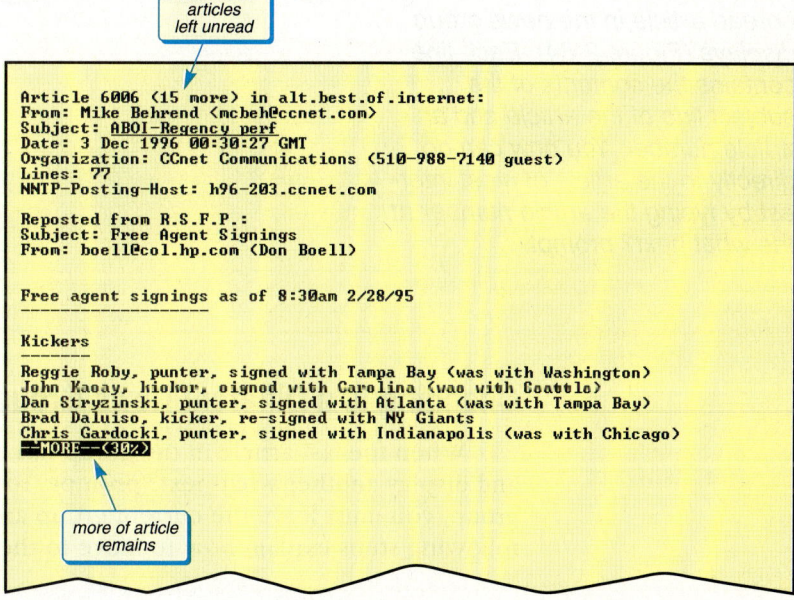

FIGURE 2-83

Displaying a Summary of Articles

It is not necessary to read each article, one after the other. Just as the h command in the electronic mail program displays a summary list of mail messages, you can enter a command to display a brief summary of all the unread articles in a group. The more interesting articles then can be selected for reading. The steps on the next page show how to display the article summary.

TO DISPLAY A SUMMARY OF ARTICLES

STEP 1 ▶

If you have not already done so, press the SPACEBAR to get to the end of the current article.

The what next? prompt displays.

STEP 2 ▶

Type = (the = will not display).

A one-line summary of each unread article in the news group displays (Figure 2-84). Each line contains the contents of the subject line of the article and an article number. You now can go directly to the article of most interest by typing the article number at the what next? prompt.

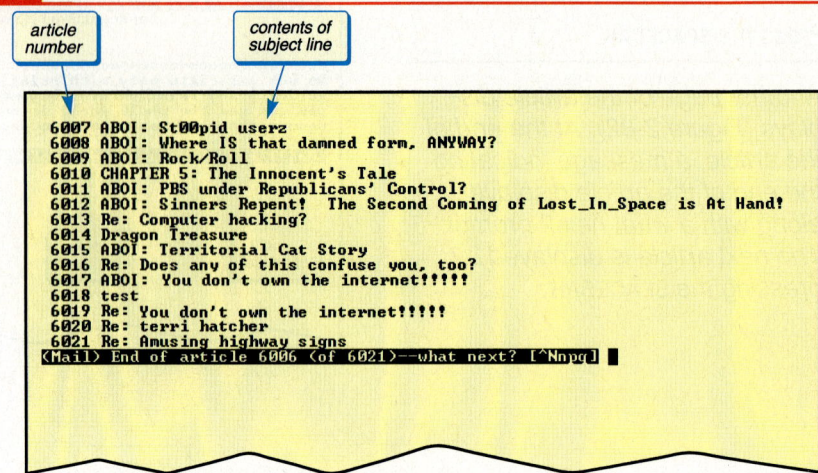

FIGURE 2-84

Changing to a Different News Group

When the last article in the group has been read, the computer will indicate it and display another what next? prompt. To read the articles from the next news group, you must leave the current group and enter the next news group. The following steps explain how to move to the next news group.

TO ENTER THE NEXT NEWS GROUP

Step 1: Type q (the q will not display) to go to the next news group.

A message indicating the number of unread articles in the next news group, comp.graphics, displays. This is followed by the read now? prompt.

Step 2: Type y to indicate you wish to read the first article.

The first article from the comp.graphics news group displays.

You do not have to move through the news groups in the order they are displayed. The following steps show how to skip past news groups without reading the articles.

TO SKIP A NEWS GROUP

STEP 1 ▶

If you are not at the end of the current article, press the SPACEBAR until the end of the current article is reached.

STEP 2 ▶

Type q to go to the next news group.

A message indicating the number of unread articles in biz.jobs.offered displays and is followed by the read now? prompt. You have exited the comp.graphics news group but have not actually entered the biz.jobs.offered group.

STEP 3 ▶

Type n to indicate you do not wish to read any biz.jobs.offered articles.

A message containing the name of the misc.invest.stocks news group, the number of unread articles in that group, and the read now? prompt displays (Figure 2-85).

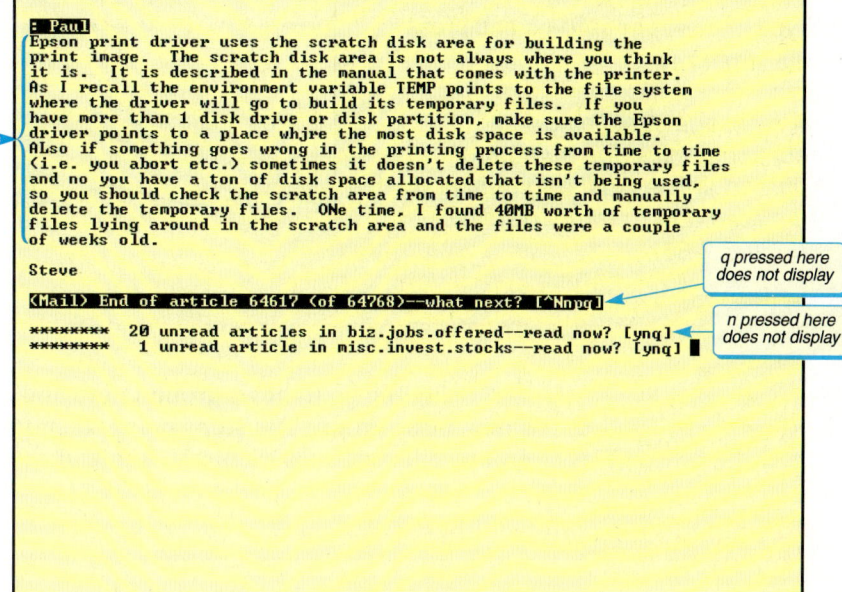

FIGURE 2-85

Note that you have a choice of y (yes, I want to read the articles), n (no, I do not want to read the articles), and q (I want to exit this procedure). Think of the n command as taking you to the next news group. You have skipped the biz.jobs.offered news group. Pressing y will display the first article from misc.invest.stocks.

It also is possible to move directly to the news group in which you are interested. This is desirable when you have several groups in your .newsrc file, and you do not want to skip over several news groups to get to the one you want to read. The step on the next page illustrates how to move directly to the comp.graphics news group.

TO MOVE DIRECTLY TO A NEWS GROUP ▼

STEP 1 ▶

Type `g comp.graphics` **and press the ENTER key.**

A message containing comp.graphics, the number of unread articles in that group, and the read now? prompt displays (Figure 2-86).

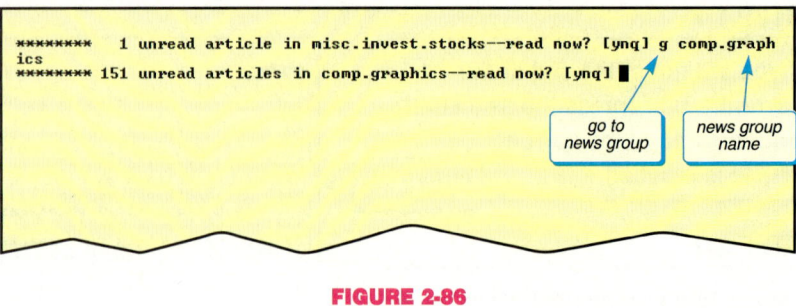

FIGURE 2-86

Using the go to news group command (g) is also the best way to subscribe to a new news group. The steps below demonstrate how to subscribe to a news group called alt.binaries.pictures.fractals.

TO SUBSCRIBE TO A NEW NEWS GROUP ▼

STEP 1 ▶

Type `g alt.binaries.pictures.fractals` **and press the ENTER key.**

A message indicates the group is not in your .newsrc file and asks if you want to subscribe (Figure 2-87).

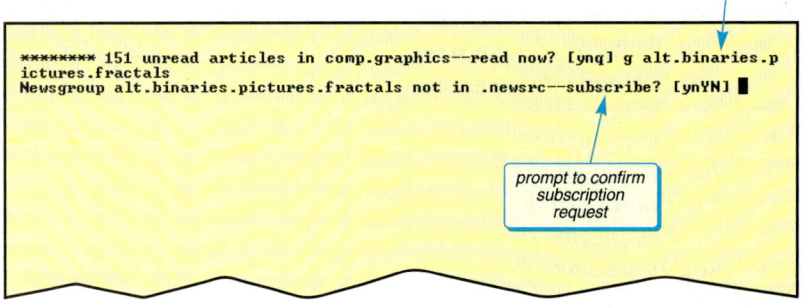

FIGURE 2-87

STEP 2 ▶

Type `y` **to subscribe.**

A message displays that asks where to place the new news group in your .newsrc file.

STEP 3 ▶

Press the ENTER key to add the group to the end of your .newsrc file.

A message displays indicating how many unread articles are available to be read. This is followed by the read now? prompt (Figure 2-88).

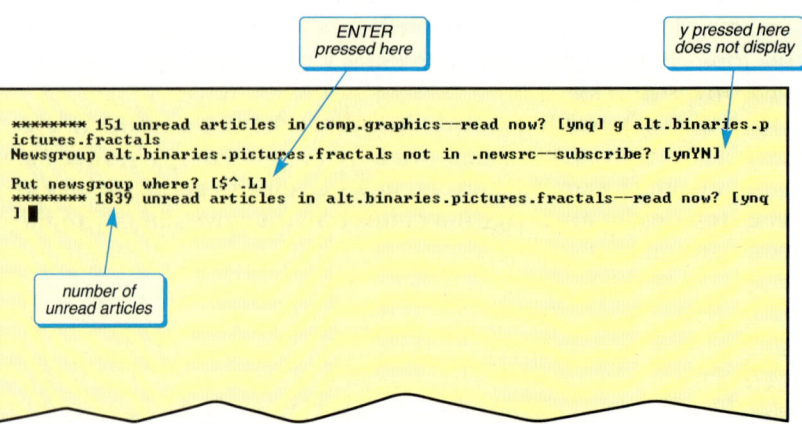

FIGURE 2-88

New news groups also can be added to your .newsrc file with any text editor. The news reader program makes those groups available the next time you start it.

Usually, when subscribing to a new news group, there will be several hundred unread messages. Figure 2-88 shows the alt.binaries.pictures.fractals news group has 1,839 unread articles. You can, of course, attempt to read all of them, or you can mark them all as read and start fresh with any new articles that may be posted. The following steps show how to mark all the unread articles as read in the alt.binaries.pictures.fractals group.

TO MARK ALL ARTICLES AS READ

STEP 1 ▶

Type c (the letter will not display on the screen) to mark all articles as read.

A message displays asking if this is really what you want to do.

STEP 2 ▶

Type y to confirm the choice.

A message displays indicating all the messages are being marked as read (Figure 2-89). Another message displays indicating the end of the news group. It is followed by the what next? prompt. Think of the c command as catching up on unread articles.

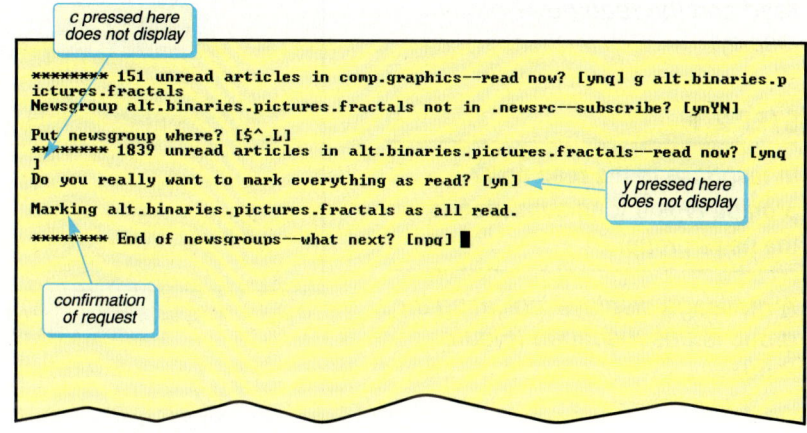

FIGURE 2-89

There may come a time when you no longer want to participate in a news group. The steps on the next page show how to unsubscribe from the news group alt.binaries.pictures.fractals. You must be at the news group level for the unsubscribe request to work correctly. The read now? prompt displaying is the indication that you are at the news group level. Refer to Figure 2-78 on page I.77 for an explanation of news group levels. The g command can be used to move back to the proper level.

TO UNSUBSCRIBE FROM A NEWS GROUP

STEP 1 ▶

Type `g alt.binaries.pictures.fractals` **and press the ENTER key to go to the alt.binaries.pictures.fractals news group.**

A message indicating how many unread articles are available to be read and the read now? prompt display.

STEP 2 ▶

In response to the read now? prompt, type `u` **to unsubscribe to the news group.**

A message displays indicating the group is unsubscribed (Figure 2-90).

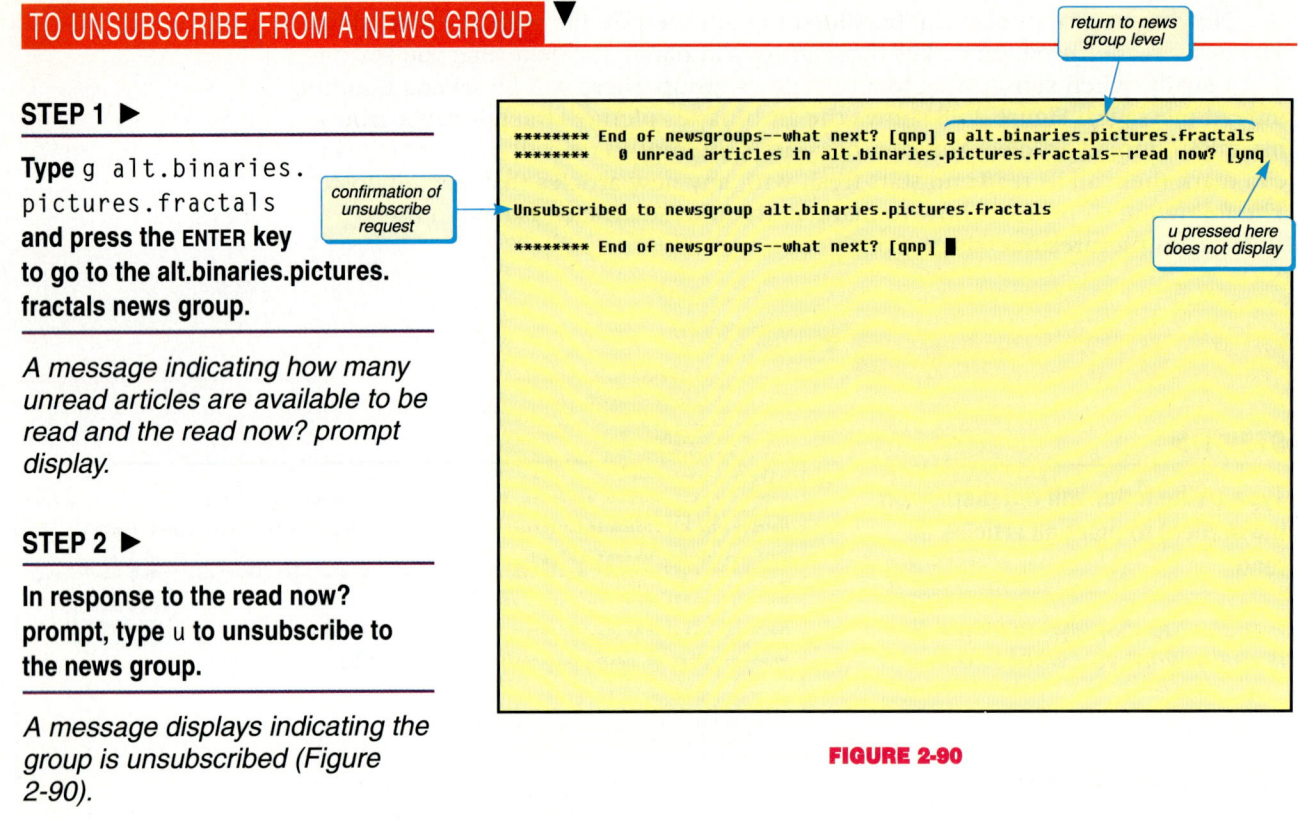

FIGURE 2-90

You can also unsubscribe from a news group by removing that news group entry from your .newsrc file with any text editor. The next time the news reader program starts, that group will not be listed in the news group summary.

Saving an Article to Disk

Just as you may wish to save certain mail messages, you almost certainly will want to preserve certain news articles that contain interesting or important information or files. When saving articles, the news reader program will create a separate file for each news group with the news group name as the name of the file. Only articles from that particular group will be stored in the disk file with the corresponding news group name. The following steps show how to save an article from the misc.invest.stocks news group to a disk file.

TO SAVE ARTICLES TO DISK ▼

STEP 1 ▶

Type g misc.invest.stocks and press the ENTER key to go to the misc.invest.stocks news group. Press the ENTER key again to display the first article. Press the SPACEBAR to move to the end of the article.

The end of the article message displays (Figure 2-91).

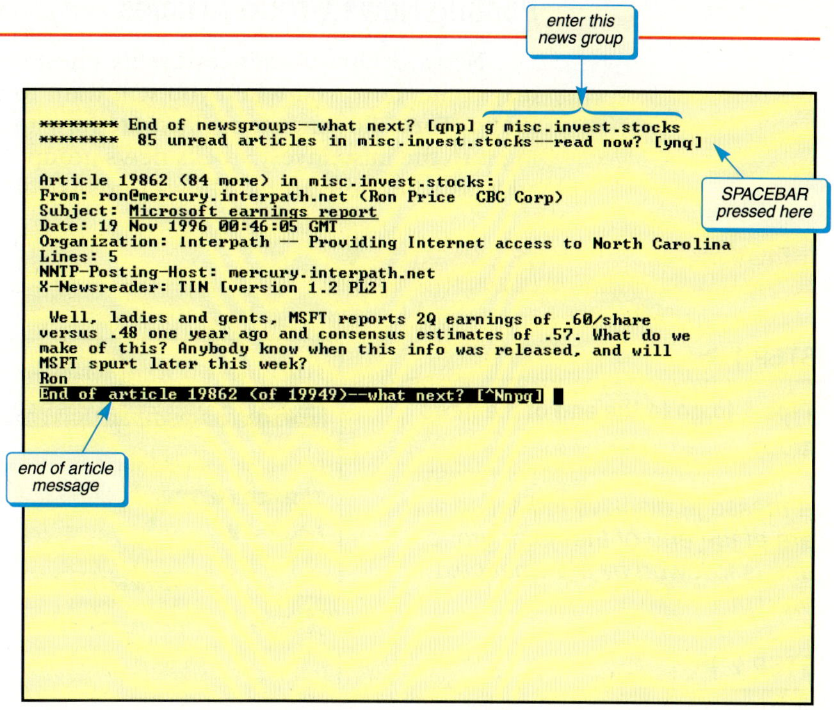

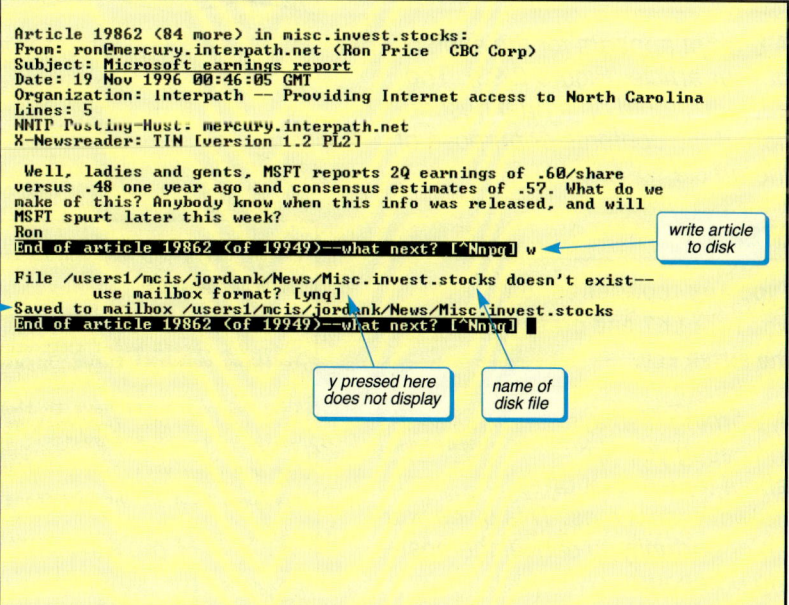

FIGURE 2-91

STEP 2 ▶

Type w and press the ENTER key to write the article to a disk file.

A message displays indicating that the file, /users1/mcis/ jordank/News/Misc.invest.stocks, doesn't exist. This is followed by a prompt asking whether to use mailbox format. **Mailbox format** *means the mail heading lines at the top of the message will be preserved as part of the article when it is written to the disk file.*

STEP 3 ▶

Type y to use mailbox format.

A message indicating the article has been stored (Figure 2-92) followed by a what next? prompt displays.

FIGURE 2-92

Any other articles saved from this news group will be appended, or added, to the end of the Misc.invest.stocks file.

Posting News Group Articles

News groups contain a treasure chest of information and amusement. A time may come, however, when you will want to **post**, or send, an article to a news group. The following steps illustrate how to submit a news group article by posting it to the misc.invest.stocks news group. You will have to substitute your e-mail address where the article shows jordank@alpha.acast.nova.edu.

TO POST A NEWS GROUP ARTICLE ▼

STEP 1 ▶

Type $ to go to the end of the news group.

A message displays indicating you are at the end of the news group and is followed by the what next? prompt.

STEP 2 ▶

Type f to start submission of your article.

A prompt appears for the subject of your article (Figure 2-93). The subject should be a brief description of the contents or purpose of the article.

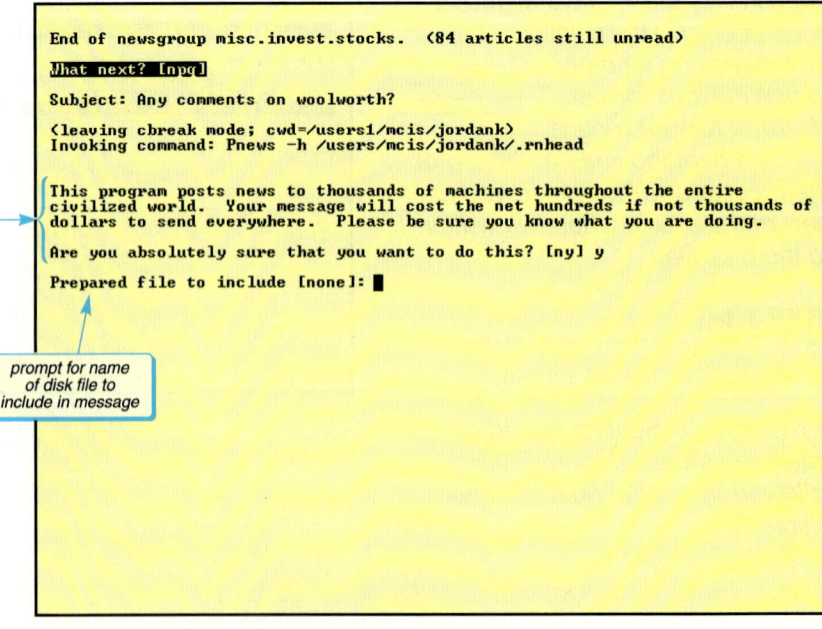

FIGURE 2-93

STEP 3 ▶

Type Any comments on woolworth? and press the ENTER key.

A warning displays indicating you are about to use a lot of network resources. This gives you an opportunity to cancel the posting procedure.

STEP 4 ▶

Type y to confirm you still want to post your message.

A prompt appears asking for the name of any disk file you may want to include (Figure 2-94). A disk file can be included here just the same as including a disk file in an electronic mail message.

FIGURE 2-94

STEP 5 ▶

Press the ENTER key.

A text editor session appears with several heading lines already filled in (Figure 2-95). The news reader program obtained the information on these lines from the local host computer. Text editor commands must be used to move to the appropriate lines and type the rest of the entries.

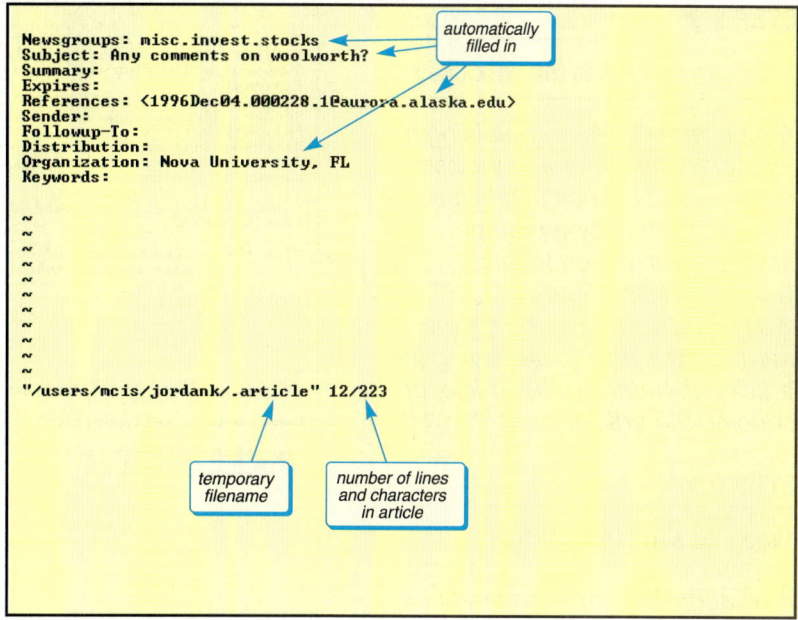

FIGURE 2-95

STEP 6 ▶

On the summary line, type soliciting woolworth comments. **On the sender line, type your e-mail address. On the distribution line, type** na. **On the keywords line, type** woolworth **(Figure 2-96).**

STEP 7 ▶

Move down to the body of the message and type I bought Woolworth a couple of years ago at $25 (and obviously took a bath). With the restructuring, and new management, does anyone think it will be wise to keep holding it?

Thanks
Kurt Jordan.

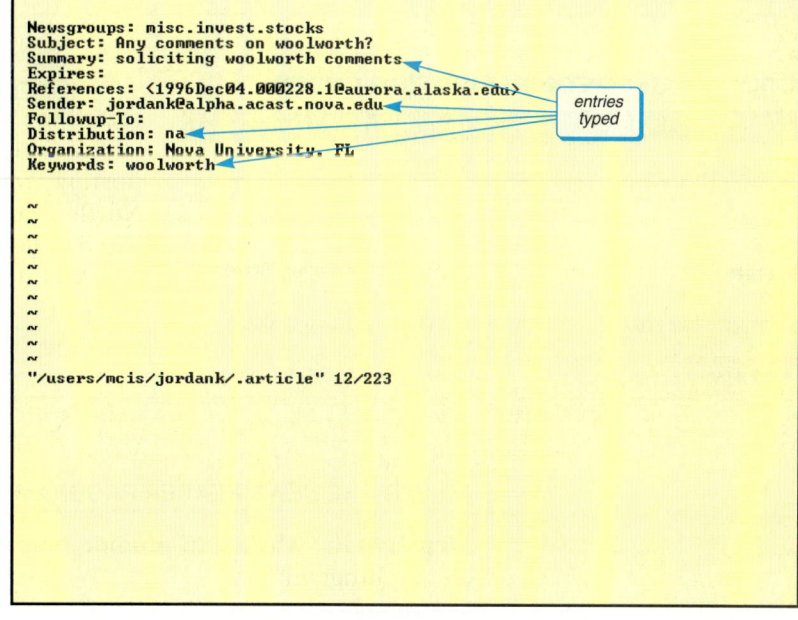

FIGURE 2-96

STEP 8 ▶

Type `:wq` **and press the ENTER key**

A message displays containing a temporary filename and the size of the article in lines and bytes. This is followed by a prompt asking which action to take with the article (Figure 2-97). You now have the choice of reediting the article, displaying the article, abandoning the article, or sending the article.

STEP 9 ▶

Type `s` **to send the article.**

A *what next?* command prompt displays. Other people with access to news reader programs can now read your article.

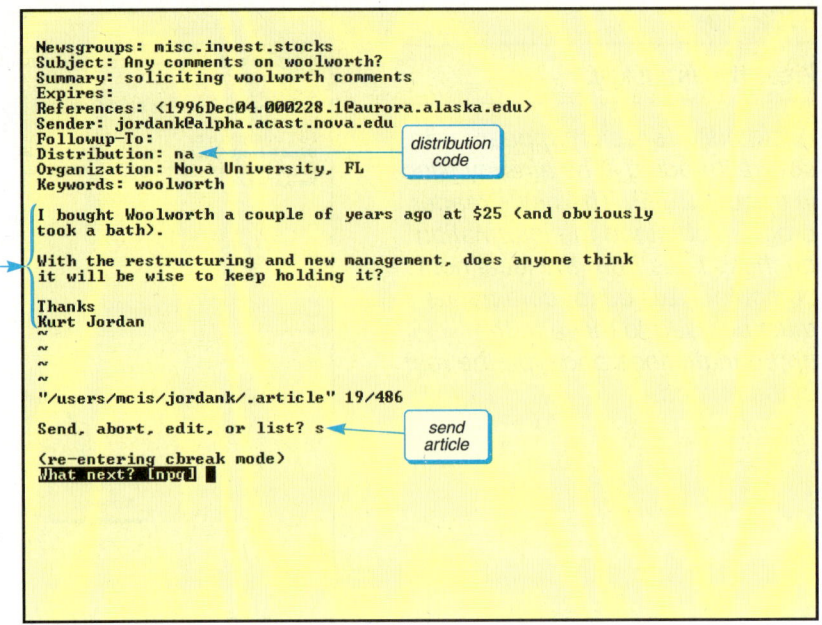

FIGURE 2-97

COMMON USENET DISTRIBUTION CODES

NAME	DESCRIPTION
world	Worldwide distribution
na	Limited to North America
usa	Limited to the United States
organization	Limited to a group of users
state	Limited to a particular state

FIGURE 2-98

In Step 8 above, the :wq saved the file and exited the text editor. The distribution line allows you to limit the number of people who see your posting. You entered na to limit distribution to North America. Available distribution codes are listed in Figure 2-98.

When you have finished reading news articles, you can exit the news reader program. The following steps summarize this procedure.

TO EXIT THE NEWS READER PROGRAM

Step 1: At the what next? prompt, type q to begin exiting the news reader program.

A message indicating you are at the end of the current news group and a what next? prompt display.

Step 2: Type q again to exit.

The UNIX command prompt (%) displays.

News readers have many other features and commands available. The commands and functions that were covered in this section are summarized in Table 2-6.

You have learned how to participate in news group discussions. Another type of discussion group on the Internet you can join uses electronic mail as the means of distributing articles. These groups are called mailing lists.

▶ **TABLE 2-6**

NEWS READER COMMAND	NEWS READER TASK
h	Access help
=	Display an article summary list
q	Exit the news reader program
g news-group-name	Go directly to a news group
$	Go to the end of a list of articles
c	Mark all unread messages as read
s	Send new article to the news group
n	Skip to the next news group
f	Start submission of news group article
g news-group-name	Subscribe to a new news group
u	Unsubscribe to a news group
w	Write an article to a disk file

▶ MAILING LISTS

Mailing lists provide many of the same discussion services as news groups but use electronic mail as the delivery vehicle. Mailing lists are sometimes called **listservs**. To use a mailing list, you must ask to be included in the list of participants. This is called **subscribing**. It is very similar to subscribing to a news group. When you want to leave the list, you must unsubscribe by asking to be removed from the list of participants.

A global list of all available mailing lists can be obtained through electronic mail simply by sending an electronic mail message that says: *list global* in the body of the message to *listserv@bitnic.bitnet*. You do not include a subject. Figure 2-99 shows some of the mailing lists that are available at ccvm.sunysb.edu. Sunysb is the computer system at State University of New York, Stony Brook campus.

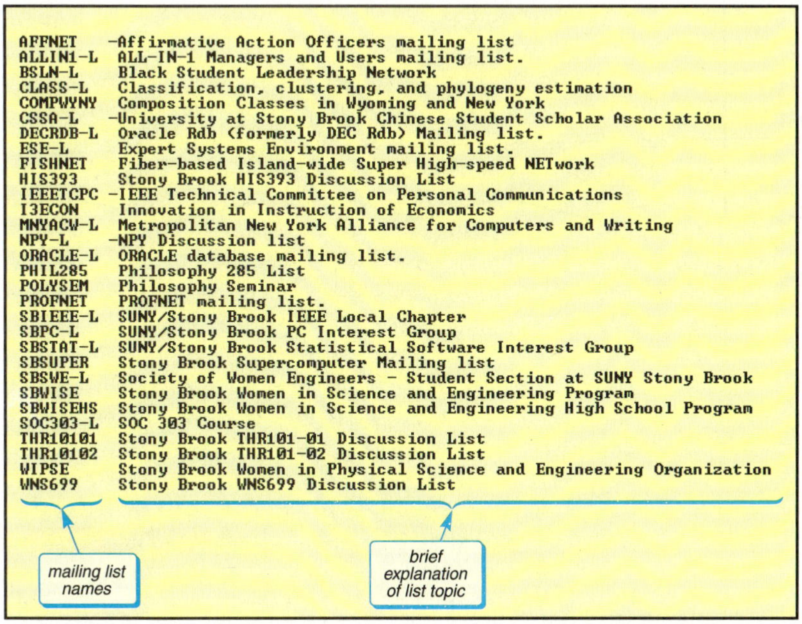

```
AFFNET     -Affirmative Action Officers mailing list
ALLIN1-L    ALL-IN-1 Managers and Users mailing list.
BSLN-L      Black Student Leadership Network
CLASS-L     Classification, clustering, and phylogeny estimation
COMPWYNY    Composition Classes in Wyoming and New York
CSSA-L     -University at Stony Brook Chinese Student Scholar Association
DECRDB-L    Oracle Rdb (formerly DEC Rdb) Mailing list.
ESE-L       Expert Systems Environment mailing list.
FISHNET     Fiber-based Island-wide Super High-speed NETwork
HIS393      Stony Brook HIS393 Discussion List
IEEETCPC   -IEEE Technical Committee on Personal Communications
I3ECON      Innovation in Instruction of Economics
MNYACW-L    Metropolitan New York Alliance for Computers and Writing
NPY-L      -NPY Discussion list
ORACLE-L    ORACLE database mailing list.
PHIL285     Philosophy 285 List
POLYSEM     Philosophy Seminar
PROFNET     PROFNET mailing list.
SBIEEE-L    SUNY/Stony Brook IEEE Local Chapter
SBPC-L      SUNY/Stony Brook PC Interest Group
SBSTAT-L    SUNY/Stony Brook Statistical Software Interest Group
SBSUPER     Stony Brook Supercomputer Mailing list
SBSWE-L     Society of Women Engineers - Student Section at SUNY Stony Brook
SBWISE      Stony Brook Women in Science and Engineering Program
SBWISEHS    Stony Brook Women in Science and Engineering High School Program
SOC303-L    SOC 303 Course
THR10101    Stony Brook THR101-01 Discussion List
THR10102    Stony Brook THR101-02 Discussion List
WIPSE       Stony Brook Women in Physical Science and Engineering Organization
WNS699      Stony Brook WNS699 Discussion List
```

mailing list names

brief explanation of list topic

FIGURE 2-99

The following steps show how to subscribe to an ORACLE mailing list at ccvm.sunysb.edu using electronic mail. ORACLE is a fourth-generation database management system.

TO SUBSCRIBE TO A LIST ▼

STEP 1 ▶

Type `mailx listserv@ccvm.sunysb.edu` **and press the ENTER key.**

A Subject: prompt displays (Figure 2-100). In the command, listserv is the account name of the listserv program, ccvm.sunysb.edu is the domain name where the mailing list is maintained.

STEP 2 ▶

Press the ENTER key to leave the subject line blank.

The cursor moves down to the next blank line.

STEP 3 ▶

Type `subscribe ORACLE-L` **and press the ENTER key to indicate your desire to subscribe to the ORACLE mailing list.**

STEP 4 ▶

Press CTRL+D.

An EOT message followed by the UNIX command prompt displays (Figure 2-101).

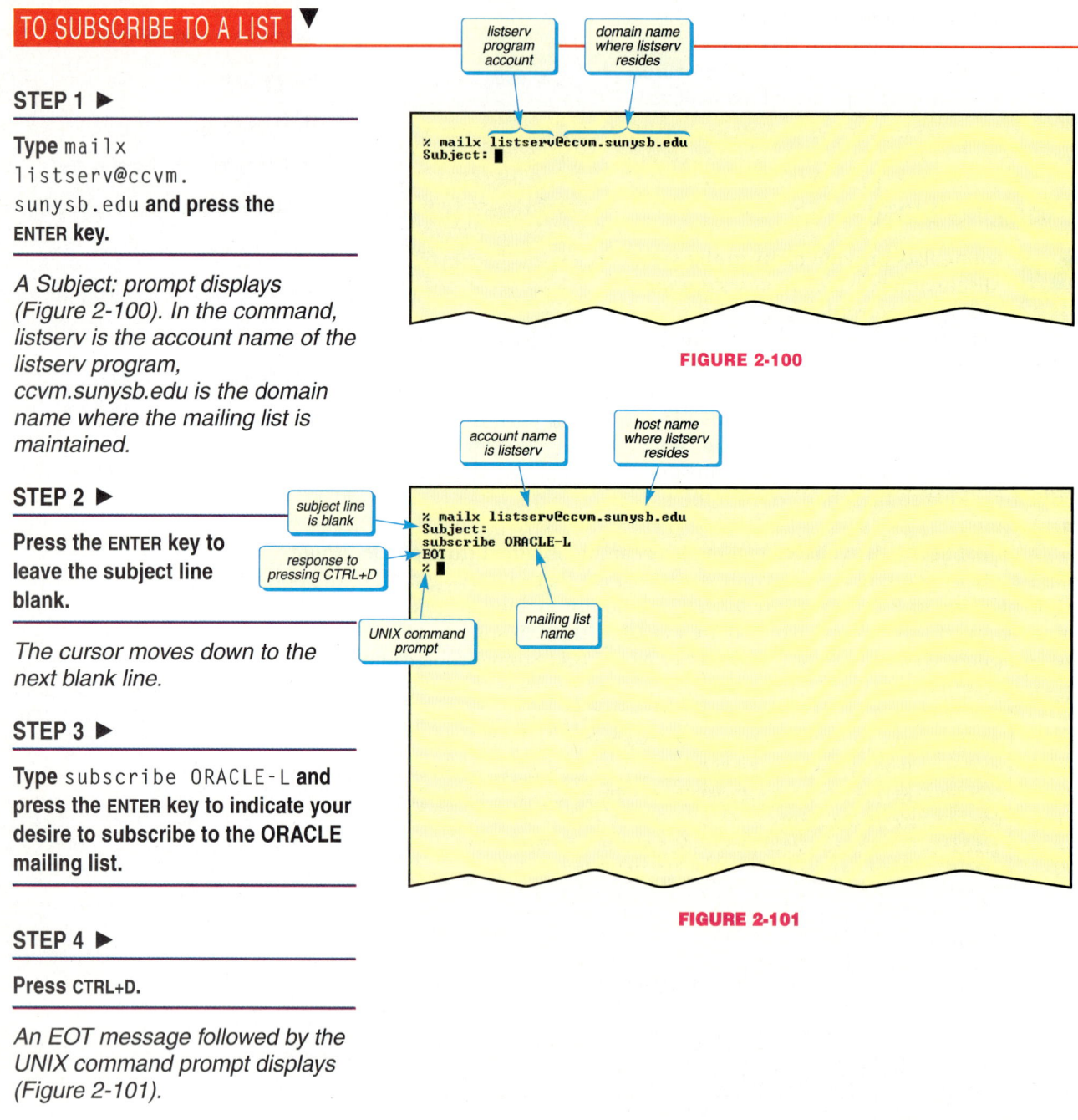

FIGURE 2-100

FIGURE 2-101

Figure 2-101 shows that the subject line should be blank. The body of the message contains only the word subscribe followed by the name of the discussion group. One listserv usually has many discussion groups it manages. You must identify which one you want to join.

The listserv program will return a confirmation message to you via electronic mail, along with instructions on how to perform frequently used functions. Figure 2-102 shows a typical confirmation message received by e-mail. You should keep this message. It tells you how to unsubscribe, should you forget later when you no longer wish to subscribe to the ORACLE mailing list.

Make sure you send your request to the listserv account. If you attempt to send a request to join a list to the mailing list account, it will be rejected because you are not yet a member.

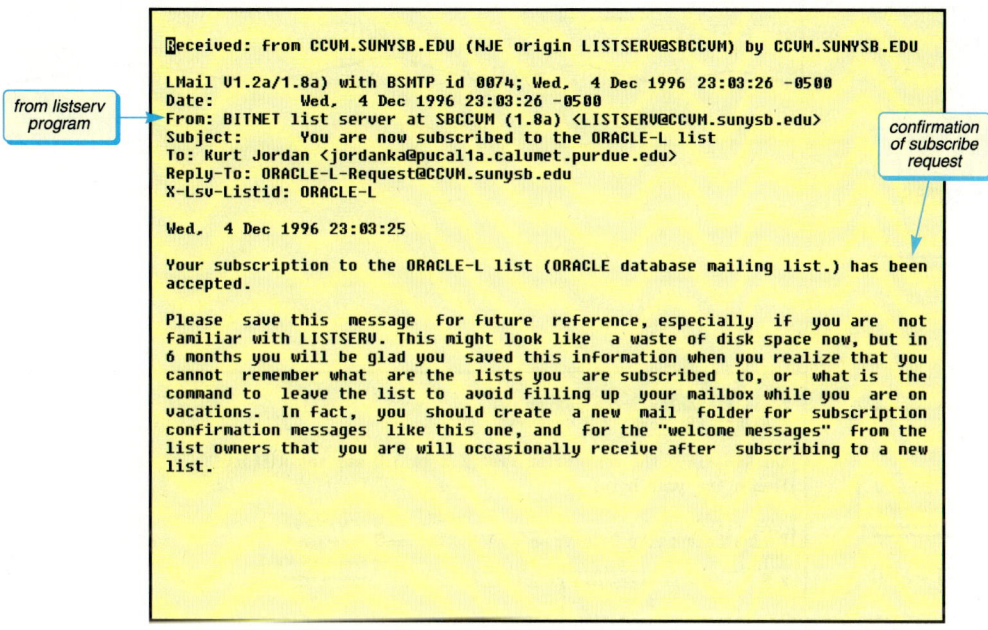

FIGURE 2-102

Reading Mailing List Postings

Because mailing list postings arrive via electronic mail, they are read like any other mail messages. Refer to the section on how to read electronic mail messages on page I.39 of this project.

Sending Mail to the List

Eventually, something in the mailing list messages you receive will make you want to respond. Diverse people contributing their thoughts and opinions make mailing lists powerful tools. Sending a message to everyone on a list is as easy as subscribing or unsubscribing. You just send your message via electronic mail to the mailing list name. This list name is not listserv. Remember, the listserv program can handle several mailing lists. You must specify which one you are using. Usually, the list name will be some descriptive name followed by the characters -L, ORACLE-L, for example.

The steps on the next page show how to send a message to the ORACLE-L mailing list. You must have subscribed and received the confirmation message from the listserv program for these steps to work properly.

TO POST A MESSAGE TO THE LIST

STEP 1 ▶

Type `mailx oracle-l@ccvm.sunysb.edu` **and press the ENTER key to begin posting your message.**

A Subject: prompt displays.

STEP 2 ▶

Type `RE: Forms 2.3 conversion` **and press the ENTER key.**

The cursor moves to the next blank line (Figure 2-103).

STEP 3 ▶

Type the following message, pressing the ENTER key at the end of each line.

```
Mr. Simpkins, the conversion
from 2.3 to 3.0 was not
difficult.
Thanks for your help.
Kurt Jordan
Purdue University Calumet
```

STEP 4 ▶

At the beginning of a blank line, press CTRL+D.

An EOT message displays and is followed by the UNIX command prompt (Figure 2-104).

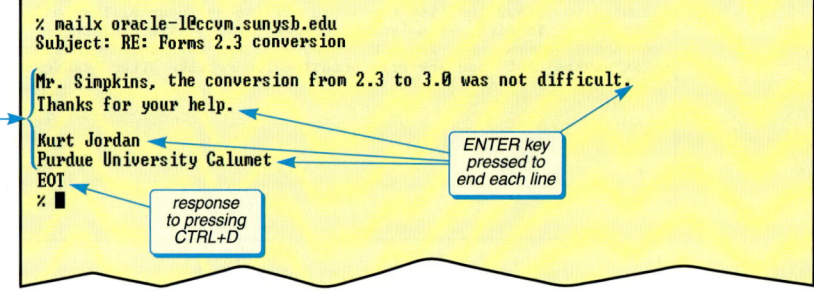

FIGURE 2-103

FIGURE 2-104

Figure 2-104 shows the completed mail message containing part of an ongoing dialog about a database upgrade that is sent to the members of the ORACLE-L mailing list at ccvm.sunysb.edu. Notice that the account name in the mail address is not listserv. If you send your posting to the listserv account, an error message will be returned from the listserv program indicating that you sent invalid commands. Confirmation is not sent by the listserv program to indicate the message has been received and sent to the other participants. This is because sending the message back to the originator wastes network resources. The person who sent the message already knows what is in it.

Unsubscribing from a Mailing List

If you will not be able to read your mailing list mail messages for an extended period of time; for example, you are going on vacation or you are graduating, you should **unsubscribe** from your mailing lists. Some lists have a high level of traffic and generate many messages daily. Your mail box quickly can become very large with so many messages you cannot possibly read them all.

Unsubscribing from a mailing list is very similar to subscribing. Instead of typing subscribe ORACLE-L in the body of the message, you type unsubscribe ORACLE-L. If you forget how to unsubscribe, the confirmation message you received when you subscribed to the mailing list contains instructions describing how to unsubscribe.

The next set of steps shows how to unsubscribe from the ORACLE-L mailing list. These steps will work only if you have previously subscribed to the mailing list.

TO UNSUBSCRIBE FROM A LIST

STEP 1 ▶

Type `mailx listserv@ccvm.sunysb.edu` **and press the ENTER key to begin the unsubscribe process.**

A Subject: prompt displays.

STEP 2 ▶

Press the ENTER key.

The cursor moves down to the next blank line (Figure 2-105).

FIGURE 2-105

STEP 3 ▶

Type `unsubscribe ORACLE-L` **and press the ENTER key. Press CTRL+D.**

An EOT message displays and is followed by the UNIX command prompt (Figure 2-106).

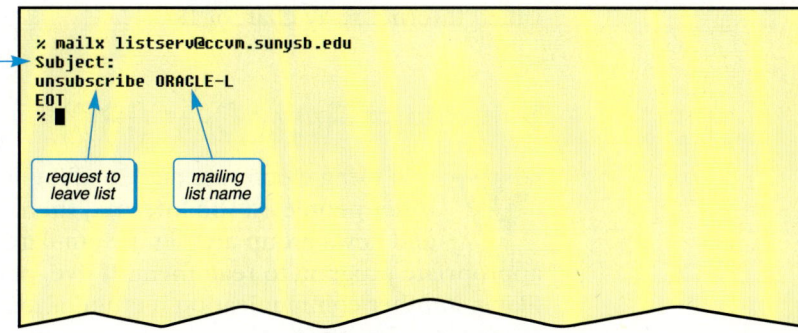

FIGURE 2-106

Figure 2-106 on the previous page shows the subject line should be blank. The body of the message contains only the words unsubscribe ORACLE-L. Figure 2-107 shows the confirmation of removal from the discussion group the listserv program will send back to you via electronic mail.

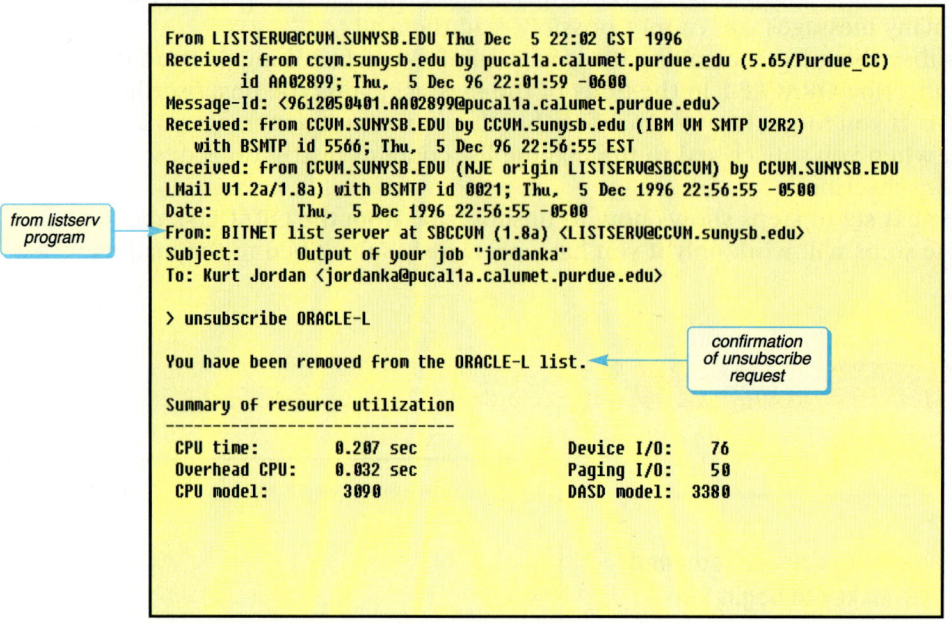

FIGURE 2-107

Make sure you send your request to leave the mailing list to the listserv account. If you try sending your unsubscribe request to the mailing list account, it will be sent to all the other participants in the list. This wastes their time and network resources and will probably generate some negative comments from other list participants about your lack of experience.

You now have learned how to subscribe to and unsubscribe from mailing lists. The last technique for communicating over the Internet discussed in this project is called Internet relay chat, or IRC.

▶ INTERNET RELAY CHAT (IRC)

When using electronic mail, mailing lists, and news groups to converse with other people on the Internet, there is a time lag between messages. Mail and news group articles accumulate over time, waiting for you to run the appropriate program to read them. If live, real-time conversation is more to your liking, another communication method is available on the Internet called **IRC**, or **Internet relay chat**.

Participating in IRC is like listening to a party-line telephone conversation. Just as everyone on the party line can hear what is being said, and can speak at the same time, everyone on a particular IRC channel can see what is being typed and can type at the same time.

When running IRC, your display screen will be split into a dialog window and a command line. These two areas are separated by an inverse-video status line. The words that IRC participants type appear in the dialog window. It composes the largest portion of the screen.

The command line is normally one line in length. On the command line, you either type IRC commands or pieces of ongoing conversations. Any entry beginning with a slash (/) is interpreted as an IRC command. Any other type of entry is interpreted as a piece of conversation and sent to other people on IRC.

Thousands of people can be participating at the same time on a particular IRC server. This could lead to chaos and anarchy, with no one being able to make any sense out of the pieces of conversation. Fortunately, the IRC server organizes conversations into topics called **channels**. By joining a channel, you would see only the conversation taking place on that channel. You can leave one channel and join another using available IRC commands.

Starting an IRC Session

To participate in IRC, you must know the IP address (or domain name) of the computer that is running an IRC service program. Three such sites are pasadena.ca.us.undernet.org on the West Coast of the United States, washington.dc.us.undernet.org on the East Coast of the United States, and ca.undernet.org in Canada. The following steps show how to start an IRC session with washington.dc.us.undernet.org using jordanka as the name that would identify your conversations. You should substitute your account name for jordanka.

TO START AN IRC SESSION ▼

STEP 1 ▶

At the UNIX prompt (%), type
irc jordanka
washington.dc.us.undernet.org
(Figure 2-108).

STEP 2 ▶

Press the ENTER key.

IRC startup messages display (Figure 2-109). Notice there are 168 people currently participating in conversations, with 456 different channels available.

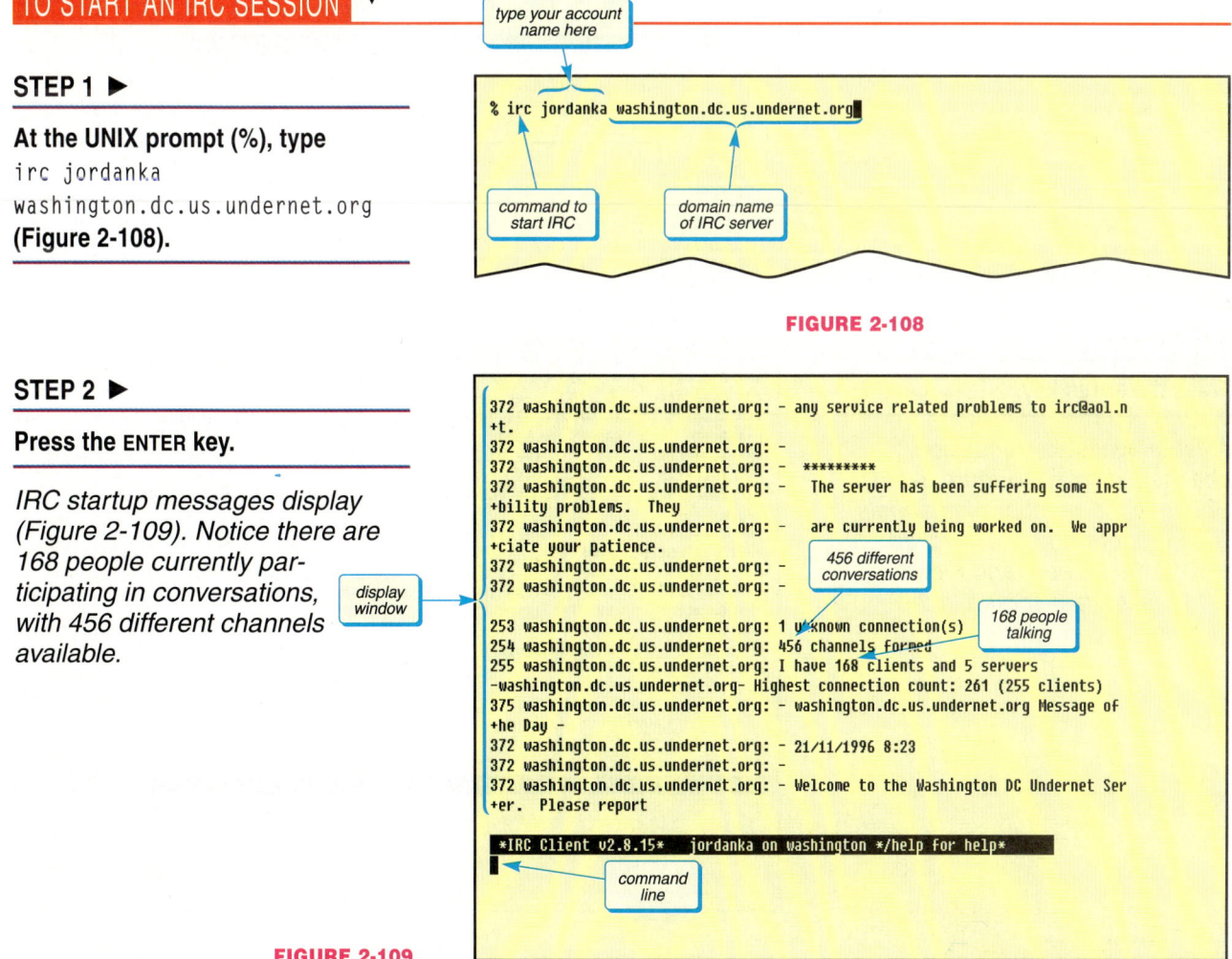

FIGURE 2-108

FIGURE 2-109

You have successfully connected to an IRC server. Available IRC commands can be displayed with the /help command. Remember, commands must be preceded by a slash (/), or the IRC server will send the command to the channel where other people would see it and no IRC function would be performed.

Displaying Channel Names

One of the available commands, /list, displays the names of the available channels that you can join. Because there are more than 400 channels at this IRC server, the channel names will scroll across the screen. To temporarily suspend the display of channel names, you can press CTRL+S. This will allow you to pause the scrolling to read the channel names. To resume the list display, press CTRL+Q. The following steps show how to list the available channels on this IRC server.

TO DISPLAY A LIST OF CHANNEL NAMES ▼

STEP 1 ▶

Type /list (Figure 2-110).

FIGURE 2-110

STEP 2 ▶

Press the ENTER key.

A list of available discussion channels displays (Figure 2-111). Because the number of channels is so great (456), they scrolled across the screen, and Figure 2-111 is the last screen in the display.

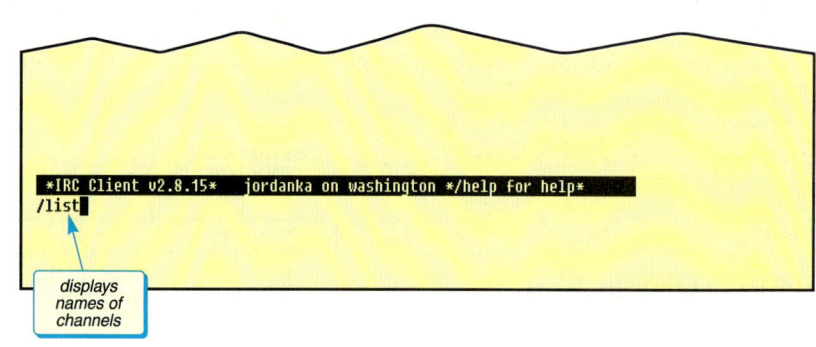

FIGURE 2-111

Figure 2-111 shows three pieces of information about each channel. The first is the name of the channel, which starts with a # (number symbol). The second is the number of people who have joined and are participating in the channel discussion. The third is an optional discussion topic.

Joining an IRC Discussion Channel

Joining an on-going discussion is as easy as specifying the channel you wish to join. The following steps show how to join a channel and participate in a real-time conversation with the people on channel #newbie, a channel for new IRC users.

TO JOIN AN IRC CHANNEL

STEP 1 ▶

Type /channel #newbie **(Figure 2-112).**

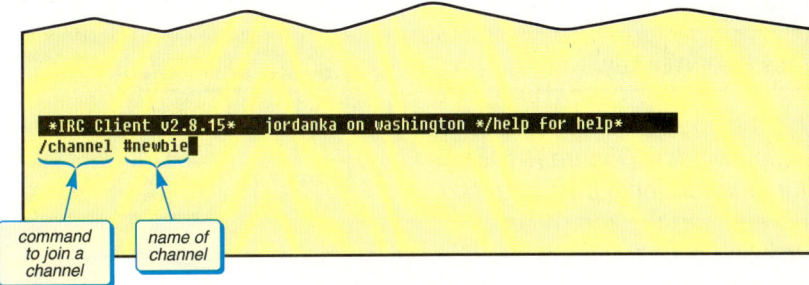

FIGURE 2-112

STEP 2 ▶

Press the ENTER key.

A message displays indicating that a change in channel status has occurred, followed by a list of the current channel participants (Figure 2-113).

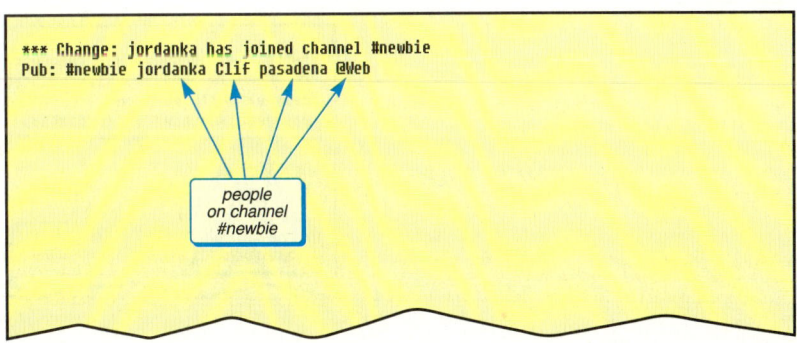

FIGURE 2-113

Figure 2-113 shows four people in this channel, jordanka, Clif, pasadena, and @Web. Now, anything that is typed by any of the four people, with the exception of IRC commands, will appear in the display window on each of their four screens.

Conversing on an IRC Channel

When you join an IRC channel, it is customary to say hello. The steps on the next page show how to participate in an IRC conversation.

TO CONVERSE ON AN IRC CHANNEL

STEP 1 ▶

Type hello everyone **(Figure 2-114)**.

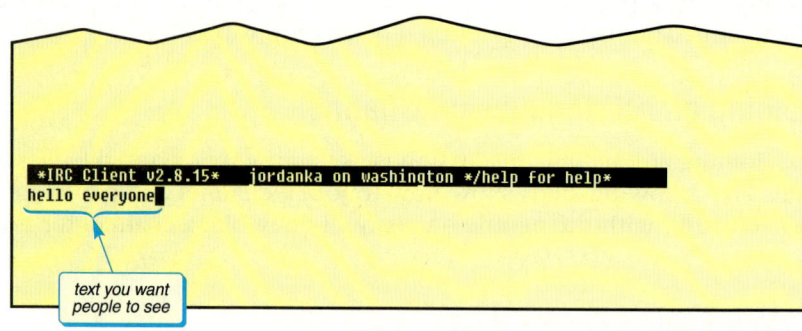

FIGURE 2-114

STEP 2 ▶

Press the ENTER key.

The line you typed appears in the display window (Figure 2-115). The other channel participants also can see the line. When someone else types a line, it appears on your screen. Figure 2-116 shows a response from a participant.

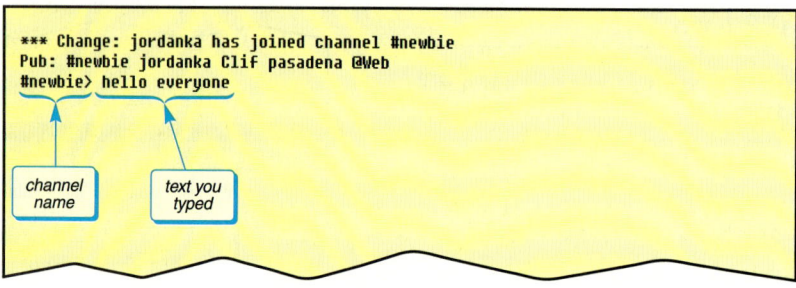

FIGURE 2-115

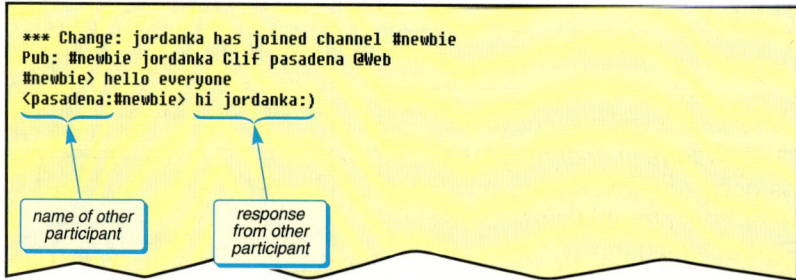

FIGURE 2-116

STEP 3 ▶

Type I see your name is pasadena, are you from california? **(Figure 2-117)**.

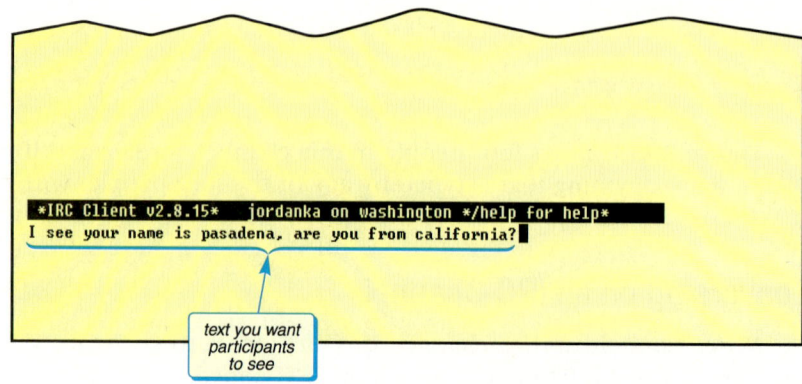

FIGURE 2-117

STEP 4 ▶

Press the ENTER key.

The line appears in the display window (Figure 2-118).

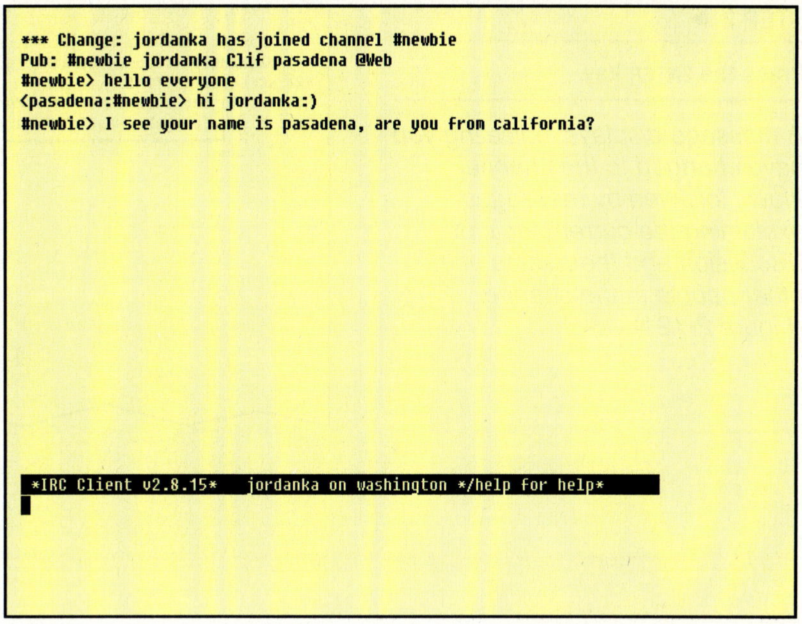

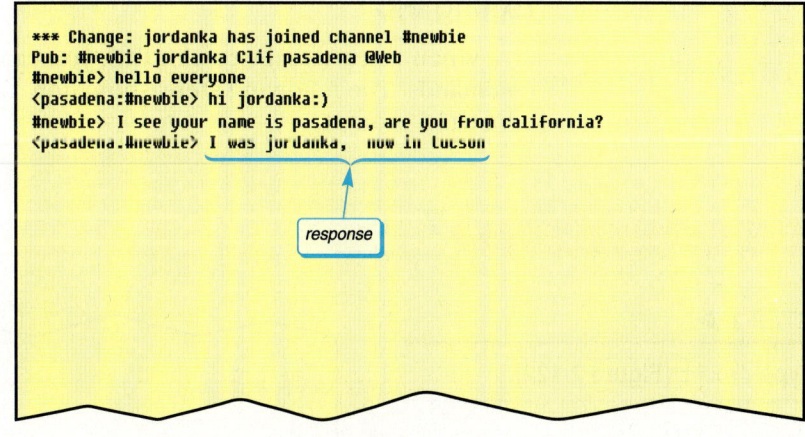

FIGURE 2-118

Figure 2-119 shows the response from pasadena. You can continue on with the conversation in this manner, reading what other people have to say and entering your own responses.

Changing to Another IRC Channel

As easily as you joined the #newbie channel, you can change to another channel. The following steps show how to leave the #newbie channel and join a channel called #love.

FIGURE 2-119

TO SWITCH TO ANOTHER IRC CHANNEL ▼

STEP 1 ▶

Type /channel #love **(Figure 2-120).**

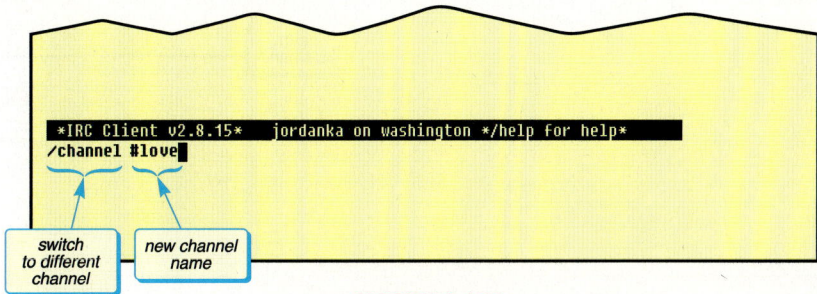

FIGURE 2-120

STEP 2 ▶

Press the ENTER key.

A message displays indicating you have changed to the channel #love, followed by messages explaining the current topic of discussion and the names of the other people in the channel (Figure 2-121).

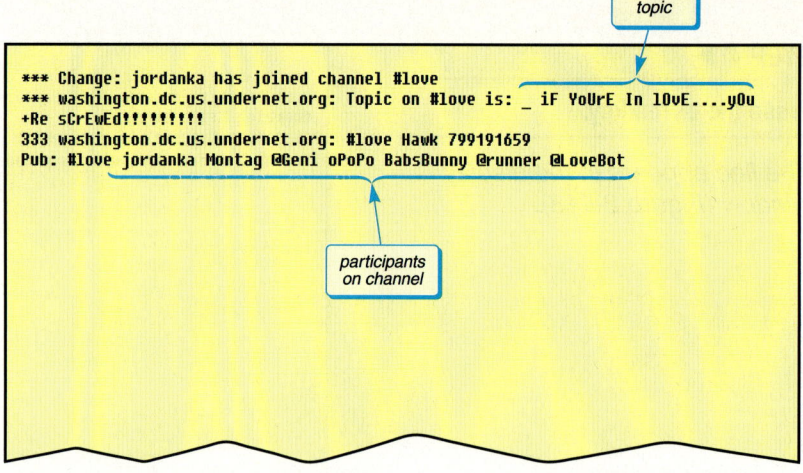

FIGURE 2-121

You can now participate in the current discussion about being in love by using the techniques just described in the section on conversing on an IRC channel.

Exiting IRC

When you are ready to exit IRC, you can do so using one of several commands. The following steps show how to exit IRC and return to the UNIX command prompt.

TO EXIT THE IRC PROGRAM ▼

STEP 1 ▶

Type /exit (Figure 2-122).

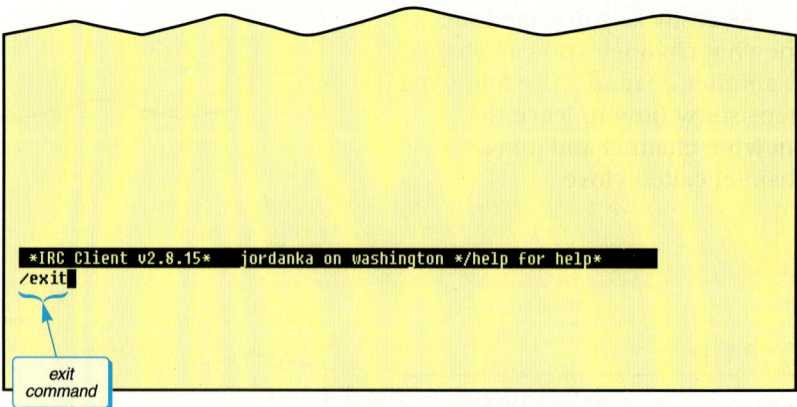

FIGURE 2-122

STEP 2 ▶

Press the ENTER key.

A message appears in the display window indicating the link has been closed, and a prompt appears at the bottom of the screen requesting that you press any key (Figure 2-123).

STEP 3

Press the SPACEBAR.

The UNIX command prompt displays.

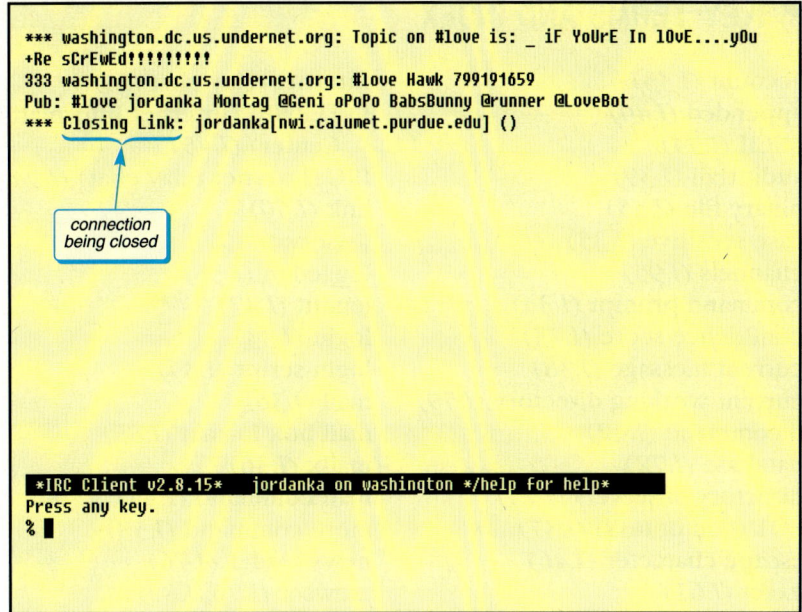

FIGURE 2-123

Using the techniques and steps just presented, you have successfully participated in Internet relay chat conversations. If you have trouble following the dialog in a channel, do not be discouraged. Some channels will have 30 to 50 people all trying to talk at the same time, and IRC will display the lines people type in the order they are received, making it difficult to follow what one person types, because the text is interspersed with text from other people who are trying to have their own conversations. As you continue to participate in IRC, you will get better at deciphering this nonsequential method of communication.

IRC is totally unregulated. People can say whatever they please, including things that may be offensive.

▶ PROJECT SUMMARY

This project introduced you to Internet service programs in a UNIX environment. You learned how to login and logout of UNIX, send and receive electronic mail messages, and manage your mail box. Displaying user account information was illustrated. You learned how to start and end a remote terminal session using TELNET. The section on FTP showed you how to send and receive files. You learned how to search for files on the Internet using archie, gopher, and veronica. You learned how to do research by displaying and retrieving WAIS documents. Finally, you learned how to subscribe to and use news groups, mailing lists, and Internet relay chat.

▶ Key Terms and Index

account (I.33)
appended (I.40)
ASCII (I.54)
audit trail (I.39)
binary file (I.55)
case-sensitive (I.35)
channels (I.95)
command prompt (I.34)
confidence score (I.73)
current message (I.38)
current working directory (I.50)
d command (I.42)
database (I.72)
directory-of-servers (I.72)
EOT (end of text) (I.37)
escape character (I.46)
exact (I.61)
GopherSpace (I.68)
highlight bar (I.72)
home directory (I.50)

Internet relay chat (I.94)
INTERNIC (Internet Information Center) (I.45)
IRC (Internet relay chat) (I.94)
link (I.50)
listserv (I.89)
logged in (I.36)
logout (I.37)
login (I.33)
login script (I.34)
mail (I.36)
mail box format (I.85)
mailx (I.36)
man command (I.35)
more command (I.53)
news reader (I.76)
.newscr (I.76, I.82)
online (I.35)
password (I.33)
policy (I.43)

post (I.86)
prompt (I.34)
regex (I.61)
repository (I.76)
selection indicator (I.65)
sequence number (I.38)
status code (I.38)
sub (I.61)
subcase (I.61)
subject line (I.37)
subscribe (I.76)
subscribing (I.89)
summary list (I.41)
TELNET (I.45)
transfer type (I.55)
unsubscribe (I.76, I.93)
veronica (I.68)
x command (I.44)

STUDENT ASSIGNMENTS

STUDENT ASSIGNMENT 1
True/False

Instructions: Circle T if the statement is true or F if the statement is false.

T F 1. It is not necessary to login to use UNIX to access the Internet.
T F 2. UNIX help documentation is stored for viewing online.
T F 3. Mail messages must be read in the order they appear in your mail box.
T F 4. IRC (Internet relay chat) allows live, real-time conversations.
T F 5. Once a mail message is deleted, it is not possible to get it back.
T F 6. To display information about a computer account on a remote system, you need to specify only the account name.
T F 7. TELNET allows you to send a file to a remote computer and give it a new name.
T F 8. Finger tests network connections.
T F 9. A link directory entry allows FTP to connect to a third remote computer to access the files located there.
T F 10. It is possible to display the contents of text files while in FTP.
T F 11. You can give archie a filename, and it will find the file and send it to you.
T F 12. Gophers can be linked together through menu entries.
T F 13. Selecting a Gopher menu choice is achieved by typing in a selection number and pressing the ENTER key.
T F 14. FTP handles binary files and text files differently.
T F 15. Veronica and archie perform roughly the same function: searching for a file.
T F 16. In a news reader program, there are several levels, each with different sets of commands.
T F 17. News groups with unread articles cannot be skipped.
T F 18. Mailing lists have a special reader program that is used only to read mailing list postings.
T F 19. WAIS allows you to search the contents of a document.
T F 20. WAIS documents cannot be retrieved because the documents are read-only.

STUDENT ASSIGNMENT 2
Multiple Choice

Instructions: Circle the correct response.

1. The command to display online help documentation in UNIX is _____.
   a. help
   b. ?
   c. doc
   d. man
2. In mail, the h command displays _____.
   a. a message summary list
   b. the next message
   c. UNIX online documentation
   d. help
3. The TELNET escape character allows you to enter _____.
   a. UNIX commands
   b. FTP commands
   c. mail commands
   d. TELNET commands
4. In FTP, the type command displays _____.
   a. the type of the remote computer
   b. a text disk file on the CRT screen
   c. the file transfer type
   d. the Internet service you are using
5. _____ is not a valid archie search type.
   a. Sub
   b. Substring
   c. Regex
   d. Subcase
6. The / at the end of a Gopher menu choice means there is another _____ under the choice.
   a. menu
   b. directory
   c. text file
   d. binary file
7. You can jump immediately to the news group you want to read by entering the _____ command followed by the news group name.
   a. h
   b. ?
   c. j
   d. g
8. When sending a mail message to request participation in a mailing list, the command placed in the body of the message is _____.
   a. subscribe
   b. g mailing list name
   c. p mailing list name
   d. list global
9. To read mailing list articles, use the _____ program.
   a. news reader
   b. TELNET
   c. man
   d. mail

(continued)

STUDENT ASSIGNMENT 2 (continued)

10. To select a WAIS database to search, position the highlight bar on the database name and then press _____.

    a. the SPACEBAR
    b. h
    c. s
    d. w

STUDENT ASSIGNMENT 3
Understanding Mail Message Headings

Instructions: Figure SA2-3 contains a sample mail message. Answer the following questions regarding the message header.

```
From jordanka@pucal1a.calumet.purdue.edu Wed Dec  4 09:07:44 1996
Status: R

          id AA11092; Wed,  4 Dec 96 09:07:38 -0500
Received: from pucal1b.calumet.purdue.edu  by solar.nova.edu (5.61uf1/4.2)
          id AA16721; Wed,  4 Dec 96 09:07:01 -0500
Received: by pucal1a.calumet.purdue.edu (5.65/Purdue_CC)
          id AA09346; Wed,  4 Dec 96 08:06:25 -0600
Date: Wed,  4 Dec 96 08:06:25 -0600
From: jordanka@pucal1a.calumet.purdue.edu (Kurt Jordan CUSS)
Message-Id: <9612041406.AA09346@pucal1a.calumet.purdue.edu>
To: jordan@alpha.acast.nova.edu
Subject: Next semester

Glad to hear you got an A in statistics.  I got an A in
System Testing.

I think I will take decision support systems next term.
How about you?
```

FIGURE SA2-3

1. Who sent the message? _____

2. Who received the message? _____

3. What is the message subject? _____

4. When was this message sent? _____

5. Do you think the subject was descriptive enough? Why or why not? _____

STUDENT ASSIGNMENT 4
Practicing Writing Subjects

Instructions: Write a short descriptive subject title for each of the following messages.

1. Fourth-quarter results for XYZ Corporation were impressive, with revenues increasing 23% over the same quarter last year. Long-term debt is low. I would strongly suggest purchasing more of this rapidly growing company. _____
_____

2. There are several places you can find directories and indexes to Internet resources. These directories can be obtained using gopher or FTP. One notable directory is the Internet Resources Guide, located at the una.hh.lib.umich.edu in the /inetdirs directory. _____
_____

3. Hi Jane! How are classes going? I hope everything is fine. How do you like dorm life? The cats are doing OK. Crusty still beats up on the others. He's so fat! It's a wonder he can catch them. Thanks for sending me that tax program. It came in real handy. Well, gotta go. Bye. _____
_____

STUDENT ASSIGNMENT 5
Managing a TELNET Session

Instructions: List the steps to establish a remote terminal session with the thomas.loc.gov government Internet site, enter the TELNET escape sequence, close the connection, and end the remote terminal session.

1. _____
2. _____
3. _____
4. _____

STUDENT ASSIGNMENT 6
Performing an Archie Search

Instructions: List the steps to use TELNET to connect to an archie server and search for Internet sites containing filenames that match exactly the filename xgif.

1. _____
2. _____
3. _____
4. _____

HANDS—ON EXERCISES

HANDS—ON EXERCISE 1
Retrieving a File Using FTP

Instructions: Login to a UNIX system and perform the following tasks.

1. Initiate an anonymous FTP session with ftp.uip.edu.
2. Change to the xevious subdirectory.
3. Retrieve a file called index.txt.
4. Display the index.txt file on the screen without exiting the FTP program by using the UNIX more command.
5. Choose a filename from the index.txt display.
6. Change the file transfer type to binary.
7. Retrieve the file you chose in step 5.
8. End the FTP session.

HANDS—ON EXERCISE 2
Participating in Mailing Lists

Instructions: Login to a UNIX system and perform the following steps.

1. Select one of the following mailing lists. The name of each list and a brief description of its purpose follows the list name.
   a. List name: fine-art   Fine art forum
      Address   listserv@rutvm1.rutgers.edu
   b. List name: vettes   About corvettes
      Address   vettes-requests@compaq.com
   c. List name: cybsys-l   About cybernetics
      Address   listserv@bingvmb.cc.binghampton.edu
   d. List name: gardens   Home gardening mailing list
      Address   listserv@ukcc.uky.edu
   e. List name: wwii-l   World War II mailing list
      Address   listserv@ubvm.cc.buffalo.edu
   f. List name: grunge-l   grunge music
      Address   listserv@ubvm.cc.buffalo.edu
   g. List name: libfem   Liberty and Feminism
      Address   libfem-request@math.uio.no
2. Subscribe to the mailing list you chose in step 1.
3. Monitor your electronic mail for submissions to the list.
4. When you have read several messages from the list, unsubscribe from the list.

HANDS—ON EXERCISE 3
Reading USENET News

Instructions: Login to a UNIX system and perform the following tasks.

1. Start the news reader program.
2. Read the first message from the first news group.
3. Exit the first news group.
4. Subscribe to the alt.best.of.internet news group.
5. Mark all the articles as read from the alt.best.of.internet news group.
6. Exit the news reader program.

HANDS–ON EXERCISE 4
Performing a WAIS Database Search

Instructions: Login to a UNIX system and perform the following tasks.

1. Start a remote terminal session with quake.think.com. Use wais as the account name.
2. Select the directory.of.servers database.
3. Search for the keyword fission.
4. Return to the Search menu.
5. Select the cold.fusion.src database.
6. Search for the keyword fission.
7. Display a document.
8. Instruct the WAIS server to mail the document to you.
9. Display the document again.
10. End the remote terminal session.

HANDS–ON EXERCISE 5
Retrieving Information Using Gopher

Instructions: Login to a UNIX system and perform the following tasks.

1. Initiate a gopher session with gopher.census.gov.
2. Choose Enter the main data bank.
3. Choose Statistical Abstract of the United States.
4. Choose USA Statistics in brief: part 1.
5. Display the document.
6. Save the document to a disk file called usapop.stats.
7. Exit the gopher server.
8. Print the usapop.stats file.

HANDS–ON EXERCISE 6
Searching for Files Using Archie

Instructions: Login to a UNIX system and perform the following tasks.

1. Initiate a remote terminal session with archie.sura.net. Use archie as the account name.
2. Set the search type to perform a substring search.
3. Search for the string plot.
4. Write down three Internet address and directory locations that contain the file xplot.
5. Terminate the remote terminal session.
6. Initiate an anonymous FTP session with one of the three Internet addresses.
7. Change to the directory location where the xplot file is located.
8. Change the transfer type to binary.
9. Retrieve the xplot file.
10. Terminate the FTP session.

THE INTERNET
Introductory Concepts and Techniques

APPENDIX

POPULAR INTERNET SITES

This appendix contains several popular Internet locations broken down into categories by topic. You should start and keep a directory of your own favorite Internet sites. Use the format shown below as a guide. It contains a brief description of what you can find at the site, what Internet service is used to connect to the site, and any navigational instructions and account names.

▶ GOVERNMENT

Members of U.S. Congress
: **gopher marvel.loc.gov**
choose *US Congress*, then *Congressional Directories*

Budget of U.S. Government
: **gopher sunsite.unc.edu**
choose *Worlds of SunSite - by Subject*, then *US and World Politics*, then *Sunsite Political Science Archives*, then *US-Budget*

U.S. Census Information
: **gopher gopher.micro.umn.edu**
choose *Libraries*, then *Electronic Books*, then *By Title*, then *1990 USA Census Information*

: **gopher bigcat.missouri.edu**
choose *Reference and Information Center*, then *United States and Missouri Census Information*, then *United States Census Data*

National Archives and Records
: **gopher gopher.loc.gov**
choose *Government Information*, then *Federal Information Sources*, then *National Libraries and National Archives*

Library of Congress
: **telnet locis.loc.gov**

Consumer Information
: **gopher consumer.ftc.gov**
choose *US Federal Trade Commission*, then *Consumerline*, then *Publications*

▶ Pictures

Small Collection of Various Images	`ftp ftp.nau.edu` login as anonymous; located in /graphics/gif
Works of Art Arranged by Artist Name	`gopher unix5.nysed.gov` choose *K-12 Resources*, then *Arts & Humanities*, then *Gallery*
Thousands of Images	`gopher cs4sun.cs.ttu.edu` choose *Art & Images*
OTIS Project – Original Artwork and Photographs	`ftp sunsite.unc.edu` login as anonymous; located in /pub/multimedia/pictures/OTIS
Smithsonian Institute Photographs	`gopher gopher.pipeline.com` choose *Arts and Leisure*, then *Smithsonian Photographs and viewing software*
Outer Space Photographs	`ftp sseop.jsc.nasa.gov` login as anonymous; get README.txt for descriptions of pictures
Weather Photographs	`gopher gopher.gsfc.nasa.gov` choose *Nasa information*, then *space gifs from Hubble etc*, then *images*

▶ Sound

Special Effects, Movie Voices, Cartoon Characters, Classical, Rock	`ftp sunsite.unc.edu`
	login as anonymous; located in pub/micro/pc-stuff/sounds
	
	`ftp plan9.njit.edu`
	login as anonymous; located in /pub/sounds
	
	`ftp valhalla.ee.rochester.edu`
	login as anonymous; located in /pub/sounds
	
	`gopher gopher.med.umich.edu`
	choose *Entertainment*

▶ Books

Index of Electronic Books	`ftp ftp.spies.com` login as anonymous; located in /Library/Classic
Online Book Initiative	`gopher wiretap.spies.com` choose *Electronic Books at Wiretap*
Project Gutenburg	`gopher gopher.std.com` choose *OBI the Online Book Initiative*

Online Library Search	**ftp mrcnext.cso.uiuc.edu** login as anonymous; located in /gutenberg **telnet eureka-info.stanford.edu** **telnet library.wustl.edu**

▶ GAMES

Dungeons and Dragons	**ftp ftp.cs.pdx.edu** login as anonymous; located in /pub/frp
Chess Programs	**ftp chess.uoknor.edu** login as anonymous; located in /pub/chess
Many PC Games	**ftp ftp.wustl.edu** login as anonymous; located in /pub/MSDOS_UPLOADS **ftp ftp.cdrom.com** login as anonymous; located in /.17/games/Games
Games for SCO UNIX	**ftp ftp.sco.com** login as anonymous; located in /Games

▶ JOBS

Federal Jobs	**gopher dartmouth.edu** choose *Career Services*, then *Job openings in the Federal Government*
Career Center Database	**gopher garnet.msen.com** choose *Msen Career Center*, then *Internet Employment Network*
Resume Database Make Your Resume Available Online	**gopher garnet.msen.com** choose *Msen Career Center*, then *Online Career Center*, then *How to enter a resume*

▶ INTERNET RESOURCES

Anonymous FTP Site List	**ftp ftp.shsu.edu** login as anonymous; located in /pub/ftp-list
Internet Services List The Yanoff List	**ftp ftp.csd.uwm.edu** login as anonymous; located in /pub/inet.services.txt
RFC (Request for Comments) Archives Try rfc1118.txt, the Hitchhiker's Guide to the Internet	**ftp ftp.wustl.edu** login as anonymous; located in /doc/rfc

Index

? command, mail commands and, I.43

Access to Internet, I.28
  using UNIX, I.33-102
Account, **I.33**
  anonymous, I.48, I.49
  displaying information about, I.44
Address, **I.13**
  archie search for, I.19
  e-mail, **I.13**
  IRC and, I.95
  list of, I.108-110
  UNIX and, I.36
  URL and, I.26
Addressing, **I.9**-10
Advanced Research Projects Agency NETwork (ARPANET), **I.3**
America Online, I.6
Anchors, **I.25**-26
Appended, **I.40**
archie, I.18, **I.19**
  displaying information about file, I.60-61
  exiting session, I.63
  search type and, I.61-62
  UNIX and, I.59-64
archie server, **I.19**, I.45
ARPANET (Advanced Research Projects Agency NETwork), **I.3**
Article, saving to disk, I.84-85
ASCII (American Standard Code for Information Interchange), **I.54**
Audit trail, **I.39**

Binary file, **I.55**, I.56
Books, Internet addresses, I.109-110
Bridge, **I.4**
Browser, Internet, I.22, **I.26**, **I.27**

Case-sensitive, **I.35**
Category names, news group, I.21
Channel(s), **I.24**, **I.95**
Channel names, displaying in IRC, I.96-97
Character string, search and, I.72
Classes, I.11
Client/server computing, **I.12**
Coaxial cable, **I.7**
College computer networks, I.4-5
Command prompt, **I.34**, I.35
Commercial software, **I.17**
CompuServe, I.6
Computer
  destination, I.8
  host, **I.8**, I.45-48
  remote, I.12, I.15, I.45-48
  source, I.8
  terminal sessions on remote host, I.45-48
Computer account, finger providing information about, I.14
Computing, client/server, **I.12**
Confidence score, **I.73**
Confidentiality, I.14
Connecting to Internet, I.5-10
Copyright, **I.17**-18
Current message, **I.38**-39
Current working directory, **I.50**-54

DARPA (Defense Advanced Research Projects Agency), **I.3**
Data, sending, I.8-10
Database, **I.72**-76
Data lines, **I.5**
  types of, I.5-6
  types of media for, I.7
d command, **I.42**-43
Default address, I.9
Defense Advanced Research Projects Agency (DARPA), **I.3**
Deleting mail message, I.42-43
Demon, **I.12**
  FTP, **I.16**
Destination computer, I.8
Directory, link to, I.51
Directory-of-servers, **I.72**
Directory path, URL and, I.26
Directory structure, FTP archives, I.50-51

Discussion channels, IRC, I.96-100
Discussion groups, I.18, I.21-22
Disk, saving article to, I.84-85
Disk file
  including in message, I.40-41
  saving messages to, I.39-40
Document(s), searching for with WAIS, I.70-76
Document retrieval system, I.20
Documentation manual page, I.35-36
Domain name/domain naming, **I.9**-10
  e-mail and, I.12-13
  FTP and, I.16
  information about account and, I.44
  IRC and, I.95
  TELNET and, I.15
Dotted decimal format, addressing and, **I.9**
Downloading files, I.16-17

Electronic mail, *see* E-mail
E-mail (electronic mail), **I.11**, **I.12**-14
  archie search results and, I.62-63
  courtesy, I.14
  deleting, I.42-43
  electronic carbon copies and, I.22
  exiting, I.43-44
  including disk file in, I.40-41
  mailing lists and, I.18, I.22-23
  managing, I.38-39, I.43
  managing mail box and, I.38
  reading other messages, I.41-42
  redisplaying, I.42
  saving, I.39-40
  sending to mailing list, I.91-92
  summary of commands, I.44
  UNIX and, I.36-44
  WAIS search results, I.75
E-mail address, **I.13**
  gopher and, I.20
End of text (EOT), **I.37**
EOT (end of text), **I.37**
Error message, routing message and, I.9
Escape character, **I.46**
Exact search type, **I.61**
Exclamation point (!), UNIX commands within FTP and, I.53
Exiting
  archie session, I.63
  IRC, I.100
  mail program, I.43-44
  news reader program, I.88
  TELNET, I.47-48
  WAIS server, I.75

Fiber-optic cable, **I.7**
File(s)
  archie search for, I.19
  binary, **I.55**, I.56
  compressed, I.17
  displaying information about, I.60-61
  downloading, I.16-17
  finding, *see* Finding files
  link, I.51
  login scrips, I.34
  Mosaic directory, I.52
  README, I.18, I.49, I.51, I.52
  receiving, I.16-17
  retrieving with gopher, I.64-70
  sending, I.8-10, I.16
  sending using FTP, I.57-59
  text, I.54
  transferring with FTP, I.48-59
  transferring with new name, I.58-59
  transfer types, **I.55**-57
  unzip and, I.17
  See also Searches
Filenames, I.17
  changing during transfer, I.58-59
  searching for, I.62
  UNIX and, I.35
File transfer protocol (FTP), *see* FTP
Finding documents, using WAIS, I.70-76
Finding files
  using archie, I.18, I.19, I.59-64
  using veronica, I.20-21, I.68-70
  using WAIS, I.70-76

Finding information about people, using UNIX, I.44-45
Finding people, using finger, I.14, I.45
finger, finding people using, **I.14**, I.45
Flaming, **I.14**
Fraud, I.14
Freeware, **I.18**
FTP (file transfer protocol), **I.11**, **I.16**
  displaying current directory, I.50-54
  displaying information about, I.35-36
  file transfer types and, I.54-57
  sending files using, I.57-59
  starting session, I.48-49
  transferring files with, I.48-59
FTP demon, I.12, **I.16**

Games, Internet addresses, I.110
Gateways, **I.4**, I.9
gopher, I.18, **I.20**
  WAIS services and, I.68, I.71
Gopher menus, navigating, I.65-68
GopherSpace, **I.20**, **I.68**
  search of using veronica, I.20-21, I.68-70
Gopher Web, **I.20**
go to news group command, I.82
Government, Internet addresses, I.108

Help, UNIX and, I.35-36
Highlight bar, **I.72**
History tracking, Netscape and, I.27
Home directory, **I.50**
Home page, World Wide Web and, **I.26**
Host computer, **I.8**
  terminal sessions on remote, I.45-48
Hotlists, **I.27**
HTML (hypertext markup language), **I.25**
Hypermedia, **I.25**
Hypertext, **I.25**-26
Hypertext markup language (HTML), **I.25**

Illegal activities, I.14
Information Superhighway, **I.4**
INTERconnected NETworks, **I.4**. *See also* Internet
Internet (INTERconnected NETworks), I.2, **I.4**
  access to, I.28
  connecting to, I.5-10
  devices attached to, I.4-5
  history of, I.3
  introduction to, I.2-28
  rights and responsibilities and, I.17-18
  sending information over, I.8-10
  services provided on, I.10-18
  tools, I.18-24
  UNIX and, I.33-101
Internet browser, I.22, **I.26**, **I.27**
Internet Information Center (INTERNIC), **I.45**
Internet relay chat (IRC), *see* IRC
Internet resources, addresses, I.110
Internet service programs, I.12-15
  documentation about, I.36
Internet services, accessing from UNIX, I.33-102
Internet sites, I.11
INTERNIC (Internet Information Center), **I.45**
IP address, **I.9**-10
  IRC and, I.95
IRC (Internet relay chat), **I.24**, **I.94**-101
  changing to another channel, I.99-100
  conversing on discussion channel, I.97-99
  displaying channel names, I.96-97
  exiting, I.100
  joining discussion channel, I.97
  starting session, I.95-96
IRC server, available channels on, I.96-97
Jobs, Internet addresses, I.110

Keyword, I.70

Leased line, **I.5**-6
License, **I.17**-18
Link, **I.51**
  hypertext, I.25-26
listserv, **I.22**, **I.89**-91
Login, **I.33**
Login prompt, **I.34**
Login scripts, **I.34**
Logout, **I.36**

I.111

Mail, *see* E-mail
Mail box, **I.13**
   managing in UNIX, I.38
Mailbox format, **I.85**
Mail command, **I.36**
Mail demons, I.12
Mailing lists, I.18, **I.22**-23, I.89-94
   global list of, I.89
   reading postings, I.91
   sending mail to, I.91-92
   subscribing to, I.89
   unsubscribing from, I.93-94
Mailing search results, I.62-63
Mail messages
   deleting, I.42-43
   managing, I.38-39, I.43
   saving, I.39-40
   summary list of, I.38
Mail program, I.13
   exiting, I.43-44
Mailx command, **I.36**
man command, **I.35**-36
Manual page, documentation, I.35-36
Messages
   current, **I.38**-39
   deleting, I.42-43
   including disk file in, I.40-41
   managing, I.38-39, I.43
   reading other, I.41-42
   saving, I.39-40
   summary list of, I.38, **I.41**
Microwave, **I.7**
Microwave tower, I.7
Modem (<u>mo</u>dulate/<u>dem</u>odulate), **I.6**
more command, **I.53**
Mosaic software, I.3, I.27
   retrieving latest version of, I.48-49, I.51

Naming, domain, **I.9**-10
National Center for SuperComputing Applications, I.26
National Center for SuperComputing Applications FTP archives, I.48-49
Navigation, Netscape and, I.27
Netscape, I.22, **I.27**
Netscape Communications Corporation, I.26
Netscape Navigator software, I.3, I.26
Network, **I.4**
Network capacity, I.14
News articles, saving to disk, I.84-85
News group, I.18, **I.21**-22
   changing to different, I.80-84
News group articles
   posting, I.86-89
   reading, I.78-79
   summary of, I.79-80
.newsrc data file, **I.76**, I.82-83
News reader, **I.22**, **I.76**

Online, **I.35**
Online service providers, **I.6**
ORACLE mailing list, I.90-91

Packets, **I.8**
Packet switching, **I.8**
Password, **I.33**
   FTP and, I.48, I.49
People
   finding information about using UNIX, I.44-45
   finding using finger, I.14, I.45
Pictures, Internet addresses, I.109
Policy, **I.43**
Post, **I.86**
Posting news group articles, **I.86**-89
Posting to news groups, I.21

Programs, running, I.11
Prompt
   FTP and, I.49
   login, I.34
Protocol, **I.3**
   file transfer, **I.11**, **I.16**
   TCP/IP, **I.3**
   URL and, I.26
Providers, **I.6**
Public domain software, **I.18**

q command, I.43
Query, archie and, I.60-61

README file, I.18, I.49, I.51, I.52
read now? prompt, I.82, I.83
Receiver, I.12
Receiving files, I.16-17
Regex search type, **I.61**
Remote computer, I.12, I.15
Repository, **I.76**
Research, I.11, I.15
   mailing list and, I.23
Retrieving files, using gopher, I.64-70
Route table, **I.9**
Routing decisions, I.8

Satellite, **I.7**
Saving
   article to disk, I.84-85
   mail messages, I.39-40
Searches
   archie and, I.19
   gopher and, I.18, I.20
   veronica and, I.18, I.20-21
   Wide Area Information Service and, I.18, I.23-24
Searching for documents, using WAIS, I.70-76
Search results, mailing, I.62-63
Search type, archie and, I.61-62
Selection indicator, Gopher menu, **I.65**
Sender, I.12
Sending files, I.16
   using FTP, I.57-59
Sending information, I.9-10
Sending to news groups, I.21
Sequence number, **I.38**
   packets and, I.8
Server, archie, **I.19**, I.45
Service programs, I.12-15
Services, types of, I.10-18
Shareware, **I.18**
Shopping, I.11
Sniffer, **I.14**
Software
   commercial, **I.17**
   public domain, **I.18**
   rights and responsibilities and, I.17-18
Software packing, I.16-17
Sound, Internet addresses, I.109
Source computer, I.8
Source Selection menu, I.73
Status code, **I.38**
Subcase search type, **I.61**
Subject line prompt, **I.37**
Subnetworks, I.4
Subscribe to news groups, **I.76**
Subscribing, **I.76**, **I.89**
Sub search type, **I.61**
Summary list, of messages, I.38, **I.41**
Summary of news group articles, I.79-80
sura.net archie public access site, I.45
Switched line, **I.5**-6

Table, route, **I.9**
TCP/IP (<u>T</u>ransmission <u>C</u>ontrol Protocol/<u>I</u>nternet <u>P</u>rotocol), **I.3**, I.5
   bridge and, I.4
   sending data and, I.8
   sniffer displaying packets, I.14
Telephone lines, I.7
TELNET, **I.11**, **I.15**, **I.45**
   archie server and, I.59-64
   connecting to WAIS and, I.71
   ending session, I.47-48
   gopher and, I.64
   managing, I.46-47
   starting session, I.46
TELNET demons, I.12
Terminal sessions, on remote host computers, I.45-48
Text editor session, I.87
Text file, I.54
   finding using WAIS, I.70-76
Thread, **I.21**
Topics
   Internet relay chat and, I.24, I.94
   mailing list and, I.23
   news group, I.21, I.76
Transferring files, with FTP, I.48-59
Transfer type, **I.55**-57
<u>T</u>ransmission <u>C</u>ontrol Protocol/<u>I</u>nternet <u>P</u>rotocol, *see* TCP/IP
Twisted pair wire, **I.7**

Universal Resource Locators (URL), **I.26**
University library catalogs, I.15
UNIX
   accessing Internet services from, I.33-102
   e-mail and, I.36-44
   finding files with archie, I.59-64
   finding information about people using, I.44-45
   help in, I.35-36
   login and, I.33
   mailing lists and, I.89-94
   managing mail box in, I.38
   retrieving files using gopher and, I.64-70
   searching for documents with WAIS, I.70-76
   sending files using FTP, I.57-59
   terminal sessions on remote host computers and, I.45-48
   transferring files with FTP, I.48-59
   USENET news groups and, I.76-89
UNIX command prompt, I.34, I.35
Unsubscribe, **I.76**, I.83, **I.93**-94
Unsubscribe to news groups, **I.76**, I.83
Unzip, **I.17**, I.62-63
URL (Universal Resource Locators), **I.26**
USENET, **I.22**, I.76-89

veronica, I.18, **I.20**-21, **I.68**
   searching GopherSpace using, I.20-21, I.68-70

WAIS (Wide Area Information Service), I.18, **I.23**-24
   searching for documents with, I.70-76
WAIS commands, list of, I.75, I.76
WAIS databases, **I.72**-76
WAIS server
   connecting to, I.71
   exiting, I.75
Web sites, **I.3**
whatis command, I.60-61
whois command, I.44, I.45
Wide Area Information Service, *see* WAIS
Windows, using TELNET in, I.15
Windows directory, I.52
Worldwide Gopher and WAIS Servers menu, I.68, I.71
World Wide Web (WWW), **I.3**, I.25, **I.26**-28

x command, **I.44**

Photo Credits

PROJECT 1
Figure 1-7a, Bruce Ando/Tony Stone Images
Figure 1-16, Courtesy IBM Corp.
Figure 1-27, Phil Matt Photography